Languages of Theatre Shaped by Women

Jane de Gay and Lizbeth Goodman

intellect™
Bristol, UK
Portland, OR, USA

Reprinted in Paperback in Great Britain in 2003 by
Intellect Books, PO Box 862, Bristol BS99 1DE, UK

Published in Paperback in USA in 2003 by
Intellect Books, ISBS, 5824 N.E. Hassalo St, Portland, Oregon 97213-3644, USA

Consulting Editor:	Robin Beecroft
Cover Illustration:	Mark Mackie
Copy Editor:	Holly Spradling
Typesetting:	*Macstyle Ltd*, Scarborough, N. Yorkshire

A catalogue record for this book is available from the British Library

ISBN 1-871516-78-1

Printed and bound by The Cromwell Press, Trowbridge, Wiltsire

Contents

List of Illustrations

Notes on Contributors

Patience Agbabi was born in London in 1965 and educated at Pembroke College Oxford. She has published two collections of poetry: *R.A.W.* (Gecko Press, 1995) and *Transformatrix* (Payback Press, 2000). Renowned for live performances, her poems have been featured on radio and TV worldwide. Having been Writer in Residence at the Poetry Cafe during 1999 and Flamin' 8 Tattoo Parlour in 2000, she is currently Writer in Residence at Oxford Brookes University (Humanities and Health Care).

Adeola Agbebiyi was born in Toronto and brought up in Burnley and the Midlands. As a singer/songwriter, she has played gigs with Labi Siffre, Linton Kwesi Johnson, Desree and Andy Fernbach among others. She released an album *Crystal Visions* (Shango Music, 1993) before featuring as 'The Jazz Singer' in the short film *B.D. Women* (Channel Four and various film festivals 1994). Having worked as an actress for two years, she is currently writing and recording a new album.

Lindsay Bell is a PhD candidate at the Graduate Centre for Study of Drama at the University of Toronto. Her doctoral thesis focuses on feminist strategies of adaptation in four plays by Sally Clark. Other adaptations include *Priest* (from the screenplay by Jimmy McGovern, 1997), and a Shaw Festival/CBC radio adaptation of Emily Carr's *Klee Wyck* (produced at the Shaw Festival August 2001, and was broadcast on CBC in April 2002).

Jane de Gay is Lecturer in English at Trinity and All Saints, University of Leeds. She was a key contributor to *Feminist Stages* (Harwood Academic Press, 1994) and co-editor, with Lizbeth Goodman, of two performance readers for Routledge. She has published articles on Bryony Lavery, Louise Page and Caryl Churchill. Her research interests also include intertextuality and she is currently writing a book on Virginia Woolf's responses to the literary past.

Jools Gilson-Ellis is a writer, choreographer, performer and installation artist. She is co-director of the performance production company half/angel, founded in 1995 with Richard Povall. half/angel develops projects involving new technologies, poetic text and performance. She teaches performance at University College Cork in Ireland.

Lizbeth Goodman is Director of the SMARTlab Centre for Site Specific Media, Performing and Digital Arts at Central Saint Martin's College of Art and Design, the London Institute. She also directs the Practice-based PhD programme for CSM. She is the Principal Investigator of the SMARTshell Project (creating innovative tools for synchronous and asynchronous online/integrated performance and learning), and of the Virtual Interactive Puppetry Project, the British Council's Cultural and Media

Studies development programmes in North Africa, and the European Commission's RADICAL project (Research Agendas Developed in Creative Arts Labs). She is also the UK Executive Producer of Sara Diamond's Code Zebra Project, working with international partners at the Banff New Media Institute, BBC Imagineering, V2, UCLA, UC Berkeley, et al. Dr Goodman has written and edited some 12 books including a range of titles on women and theatre, the arts, representation and creativity. Her books have been translated into several languages and are set on courses internationally.

Leslie Hill is a writer and performer whose work has been widely shown in a variety of venues across the US and UK and commissioned by major institutions such as the Arts Council of England, the National Endowment for the Arts and the Institute for Contemporary Arts. Articles by and about Hill have appeared in two dozen publications over the past few years, including *Performance Research* and *New Theatre Quarterly* and *The Routledge Reader in Politics and Performance*. Hill is artistic director, with Helen Paris, of London-based curious.com Performance and Multimedia Company. Hill is currently Head of Media at the London College of Music and Media.

Helen Paris is a nationally and internationally commissioned performance artist of solo and collaborative works. Her work has been supported by, amongst others, the Arts Council of England, the London Arts Board, the National Endowment for the Arts, The London Filmmakers Co-op, London Electronic Arts, the Institute for Contemporary Art, South East Arts and Artsadmin where she is an Associate Artist. With Leslie Hill she is co-artistic director of curious.com performance and multimedia company: www.placelessness.com. Hill and Paris's recent book, *Guerilla Performance and Multimedia* is published by Continuum. curious.com are currently working on a live art installation and TV documentary *On the Scent* exploring live performance and the olfactory, funded by the Wellcome Trust. Paris holds a PhD from the University of Surrey and is Lecturer in Drama at Brunel University, London.

Jane Prendergast is a performer, writer and teacher of theatre. She is presently teaching drama in Singapore, at the National Institute of Education, a section of The Nanyang Technological University. Her current performance research is a solo performance called 'Tempes[t]sepmet', based upon Shakespeare's *The Tempest*. Her project combines Asian and Western theatre styles, and the discourses of postcolonialism and feminism. The project will be toured internationally.

Dorothea Smartt, a poet, writer and live artist, was Brixton Market's first Poet-in-Residence, and a former Attached Live Artist at London's Institute of Contemporary Arts. She has been awarded several commissions and bursaries; lectures part-time at Birkbeck College; provides workshops to diverse communities; and performs nationally and internationally. In 2000 her commissioned multi-media children's play, *Fallout* (Theatre Venture), successfully toured London schools. Her poetry collection, *Connecting Medium*, was published by Peepal Tree Press in 2001.

Introduction: Speaking in Tongues – Making (Sense of) Women's Languages in Theatre

Jane de Gay and Lizbeth Goodman

The notion of 'speaking in tongues' (as it is found in the Biblical story of the Christian apostles speaking many languages and being understood by an international crowd of onlookers) articulates an ideal of communicating across national and linguistic boundaries. This is something to which theatre, and international performance in particular, has often aspired. Theatre is a place and space in which we can dream such large dreams and attempt to realise them, which is one reason why women whose energies are often blocked in other areas of life and forms of expression will turn to the theatre.

In practice, however, speaking with the languages of theatre often results in a disappointing Babel-like failure to communicate. Indeed, the phrase 'speaking in tongues' has often been used to imply incomprehension, ignorance and disdain, recalling the racist stereotypes of First Nations peoples which imply that a multiplicity of languages and indirectness of expression have not traditionally been valued highly in the West.

We can attempt to embrace and 'replay' this negative association in an empowering light, though, if we take the language and its associations and transport them into a different context which is open to exploration of diversity, articulation of difference and division within a framework of communication. This space can be found in the theatre: not on the stage but in the contemporary field of Performance Studies which has created – sometimes by force – spaces for the exploration of languages of theatre, and in particular of women's languages in theatre.

Performance is a means of expression and articulation of greater ideas yet it can be appropriated and utilized to political ends and personal aims as well. So female artists and students working in many different disciplines and spaces – from the home to the street to the office to the lecture 'theatre' – have long sought avenues for group collaboration and for embodied engagement in a shared sense of striving for language: in an exercise of making meaning which is not so much about reaching an 'understanding' in any traditional sense, but more about reaching beyond the quotidian use of language and body language, towards a new form of communication that might be at once broader and also deeper, more resonant to an individual's personal sense of agency and identity.

So, we ask a lot of the theatre. And we ask a lot of each other when we come together to explore this process of asking. This book asks questions about that process of asking, searching, attempting to define suitable spaces for the process which has no one clear, definable or 'deliverable' end.

The very process of communication cries out for attention. Speaking across and about gendered uses of language raises the question of whether the languages of theatre are patriarchal: that is, whether the linguistics of the play-text and the conventions of gesture and symbol alike are sign-systems that render women objects not subjects, spoken for and not speaking (Case, 1988: 120). If that is so, then can women speak those languages at all, or, if they do, will they only be misinterpreted? If, as a solution, we set ourselves the task of exploring a 'women's language in theatre' do we thereby imply that there is one such language which we should all search for and find – or pretend to find? Alternatively, is the idea of a 'women's language' in theatre an essentialist one, the product of an outmoded view of gender difference based on binary opposition? It is probably more realistic to say that are there many languages or modes of expression to be found for many different women, but if this is so, what is to be gained from projects which bring many women together, unless we find a way to value many different forms of communication and to seek deep and broad communication within the women's space as well as beyond it?

The last question is a basic, and huge, one for women's theatre. The dilemma is often acknowledged privately, and sometimes complained about when individuals who had hoped for deep connection feel silenced by or within what they anticipated would be a safe group of like-minded women. Yet the dilemma itself can be turned on its head as a symptom of the 'women's theatre' situation, rather than as the cause of its (sometimes perceived) failure. The many languages and cultural backgrounds imported into any gathering of women from around the world, combined with the differences in educational access and in training (both academic and practical), all contribute to a wonderful, complex hybrid: dancers from Ireland, theatre-makers from Poland and Brazil, singers from Wales, visual and media artists from Australia, all coming to a space from their own generations, class and race backgrounds. How can such a group be expected to communicate to each other in a 'shared language' in order to achieve a group understanding and then to articulate one shared notion of a 'women's language'?

If we set such a huge and impossible task for ourselves and our sisters, of course we set up situations where individuals will feel silenced or confused. But if we take the notion of 'speaking in tongues' as an empowering phrase to embrace and allow for much difference of opinion and expression within a larger theme, then each voice may find its own level: whether in words, sound, image or movement. Then we may be getting somewhere worth going, together and apart.

When any individual's perceived 'failure' to understand the group is acknowledged and woven into a group discussion of the meaning of understanding and the importance of communication, the potentially divisive becomes strong. Yet even in an ideal grouping where Babel finds its own communicative level, there are more problems – or in business-speak, more 'challenges' – to be addressed.

One set of problems, which exercises many of the contributors to this volume, concerns the performing body. Physical exchange, physical giving, bodily movement and the flow of energy are key components in performance work. Yet how can the lived reality of bodily experience be made concrete in the theatre? Additionally, how can bodily presence and body language be incorporated into multimedia performance, when new media technology by definition would seem to place any experience at a second or third remove? In how many different ways might the performing female body be read by different spectators? And to what extent can the physical experience of theatre be captured in text and photographs – or even recordings?

The chapters of this book explore the nature of these problems but also, crucially, examine some of the ways in which performers have sought to address them. The book discusses a range of performance pieces by women, many of which have specifically avoided communicating a simple, unequivocal meaning to their audience. These are multi-layered performances, some of them created and shared in multimedia, and all of them multivalent. The chapters – and many of the performances they discuss – are concerned with how the (female) body might be presented and re-presented in performance. Many of the contributors are concerned with how these processes might be theorized (specifically, how they might be theorized in gendered terms), not only in writing but in performance itself.

The selection of performances chosen for attention is not meant to be exhaustive or representative of the range of theatre work being undertaken by women around the world. Rather, the performances discussed are offered as case studies in addressing issues of women's performance and the languages of theatre. The collection aims for the most part to discuss performances with which the authors have been closely involved: seven of the contributors discuss their own work and so can draw on personal experience of the process of tackling these issues. Jane de Gay's chapters are written from the point of view of an invited observer watching the gestation of several of the projects she discusses. Lizbeth Goodman was both invited observer and academic adviser to the two Shakespearean adaptations considered in her chapter. Leslie Hill's article on Helen Paris is written with close knowledge and understanding of Paris's work and methods, for the two have frequently collaborated, notably on the project, *I Never Go Anywhere I Can't Drive Myself,* a tour of Route 66 in the United States which they recorded and documented – that is, *performed* – on an interactive website. These chapters therefore present personal experiences and insights to offer a range of perspectives on shared issues and concerns.

Theory into Practice: Feminist Theories of Women's Language(s) as Articulated in Performance

At the outset of this collection of voices and arguments, it is worth setting the discussion in context by outlining in brief some of the major points made by feminist critics and theorists who have addressed the question of 'women's language' over the years. The discussion here must be truncated and inevitably simplified, but it may serve as a starting point, from which the authors of each chapter have taken their various cues.

Feminist thinking about language was dominated for many years by concerns about unequal access to the right to speak. In the early stages of second-wave feminism, those women who wrote and performed pieces about issues such as motherhood, childcare, sexuality and the gendered division of labour – and also, crucially, women who convened and took part in post-show discussions – were seen as breaking a silence which had hitherto seemed to surround crucial aspects of women's lives. Such projects were informed by the idea that the personal is political – or at least that the personal is important and significant and worthy of representation on stage and in performance. Although the feminist theatres that flourished from the 1960s to the 1980s have for the most part ceased to operate, there is still evidence of a need to give voice to experiences which may otherwise be lost to silence. Yet the process has also undergone some major shifts. Firstly, the notion of 'women's issues', in the sense of concerns which all women might share, is no longer tenable: instead, recent performances have tended to speak of particular experiences (sometimes experiences specific to certain social or cultural situations), which may not strike a chord with all female audience members. Secondly, now that there are relatively few forums in which work by women is staged for predominantly female audiences, the challenge of maintaining a feminist or gender-aware stance in wider or more 'mainstream' media contexts becomes more pressing.

The first, very broad, question that arises in exploring the role of feminist approaches in these wider contexts concerns the relation of women performers to the languages of theatre tradition. Although feminist critics from Kate Millett onwards have criticized the patriarchal nature of the canon and the prevalence of 'dead white male' writers within it, there has been an ongoing interest in asserting women's right to act in the canonical plays by men – and in discovering how to do so on their own terms. The Shakespearean canon has attracted the most attention in this respect. Although some feminist critics have deplored the lack of female parts in Shakespeare's plays and argued that these female roles perpetuate stereotypical views of women, from the demonized Lady Macbeth to the sad and saintly Ophelia, feminist actors in the 1980s showed that it was possible both to recuperate Shakespeare's female characters and to critique Shakespeare's plays by performing in them. Harriet Walter and Frances Barber are two of many actors who have sought to do this in performance, and have also published articles arising from their experiences (see Walter, 1993 and Barber, 1988). A further set of examples may be found in *Clamorous Voices*, a collection of interviews published by Carol Rutter in 1988. The reflective and reflexive approach taken by these actors suggests that it may be possible to *perform* criticism. This idea has inspired several of the performers who contribute to this book: Jane Prendergast's *I, Hamlet*, an adaptation of Shakespeare's play, may be set in this tradition, although Prendergast goes further firstly by exploring how a female actor may critique a male role in performance and secondly by underpinning her performance practice with feminist and cultural theories as well as literary criticism.

Closely aligned with the idea of performing a critique of plays is that of writing original creative material, which holds earlier plays up to scrutiny. As Deborah Novy's two edited collections – *Women's Revisions of Shakespeare* (1990) and *Cross-Cultural*

Performances (1993) – have demonstrated, women writers and theatre-makers have over the years attempted to rewrite motifs from Shakespeare, or to enlarge upon the lives and experiences of his female characters which seem to receive scant attention in the original plays. *Lear's Daughters* was a notable piece of work in this tradition, and indeed was discussed in the second Novy collection; Bryony Lavery's *Ophelia* is a more recent contribution to this process. Works such as these may be seen as examples of parody – something which has often been seen as a feminist tool. Yet, as Linda Hutcheon has noted, while parody can have a critical function, it is paradoxical, because it may perpetuate tradition even as it undercuts it (1985: 68–9). The chapters in Part 1 of this book explore the fine line which some of these writers and performers may walk in trying to parody and critique tradition.

Underlying these questions is the more fundamental issue of women's relationship to language, which has been hotly debated for many years. Much feminist thinking on this issue has taken its cue from Lacanian psychoanalytic approaches to language acquisition, in which entry into the symbolic order of written language is figured as a male privilege: such language represents 'woman' as the desired other and thus fails to embody her. Language becomes a tool that objectifies women and cannot convey their perspectives or experiences. The search for a 'woman's language' may thus be seen as an attempt to circumvent this perceived problem. The most influential contributions to this debate were made by the 'new French feminists', Luce Irigaray, Hélène Cixous and Julia Kristeva. Irigaray and Cixous formulated slightly differing accounts of *écriture féminine*, a 'feminine writing' which would deconstruct the assumptions of symbolic language – not least its reification of gender differences – through a variety of strategies including the use of gaps and silences, word-play and puns, confusion, multivalency and meaninglessness, and a resistance of binary oppositions to champion the spaces 'in between'. Kristeva, while resisting ideas of a 'woman's writing', places similar emphasis on linguistic disruption and confusion and the resistance of binary oppositions in her theory of 'semiotic' language.

Recent feminist theorists have disagreed about the value of *écriture féminine*. Detractors accuse the French theorists of essentialism, because *écriture féminine* is closely aligned with thinking about the female body, implying a causal relationship between biological make-up and language-use. The theories of Irigaray, Cixous and Kristeva draw closely on images of the female body and of motherhood in particular: for example, Cixous (1975) describes *écriture féminine* in terms of writing with mother's milk and Kristeva (1984) associates the 'semiotic' with pre- and post-partum connections between mother and child. However, other feminists have shown that *écriture féminine* may be recuperated from charges of essentialism, for example by pointing out that Cixous characterized it as a resistant, playful form of writing which might become a tool for anyone wishing to challenge the status quo. Viewed in this way, Cixous's *écriture féminine* has continuing relevance in an age when many feminist approaches have sought to recognize cultural diversity and to resist universalizing conceptions of womanhood. Something of this spirit of resistance may be seen in Chapter 6, on *Fo(u)r Women*, where the authors' rejection of racial and sexual labels articulated in Adeola Agbebiyi's introduction finds a mirror in the playful, experimental nature of their text.

As Jeannette Laillou Savona has demonstrated, fruitful connections may be made between French feminist theories and theatre, because a 'proclamation of a feminist poetics of theatre' is 'implicit' in Cixous's writing (1984: 541). Julia Kristeva's writing, too, lends itself to a feminist theory of performance, for her conception of the semiotic order has more than a semantic link with theatre semiotics. For Kristeva, the semiotic ruptures the symbolic order of textual communication, and this is achievable in the theatre and performance spaces where visual signs speak for themselves, perhaps detracting attention from the text, eliciting meanings which counter those in the text, or even replacing text altogether. This theory of rupture may help point to moments at which performance is at its most radical and challenging: that is, where women reshape the languages of theatre in performance.

However, although many feminists are attracted by the idea that 'the utilization of the body in performance may ... provide an alternative order to the symbolic order or language itself' (Carlson, 1996: 169), there is still room for doubt that the body *can* speak, for it may still be used as a *tabla rasa* on which patriarchal notions are inscribed. The problem of the male gaze, identified by Laura Mulvey in her classic essay, 'Visual Pleasure and Narrative Cinema' (1975), still persists as the female performer risks being denied subjectivity and rendered the object of the male spectator's fantasies. Two chapters in particular explore possible solutions to this problem. Lindsay Bell discusses the liberating potential of radio in chapter five, 'Transmitting the Voices, Voyages and Visions: Adapting Virginia Woolf's *To the Lighthouse* for Radio'. Helen Paris in chapter eight, 'One to One: Lone Journeys', explores how the possibilities opened up by new media technology might offer ways of subverting the binary opposition between spectator and participant in order to create a safer, more comfortable space for the female performer to occupy.

However, it may not be enough simply to 'hide the body', for the body may be objectified even when it is not there. As Judith Butler demonstrates in *Bodies that Matter* (1993), sex and gender are linguistic categories which we can scarcely think beyond: gendered language, and the gender 'norms' it carries, influence our thinking. Thus, even 'virtual' bodies created in multimedia may be gendered in ways which are more coercive than we may realise. Butler suggests that a way forward may be to 'cite' norms ironically in order to produce them differently: voicing words in contexts which undercut their meaning. Although Butler's theory is rooted in philosophy and linguistics, its applicability to theatre performance has not gone unnoticed, for physical action in theatre can undercut the power of words and unseat meanings.

For these reasons, many feminist practitioners (including several contributors to this volume) recognize the potential usefulness of postmodern techniques for feminist performance. The relationship of postmodernism and feminism is a matter of some debate (see Nicholson, 1990: 1–16), and some have argued that the notion of the decentred self as proposed by postmodernists is inimical to feminist arguments for subjectivity and self-determination. However, others have argued that these are precisely the qualities that help to overcome problems of essentialism by holding traditional understandings of womanhood up to scrutiny. Postmodern irony has helped feminists distance themselves from earlier conventions and understandings: for example, as Elin Diamond has noted, feminist performance has often taken traditional representations of women and subjected them to 'ironic disturbance' or 'mimicry' (1989: 59–60), to undercut their effect. The multiple perspectives enabled by postmodern approaches (not least the kinds of non-linearity enabled by the CD-ROM, the world-wide web and 'replay culture') support difference and facilitate deconstruction of traditional notions. Thus postmodern techniques are some of the range of tools used by feminist theatre-makers unmaking and remaking language to elicit new meanings.

The contributors to this volume engage with these debates in various ways, claiming for women the right to use all the languages of theatre and to invent languages and communicative forms of their own as well. The chapters of Part 1 explore how women performers can take on board writing by men or theatrical tropes traditionally associated with male playwrights while asserting the subjectivity and dignity of the female performer. In chapter one, 'Seizing Speech and Playing with Fire: Greek Mythological Heroines and International Women's Performance', Jane de Gay looks at how female performers have interpreted the heroines of Greek mythology. The strategies she identifies include the use of irony and metatheatre to hold old stereotypes up to scrutiny. The remaining chapters in Part 1 present four case studies of feminist actors' and playwrights' responses to Shakespeare. In '*Lear's Daughters* on Stage and in Multimedia and Fiona Shaw's *King Lear* Workshops as Case Studies in Breaking the Frame', Lizbeth Goodman discusses *Lear's Daughters* by Elaine Feinstein and the Women's Theatre Group as a performed critique of *King Lear,* and also looks at Fiona Shaw's experimental direction of selected scenes from *King Lear* for video. Shaw's project, it emerges, is particularly successful in opening up new perspectives on the play and inviting the audience to re-play it with new insights, not least because her finished product incorporates a variety of different 'cuts' of the same performance material. In 'Playing (with) Shakespeare: Bryony Lavery's *Ophelia* and Jane Prendergast's I, *Hamlet*', de Gay discusses Bryony Lavery's play *Ophelia*, which both critiques Shakespeare's plays and, in a more positive way, reclaims the power of heroines inherent in Shakespeare's original. This works as a recuperation of Shakespeare: as Lavery herself commented, she came to see Shakespeare as 'an old friend with an old friend's strengths. He writes beautifully', and an old friend's faults: 'he never puts in enough women!' In the same article, de Gay also discusses I, *Hamlet,* Jane Prendergast's adaption of Shakespeare's play which takes up an even more rigorous challenge of how a woman can play one of the classic male roles, and how the text might be adapted to accommodate a female body. As Prendergast herself shows in chapter four, 'Theorizing Practice-based Research: Performing and Analysing Self in Role as "I, Hamlet"', the process of developing I, *Hamlet* involved reshaping Shakespeare's linear, five-act structure to create a more fluid and open pattern based on the octave, which is associated with music rather than text.

Where Part 1 concentrates on how female performers have shaped the language of male playwrights (or the patriarchal theatrical tradition), Part 2 places female writers centre-stage. Lindsay Bell discusses her own process of adapting Virginia Woolf's novel, *To the Lighthouse,* for radio in chapter five. Like Prendergast, Bell draws on music to re-produce Woolf's text in a contrapuntal style which is both true to the spirit of the novel and consistent with Woolf's own theories of performance and writing. In chapter six, 'Voicing Identities, Reframing Difference(s): The Case of *Fo(u)r Women*', Adeola Agbebiyi describes the process by which she collaborated with Patience Agbabi and Dorothea Smartt to develop the performance *Fo(u)r Women*. Visual cues play a part in this piece, for the performance was staged on a set which consisted of four large frames (one for each performer, one left empty), which enabled the performers to move around and literally frame and re-frame their own experience as Black British women as they challenged stereotypes and spoke for themselves. Creative writing by women is given prominence in this section: Bell's chapter includes some lengthy extracts from her script, whilst the play-text of *Fo(u)r Women* is reproduced here in its entirety.

Where Lindsay Bell's piece is concerned with the process of translating prose text into performance, a further question underlying many of the chapters concerns the reverse process: how to translate performance into text by documenting live performance. There is a danger that much may be lost in documentation, as live performance, with all its subtlety, unpredictability and energy is collapsed back into two dimensions as printed text and still pictures. A play-text is only a husk devoid of the inscription of the human voice and body. Dorothea Smartt, Adeola Agbebiyi and Patience Agbabi find innovative ways of tackling this difficulty in chapter six, for the performance text of *Fo(u)r Women* makes creative use of fonts and of the spatial arrangement of text on the page to find a way of moving gracefully between the 'trace' of the play-text and the three dimensions of performance.

The chapters of Part 3 are concerned with moving from documentation to theorization of performance. Here again, there is an interest in exploring how to make text perform. Leslie Hill's 'Scratch in the Record' (chapter seven) is concerned with the voice and languages of virtual technology. Hill's article interweaves critical and creative writing in a way which breaks down the boundaries between the two as she documents Helen Paris's performance of the same name. Like Smartt, Agbebiyi and Agbabi, she makes creative use of fonts as textual performance or a form of 'performative writing'. As Hill notes, Paris's work is concerned with breaking down the binary opposition between the visceral and the mediated, for example, where strips of film are both projected to show moving images *and* offered as physical artefacts which the audience is invited to touch. Helen Paris, in her chapter 'One to One: Lone Journeys' (chapter eight), discusses how she also sought to break down the audience/spectator binary in her performance 'Vena Amoris' by using the modern technology of the mobile phone as a way of giving the two roles equal status: both have subjectivity, but both become subject to objectification. The one-to-one performance dynamic is here both embraced and exploded as Paris demonstrates the possibilities of many-to-many and one-to-many performance potentials contained within the imaginary space of the audience/performer dynamic.

Helen Paris's work is thus underpinned by theoretical questions of breaking down binary oppositions and exploring spaces 'in between'. These questions are picked up and explored further in the final chapter, 'Mouth Ghosts: The Taste of the Os-Text', by Jools Gilson-Ellis. This chapter champions women's right to write, to speak, and to interpret and perform texts written by others – including men – while also insisting that the body matters. Gilson-Ellis discusses French feminist theories of language in detail and uses them to build into her own account of the connections between orality and writing – the experience of speech and words as both textual and physical. Being careful not to discount the importance of written language, she aims to bridge the gap between text and performance by looking at textual delivery as a physical process.

Gilson-Ellis's attempt to accommodate the physical and the textual also contributes to the wider question of finding a language for documenting and theorizing performance. Gilson-Ellis, like Hill and Paris (and Prendergast in Part 1), is concerned with devising a performed, critical language. The need to find ways of describing performance in words thus becomes a necessary counterpart of the quest to use performance as a critical tool.

Onwards

This book presents a variety of voices reflecting upon a variety of experiences, but the contributors nonetheless share certain important common aims. All the writers share a commitment to finding spaces and languages for female performers. They exhibit at some level a scepticism towards old or outdated, essentialist arguments – a reluctance to see verbal language, writing and text as antithetical to women, a resistance to generalizations about female experience, and a scepticism about the value of archetypes. They often pay as much attention to process as to product and in doing so, they seek to point the way forward to further performative exploration.

Since process is important, it is important to close the introduction and set the scene for the main event by noting that this book has arisen out of occasions when women have met to explore and exchange views in text and performance: sharing physical spaces at conferences, performance festivals and other gatherings or sharing virtual spaces on the web made by women for interaction by women and men interested in the issues arising from the question of whether there is a 'women's language' in theatre. Yet the work is also aimed at a wider authorship and readership, and is published in print in an age when we all know that the printed word is only a passing mark on a page that 'goes live' on the world wide web and changes its inflection with each reading and utterance. The book is a snapshot of a group of women's ways of using words about women's ways of using words, gestures, performances. It communicates and yet it also encourages questioning, testing, and response. It is a beginning of a new process as well as an 'end product' of an eight-year process.

Many more women contributed to the process of exchange than those whose work is represented here. Each contributor is an author, each with her or his own way of using language, written, spoken, or performative. Our thanks go out to all who have taken part – this one's for you all.

Part 1 – Re-Shaping Theatre Traditions

1   Seizing Speech and Playing with Fire: Greek Mythological Heroines and International Women's Performance

Jane de Gay

Greek mythology has constituted a powerful and fascinating theatre language ever since it provided the subject matter for some of the earliest known scripted plays. As a source of exciting stories and dramatically powerful roles to enact, it has inspired much theatre exploration, both in scripted drama and unscripted performance work, including much work by women artists. However, as feminists have long pointed out, mythology needs to be approached with caution, for it has been used to enshrine ways of seeing the world, and of seeing women, which are both problematic and hard to shift. For this reason, female performers portraying mythological heroines face the perennial problem of becoming the objects of the male gaze – objects of desire, of fear, of pity. Women performers working with mythology must therefore face the challenge of shaping this theatre language without being shaped by it. Alicia Ostriker, writing about American women poets' use of mythology, commented that although language is an encoding of male privilege 'we [as women] must also have it in our power to "seize speech" and make it say what we mean.' (1982: 69) Ostriker's concern was obviously with text, but we can extend her comments to apply to the many languages of theatre, which present the more complex challenge of resisting encodings of inequality and privilege on many different levels. This chapter will explore ways in which women performers have sought to 'seize speech' by using classical mythology for their own purposes, in original pieces based on mythological material. It also considers the strategies they have used in order to avoid the ideological traps: in other words, how to play with fire without getting burned.

Mythology has inspired numerous productions by individual female performers and feminist theatre companies, and it has also been an important focus for collaborative projects among female artists internationally. For example, 'Embodying Myth/Embodying Women', an international collaboration co-ordinated by Research Theatre International, Canada, has worked with female mythic figures drawn from classical, European and North American cultures. The exploration of myths and archetypes was also the theme of a number of performances, workshops and collaborations initiated by the Magdalena Project during the 1980s and 1990s. Most notably, Magdalena's large-scale collective project, *Nominatae Filiae* (initiated at Holstebro, Denmark in 1988), involved the creation of contemporary characters based on female figures from mythology; and several pieces performed at the Magdalena Festival of 1994 drew their inspiration from classical mythology.

It is significant that this interest in exploring archetypes has often gone hand-in-hand with an interest in developing a women's language in theatre: for example, both questions were explored at many gatherings of the Magdalena Project. The search for feminine archetypes and for a 'women's language' may be read as part of a strategy for resisting the patriarchal ideology of myths, while seeking to create a women-centred space in which mythological heroines could be valued anew. These heroines have often been assumed to have something of value and significance to offer to all women, regardless of their culture – especially since Greek myths are known throughout the western world, so that performances based on them can be understood by diverse audiences, regardless of the language or languages spoken in the production.

Such an approach is increasingly seen to take an unhelpfully essentialist view of gender, for it implies a belief in an universal common denominator, an essence of womanhood which would be true in all cultures and places. This chapter will demonstrate that, in practice, much of the performance work on the Greek myths undertaken by women performers during the 1980s and 1990s was diverse and culturally specific. Rather than seeking to say something about all women, these performances often spoke about women in particular social or cultural situations, or, increasingly, they dealt with other axes of inequality than gender difference. Furthermore, it will demonstrate that the performance pieces which were most successful in resisting the ideological content of myths were those which took a critical approach to the stories of the characters (often coming close to deconstructing them), rather than seeking some kind of essence within them.

The idea of an archetype, as it was discussed in theatre meetings during the 1980s and 1990s becomes unstable on close inspection. Although an archetype is, by definition, a typical example or an original model of which later versions are copies, much theatrical work on archetypes has involved developing specific and diverse attributes of a character to respond to particular contemporary concerns and conditions. Susan Bassnett once suggested that there may be a pattern to the theatrical representations of particular mythological or historical female figures. In her address to the Magdalena Festival of 1994, she suggested that certain figures may have strong resonances at particular historical moments:

In a moment of great crisis in European culture, before the First World War, there was a fascination with Salomé and Cleopatra. It was the end of the age of imperialism, it was the moment of discovery of psychoanalysis, which linked sexuality and the mind – and the theatre was full of Cleopatras and Salomés. In the 1930s and 1940s, with the rise of Fascism, the Second World War and the recovery after the war, the theatre was full of Jeanne d'Arcs and Antigones. In the 1980s and 1990s, the theatre has been full of Medeas.

We could note that these are groupings which have become clearer with hindsight: that generalizations which it may have been possible to make about the early part of the twentieth century are more difficult to make about recent work. Indeed, although Bassnett identified female archetypes for moments of historical crisis and explained their significance for wartime audiences, she did not offer an explanation for the fascination with Medea in the theatre of the 1980s and 1990s, but instead ended her talk by posing the question 'Why ... Medea now?'. Although this question is intriguing (and will be considered below), it should be noted that Medea was by no means the only mythological figure represented in performances in the 1980s and 1990s. As this era also offered representations of Philomela, Persephone, Medusa, and Cassandra, among others, it might better be seen as one that celebrated and supported diversity. The last two decades of the twentieth century were increasingly marked by social and cultural diffusion, and so it has become less important to look for universal archetypes than to recognize that women theatre-makers in different social, economic and political realities may gravitate towards different female figures or may have different responses to the same figure. Furthermore, it is important to acknowledge that audiences might respond to these representations in manifold ways: Lizbeth Goodman's description of Dempsey and Millan's *Mary Medusa* as offering a 'persona, a shifting figure on to which we can project our interpretations freely' (Goodman, forthcoming) could apply to many of the pieces discussed here. In this chapter, I will argue that the increasing diversity of response to classical mythology is a source of strength for women seeking to make mythology their own or to make mythologies of their own.

This chapter will develop these arguments through an examination of a selection of plays and performance pieces by women from Western Europe, Australasia and North America. These are: *Persephone: Bringer of Destruction, Promise of Resurrection* by Gerd Christiansen (Norway); *The Love of the Nightingale* by Timberlake Wertenbaker (UK); *Medusa* by Dorothea Smartt (UK); *Mary Medusa* by Shawna Dempsey and Lorri Millan (Canada); a performance of Heiner Müller's *Medeamaterial* by Siân Thomas (Wales); *Altri Tempi* and *La Nozze*, both written by Raffaella Battaglini and performed by Maria Teresa Telara (Italy); *Story of the Fallen Hero* written by Guandaline Sagliocco and Gerd Christiansen, and performed by Sagliocco (Norway); *Multi-Medea*, a multi-media performance/research project by Susan Kozel (UK); and *Crow Station,* written and performed by the Toad Lilies (New Zealand).

This is by no means an exhaustive account of performance work on these themes. Rather, the pieces considered here form a broad cross-section of examples, chosen mainly because they all in some way came within the research remit of the Open

University Gender in Writing and Performance Research Group, with which I was involved from 1994–98. A number of performances discussed here were presented at the Magdalena Festival held at the Chapter Arts Centre, Cardiff, in 1994, which I was invited to document, along with other group members. The original plan of producing a journal-length documentation of the Festival did not come to fruition, but my reviews of the pieces by Thomas, Battaglini, Sagliocco, Christiansen, and the Toad Lilies, and my subsequent correspondence with several of these performers have been used as a basis for discussion in this chapter. The pieces by Wertenbaker, Smartt, and Dempsey and Millan were included in Lizbeth Goodman's edited collection, *Mythic Women/Real Women* (she also discusses them at length in her forthcoming book, *Sexuality in Performance*). Some of the theatre-makers whose work is discussed here maintained close contacts with the research group. For example, Dorothea Smartt performed part of her *Medusa* cycle ('Medusa? Medusa Black!') and Susan Kozel gave a paper on the Multi-Medea project at the Gender in Writing and Performance Research Group's 1997 conference/festival, 'Gender in the Field of Vision'.

Victims, Villains and Visionaries: The Feminist Case Against Mythology

Before looking at these productions in detail, we need to form a clearer picture of the ideological problems potentially facing these performances by examining briefly the feminist case against mythology. Firstly, classical mythology may be seen as the record of the suppression of a female culture: put very simply, it provides a set of narratives in which women are the victims. This line of criticism may be traced back to the 1920s and the work of the feminist classical scholar Jane Harrison who pointed out that classical mythology and literature were produced by the patriarchal cultures which had arisen in Greece in order to cement their victory over local matriarchal, goddess-worshipping cults (see Harrison, 1922: 257–321). The goddesses of pre-classical Greece had been represented as closely tied to the earth and independent of men: for example, Hera was a maiden and Demeter and Kore were Mother and Maiden. The victorious Olympian cult re-wrote the stories of these figures into a narrative that reflected the patriarchal family, so that Hera became the wife of Zeus, the father-god, with various other gods becoming their sons and daughters. Demeter and Kore became Mother and Daughter rather than Mother and Maiden. In this view, classical mythology celebrates the submission of matriarchal power to patriarchal.

The second part of the case against mythology is that it rehearses and substantiates a fear of women: in other words, it is a set of narratives in which women are often villains or, if they are victims, their weakness also provokes fear. This view may be traced back to Simone de Beauvoir who argued that myths have been created and upheld by men who projected their own hopes and fears onto them. In myths, men worship virile figures such as Hercules and Prometheus; women play passive, secondary roles in the stories of these heroes (de Beauvoir, 1993: 152). De Beauvoir pointed out that women are made the projection of men's fears, particularly their fear of mortality which she saw as closely linked to a patriarchal view of women's reproductive function: 'The cult of germination has always been associated with the cult of the dead. The Earth Mother engulfs the bones of her children.' (de Beauvoir, 1993: 154) Female figures have been appropriated by male authors, especially because the famous classical plays were written by men. Furthermore, the cultural history of appropriation of Greek myths by a male institutions such as the public schools, may be seen to have imposed a cultural baggage on mythological material – a popular conception of female figures – which is impossible to shift.

Feminists have adopted a number of strategies for dealing with these problems, all of which appear, to some extent, in the work of the performers under consideration. Harrison's insights have often been read in a positive way, for she has inspired many writers to find imaginative ways of reclaiming positive and affirming images of women from traditions which have buried them. This became particularly popular as a tactic amongst women writers from the 1970s onwards, given the emphasis placed by the second wave of feminism on foregrounding 'women's stories' and 'women's experience'. It can involve rejecting classical mythology in favour of a construction of what might have gone before – for example inventing and celebrating matriarchal figures like the Great Mother. However (and this is more relevant to our purposes) it can involve an attempt to reclaim positive figures of women from narratives which ultimately celebrated male victory. So, for example, it can highlight instances of female intimacy in the face of male oppression, such as the relationship between Demeter and Kore. It can also involve arresting a narrative before the point at which its female protagonist becomes a victim (or a villain): for example, celebrating the prophetic powers of Cassandra before her downfall; in other words, seeing her as a visionary.

De Beauvoir's analysis presents an even tougher challenge, for it poses the question of how to re-write demonized figures as sources of strength. It raises the question of how far women performers can reclaim or recuperate passive figures such as Philomela and Persephone – the 'victims' – or fearsome figures such as Medea (who killed her own children) or Medusa (a figure of terror who turned men into stone) – the 'villains'? One response has involved trying to see these figures as rounded characters, explaining their motives and seeking sympathy and understanding, often by exploring and critiquing the circumstances which have led to their fate. This would certainly be the approach taken by actors and directors when preparing these roles for a performance of a classical play (for example, Deborah Warner did research into child-killers while preparing to direct Euripides' *Medea* (Warner, 2001: 7)), but it can also be detected in the processes of performers drawing on classical characters to develop new performance pieces.

A more radical approach (and one which has become more prevalent in recent years) is to disavow these characters and these stories – to resist identification with these figures and their predicament altogether. This approach involves deconstructing the original stories in some way: drawing attention to the constructed nature of narrative, the fabricated nature of performance, to deny that such narratives have any relationship to reality, thus paving the way for radical re-writings. Such an approach gives a performer critical distance from which to view the original character, enabling them to perform the kind of parody described by Linda Hutcheon as 'extended repetition with critical difference' (1985: 7). More radically still, performers may be able to re-produce the roles and the stories ironically to empty them of their original meaning: in Judith Butler's terms they may be able 'to "cite" the law to produce it differently' (1993: 15). Theoretically, the idea of villainy could be turned on its head and made a badge of strength in much the same way as Butler advocates a reclaiming of the term 'queer'.

The languages of theatre provide special scope for this latter approach: both the techniques of metatheatre and the capacities of new media technologies provide performers with tools to view narratives critically. However, in all but the most radical of these cases, we may still see evidence of the first approach: if a performer is seen to enact the role of a classical mythological heroine, there tends to be an element of trying to achieve a rounded, realistic presentation of the 'character' which may work to compromise or restrict the effects of a more deconstructive approach; any embodiment of a heroine also potentially subjects the performer to the 'male gaze'.

Victims: Persephone and Philomela

The stories of Persephone and Philomela both centre on female suffering caused by male violence. Persephone (also known as Kore), the daughter of the earth goddess Demeter, was attacked by Hades and taken to the underworld. Demeter neglected her duty of making the crops grow while she looked for her daughter. Demeter found Persephone, but was only allowed to bring her back to earth for part of the year: her mourning during the part of the year when Persephone was in the underworld was used as an explanation of the seasons. Although the figure of Persephone is a passive victim, and although Demeter's suffering may be seen as a challenge to female power, feminists have sought to read this story as a testimony to the strength of the love between mother and daughter.

The story of Philomela, as told by Ovid in *Metamorphoses,* similarly deals with female friendship and male aggression. Philomela is raped by Tereus, the husband of her sister Procne; he cuts out her tongue to prevent her from telling, but she lets her sister know by weaving a tapestry that narrates the event. Philomele kills Tereus' son Itys in revenge, assisted by Procne. When Tereus goes to strike the sisters, all three are turned into birds: Tereus becomes a hoopoe, Philomela a nightingale and Procne a swallow.

The challenge for women theatre-makers in retelling stories such as these lies in avoiding objectifying these female figures as victims while also preventing the audience from identifying themselves with the victims in a disempowering way. Commenting on early to mid twentieth-century responses to mythology, Susan Gubar notes that key strategies used by women writers in dealing with Persephone included emphasizing the importance of mother/daughter love and giving the protagonists interiority, in order to 'insist that the female role, while tragic, is not as passive as the original myth would imply' (1979: 306). Although Gubar's argument may appear essentialist to twenty-first century readers, her emphasis upon interiority draws attention to an important problem facing any female performer dealing with the story of a victim: how to present a suffering female figure – physically, on stage – without rendering her a powerless object of pity. A more recent theoretical approach might be to explode the mythology – to deny the reality of the myth as a narrative for women's lives, by deconstructing it as text and narrative – but this is not entirely possible (or perhaps desirable) in the performance context. This section will explore how far these challenges have been met in Gerd Christiansen's solo performance *Persephone: Bringer of Destruction, Promise of Resurrection* and Timberlake Wertenbaker's dramatization of Philomela's story, *The Love of the Nightingale*.

Gerd Christiansen's *Persephone: Bringer of Destruction, Promise of Resurrection* sought to give interiority to its protagonist in a similar way to that detected by Gubar in women writers. It did so by means of a set that reflected Persephone's mental landscape in a way that enabled the audience to share it (figure 1.1).[1] The set used predominantly autumnal colours, which were symbolic of a season in which the crops begin to die away, but also evocative of the underworld. The performance space was surrounded by moving models, which were lit from offstage by bright lights so that dark, moving shadows were projected onto the space, and onto the performer's body. This was suggestive of a dreamscape, as Christiansen noted in a letter:

> I use the shadows to refer to mental images, thus transcribing the myth to an inner state of transfixion (or winter) where the projections have taken control. In that state there is no understanding of the relation between light and darkness and the seasons have not yet been installed.
>
> (Personal correspondence, April 1996)

The dreamscape took on a nightmarish quality, with many of the mobiles taking the shape of animals that appeared to attack the performer. The performance used no text at all, and the soundtrack for the piece consisted of eerie, mechanical noises rather than music, so that the audience felt subjected to the torture that Persephone was suffering. In her programme notes, Christiansen admitted to a Jungian influence on her work, and declared that her aim was 'to enter the landscapes of some major feminine archetypes and to recapture the images of strength, chaos, and contradiction that still remain in our modern psyche.' Thus, the audience were drawn to empathize with Persephone's experience, and encouraged to relate it to their own experiences. As Christiansen noted: 'In my work it is important that an opening exists for each spectator to link the personal images to their personal experiences.' (ibid.)

Figure 1.1. Gerd Christiansen in 'Persephone: Bringer of Destruction, Promise of Resurrection'. Photo: Marit-Anna Evanger

Figure 1.2. Gerd Christiansen in 'Persephone: Bringer of Destruction, Promise of Resurrection'. Photo: Marit-Anna Evanger.

Ironically, although Christiansen's performance depicted an internal landscape, the extent to which this performance achieved interiority is debatable, because the centrepiece of the performance was the figure of Persephone (played by Christiansen), with her limbs and hair tied with ropes and trapped within a space (figure 1.2). She writhed around the space, as though fighting the shadows – animal shapes which approached her with a violence suggestive of rape and wheels that seemed to threaten to grind her down. As Christiansen noted in her letter: 'In the version told by Homer, the interpretations of the event are quite layered: it can be seen as the initiation to sexuality or as rape.' (ibid.) An audience watching this may be caught in a double bind: it can enter into Persephone's interior life and share her experience of rape, or of sexual initiation, which led to entrapment. Alternatively, the audience could objectify Persephone and gaze on a female body held in place for public consumption. Significantly, too, this performance did not include Demeter, and so the celebration of mother-daughter relations that Susan Gubar detected in many re-tellings of this myth was not present. *Persephone: Bringer of Destruction, Promise of Resurrection* depicted a woman alone, struggling with sexuality and the fear of rape without the hope of maternal protection.

Timberlake Wertenbaker's *The Love of the Nightingale,* on the other hand, took a more critical approach in order to interrogate the nature of victimization in a re-telling of Philomela's story.[2] Wertenbaker recasts Ovid's tale as drama, but more specifically as a parody of Greek drama which, as Jennifer Wagner has pointed out, enables her to make a critique both of theatrical form and of the myth itself. A key feature of this parody is Wertenbaker's use of the chorus to comment on events, urging the audience critically to consider what it sees. There are two choruses, one male, one female. The Male Chorus is a group of unnamed speakers who narrate the plot and raise moral questions. The Female Chorus is made up of named individuals, Procne's companions, who speak cryptically, but (to an audience which knows the outcome of the story) foretell events accurately. For example, they try to tell Procne that they sense danger (which the audience knows means the rape of Philomele), but Procne cannot understand them and dismisses their fears (Scene 9). However, the Female Chorus's refusal to provide a simple meaning is vindicated at the end of the play. Their final speech is suitably open-ended, for they leave the audience with 'some questions that have no answers' (Wertenbaker, 1996: 348), such as why countries wage war and why some peoples are silenced and oppressed. Thus, Wertenbaker succeeds in allowing distinctively female voices to be heard in her play. She also hints at her heroines' interiority in a similar way by showing them in intimate conversation together, such as in the second scene in the play where (before Procne's marriage) they talk freely and openly about their attitudes towards marriage and sexuality.

The play places its audience very carefully in relation to the violence that takes place. Philomele's rape is not depicted onstage, but is narrated by her servant Niobe who overhears the act ('Oh dear, oh dear, she shouldn't scream like that. It only makes it worse. Too tense. More brutal. … There. It's finished now.' (ibid.: 330). This is in keeping with the tradition of Greek drama where violence was not portrayed onstage, but it also avoids the objectification of a female character as rape victim. Instead, Philomele as rape survivor tells Procne about the incident by using the theatrical device of a puppet show (instead of the tapestry used in Ovid's story). Philomele and Niobe manipulate life-sized dolls of Philomele and Tereus to depict the rape in a manner described in the stage directions as 'gross and comic' (ibid.: 342). This acting-style treats male violence with derision.

However, the silencing is more graphically illustrated, for Tereus cuts out Philomele's tongue onstage. She depicts this in her puppet show by means of 'a very brutal illustration' of the severing of her tongue, followed by the dropping of a bloodied cloth onto the floor (ibid.). The play thus shows that the silencing of oppressed people – normally an unspoken, unacknowledged action – is a hideous crime. In the puppet-show sequence, the languages of theatre provide the means for a brutally silenced woman to speak out.

The climate of male violence against women is so clearly established that Philomele's murder of Tereus's son Itys is seen as an act of self-defence. The women are holding a private Bacchic ceremony: Itys spies on them and, on seeing a slave woman holding his sword, he rushes in to stop the meeting. His murder, like Philomele's rape, is first shown second-hand. We are introduced to it when we see a soldier spying on Itys's intrusion into the ceremony and being horrified by what he sees. In the next scene, we see the killing itself, where Itys rushes in aggressively, and Procne seizes him. The chorus gather around Philomele as she strikes him, and the truth is only disclosed gradually, when Philomele is revealed with bloodied hands and then the body of Itys is uncovered. Tereus accuses Procne of the killing, but she speaks out against him to point out that the murder is a result of his own actions: 'You bloodied the future. For all of us. We don't want it.' (ibid.: 351) The moral climate of this play prevents the female characters from appearing either as victims or as monsters and the killing of Itys acts as a warning of the sort of violence which may ensue when groups are victimized and denied a voice.

Wertenbaker makes it clear that the situation she depicts in *The Love of the Nightingale* is not unique to women. As she notes in her introduction to her *Plays: One*, the play was inspired by other manifestations of inequality:

Although it has been interpreted as being about women, I was actually thinking about the violence that erupts in societies when they have been silenced for too long. Without language, brutality will triumph. I grew up in the Basque country, where the language was systematically silenced, and it is something that always haunts me.

(Wertenbaker 1996: viii–ix)

Thus the play deals with political oppression in general in that it has resonances for many silenced groups, including women, with specific implications for Wertenbaker's experience of the situation of the Basque people. The wide-ranging relevance of the story is reinforced by the female Chorus in their final scene:

> Helen: Why are races exterminated?
> Hero: Why do white people cut off the words of blacks?
> Iris: Why do people disappear? The ultimate silence.
> Echo: Not even death recorded.

(Wertenbaker, 1996: 349)

Issues of language and silence are central to Wertenbaker's treatment of mythology in this play. In a telling exchange, the male chorus draws attention to the ways in which mythology is a form of ideology:

> – What is a myth? The oblique image of an unwanted truth, reverberating through time.
> – And yet, the first, the Greek meaning of myth, is simply what is delivered by word of mouth, a myth is speech, public speech.
> – And myth also means the matter itself, the content of the speech.
> – We might ask, has the content become increasingly unacceptable and therefore the speech more indirect? How has the meaning of myth been transformed from public speech to an unlikely story? It also meant counsel, command. Now it is a remote tale.
> – Let that be, there is no content without its myth. ...

(ibid.: 315)

Thus the play comments on the process by which something which might at one time have been public speech, and accepted fact, has now become dressed up as stories which nonetheless perpetuate 'unwanted truth' in the retelling. The metatheatrical aspects of Wertenbaker's play, in which the Chorus plays a part, draw attention to the need to be aware of the workings of ideologies and to step back and consider what we see.

The case-studies in this section show that mythological victims may be treated in different ways and with different effects. Of the two, *Persephone: Bringer of Destruction, Promise of Resurrection* took a more archetypal approach, which was problematic for threatening to disempower both performer and female viewer, while *The Love of the Nightingale* countered the ideological implications of its story by exploring the myth and the myth-making process in critical ways. *The Love of the Nightingale* was able to address the victimization of its protagonist more directly; *Persephone: Bringer of Destruction, Promise of Resurrection* was more static for it sought to explore a state of mind without reflecting on how the victimization had come about. As a result, Wertenbaker is able to put victimization in context and draw lessons from it. This is partly because she could ask direct questions and make clear points in a scripted play, where a performance piece had to rely solely on actions. In Wertenbaker's play the Chorus was particularly important in drawing attention to the messages of the play and to the audience's role. However, its success also lies in its control over the power of the gaze: thus, for example, where *Persephone: Bringer of Destruction, Promise of Resurrection* presents the spectacle of the suffering and confined female body, *The Love of the Nightingale* presents violence against women in the darkly comic sequence of the puppet show. While *Persephone: Bringer of Destruction, Promise of Resurrection* was a powerful piece which invited the audience to explore a state of mind, *The Love of the Nightingale* liberated the audience from identifying with Philomela's status as victim and pointed out the lessons to be learned from her predicament.

Villains: Medusa and Medea

The figures of Medusa and Medea are chiefly thought of as villains, as women horrifying to men, but what is often forgotten is that both were visionaries and victims too. According to Ovid, Medusa had once been beautiful but her face was made ugly and her hair was turned into snakes after she was raped by the sea god Poseidon. She was feared by men because it was said that one look from her could turn them to stone, but Perseus managed to kill her when he struck off her head without looking at her. Like the myths of Persephone and Philomela, the story of Medusa is a record of male violence against women, but may also be interpreted as celebrating female strengths. Joan Coldwell (1985) has pointed out (in an argument drawing on Jane Harrison's ideas) that the figure of Medusa represented primitive Greek matriarchal religions. The Medusa mask was worn by the women priests of a female cult to frighten men away from their ceremonies. Coldwell argues that the myth of Perseus cutting the head off a gorgon was propagated to celebrate the arrival of the patriarchal Hellenes, who tore down goddess shrines and tore masks off the priests, symbolizing the end of goddess worship and arrival of male gods and heroes (Coldwell, 1985: 423). She also notes that in the twentieth century, misogynistic views of Medusa were perpetuated by Freud, who argued that she embodied a castration threat. Feminists have sought to embrace the figure of Medusa as a figure of strength for women: Hélène Cixous's essay 'The Laugh of the Medusa' is a notable example of this, in which she argues that women can laugh at men because they have no fear of castration. As Coldwell summarizes it: 'Under the impact of feminism, a negative horror image of woman as a literally petrifying monster has been triumphantly embraced as an emblem not of abasement but of exaltation.' (1985: 423) This process has been taken further with the kind of postmodern irony described by Judith Butler (1993) as 'ironic citation' or by Elin Diamond (1996) as 'mimesis' – mimicking conventional representations to question their validity. In practice, however, even performances which took an ironic approach tended also to explore Medusa as a positive role model, as well as acknowledging her status as a victim and finding ways around seeing her as a villain.

The problem of dealing with the negative side of a character is also faced by performers who work with Medea. Like Medusa, Medea was once a figure of great power and dignity, but her story is one of defeat and revenge, in which she became a

demonic monster. In the myth, Medea was a magician who used her powers to help
Jason fulfil the tasks set for him by her father, Aeetes King of Colchis, in order to win
the Golden Fleece. She then helped him to escape from Aeetes and they married and
had two children. However, the second, more negative, part of Medea's story is better
known, because of Euripides's drama *Medea*. Jason tired of Medea and arranged to
marry Glauke, the daughter of Creon, King of Corinth. Medea's fury over this led
Creon to banish her from Corinth, but she pleaded for a day's respite, during which
time she contrived the deaths of Creon and Glauke. Then (in a twist which Euripides
added to the original myth (Just, 1989: 273, 297)) Medea killed her own children –
partly to spite Jason and partly to prevent them from being captured by their enemies –
before escaping to Athens. Of the two aspects of the story, the latter has attracted the
greater interest amongst theatre makers: the challenge of justifying Medea's crime and
eliciting sympathy for her plight proves a greater attraction than the chance to
celebrate a woman's power over a man.

Dorothea Smartt's solo multimedia performance *Medusa* both looks back to the
origins of the myth and seeks to make it relevant to issues in the present day. [3] Smartt
performs Medusa against the backdrop of a slide-show by Sherlee Mitchell in which
images of Medusa's mask are prevalent. The image of the mask points back to the ritual
mask worn by worshippers of the mother goddess to scare away men, but, as Smartt
explained, it also took on several different meanings as the performance evolved:

> To me, the mask represents being someone you're not – sometimes for
> protection, sometimes out of fear of sanction, because it may feel safer to pretend
> to be something 'safer'. Pretending comes naturally, at some level, for all of us
> who have had to fit in somehow, even when we don't look like we belong. The
> mask is a powerful disguise, especially Medusa's.
> I decided to find out what the mask of Medusa would be like. I wrote
> fragments about her image and the power it had for me, and also did research to
> find out more about her. I discovered she was a Libyan princess, a black woman,
> an outcast. … All the strands became entwined.
>
> (Goodman 1996d: 198)

Smartt thus combined her exploration of classical history with a search for its relevance
in the present day. As a woman of African parentage growing up in Brixton, London,
Smartt could relate to the historical Medusa as a black woman and also drew
inspiration from the idea of the mask as a way of hiding one's true identity in order to
fit in. Smartt also acknowledges the need for a mask as a way of 'being someone you're
not': implicitly drawing on her experience as a lesbian often faced with the challenge of
what Judith Butler (1993: 167–85) has called 'passing' in straight society. Thus, Smartt
draws on Medusa's adversities, but also on her strengths, so that at the end of the
second phase of the performance she can declare: 'Medusa is my shield, impregnable.'

The most poignant example of Smartt drawing on Medusa as a form of protection,
whilst also contending with her negative image and the threat of violence is 'Medusa?
Medusa Black!', a performance poem which forms part of the cycle. Smartt's Brixton

neighbours called her Medusa when she started wearing her hair in dreadlocks. In the poem, cosmetic processes for treating hair – in particular, the methods used to mould negroid hair into Caucasian styles – are a synecdoche for racial abuse:

fuck it wild haired woman
straighten it fry it desperately burn scalps
banish the snake-woman
the wild-woman
the all-seeing-eye woman

(Smartt, 2000: 262)

However, Smartt draws a source of power from the insult, for, as this quotation shows, the neighbours' jibes may be seen as an expression of their fear of Medusa's power. Thus, Smartt 'cites' the term of abuse, throwing it back at her tormentors so that the poem becomes a defiant celebration of her African identity: 'Medusa! Medusa black? / Medusa was a Blackwoman' (ibid.: 261). Smartt further celebrates her identity in a direct and positive way by writing the poem in the Bajan dialect of her parents: she declared that she found her voice with this poem, by using the dialect for the first time (Goodman, 1996d: 198). This celebration of identity is reinforced in performance, for Smartt wears a striking, colourful traditional Bajan costume to present this work, thus openly, publicly performing her African identity.

Smartt thus uses Medusa to perform many sides of her identity – as a woman, as an African, and as a lesbian. Her use of multi-media, combining projected images, movement, installation, costumes, poetry and movement, enhances this multi-faceted presentation of Medusa and her capacity to find ways to survive, including subterfuge. As Goodman (1996d: 191) notes, such an ability to push back boundaries was a feature of much of the performance work on Medusa in the 1990s: the figure of Medusa thus becomes a dynamic way of challenging concepts of difference and otherness.

Shawna Dempsey and Lorri Millan also use multi-media to explore different aspects of the Medusa myth in their performance *Mary Medusa*. [4] The full piece consists of a video, two slide/performance pieces, five short performances and one short story. Shawna Dempsey plays Medusa in all of these, each one offering a different perspective on the character. However, where Smartt performed Medusa openly and proudly in her African costume, Dempsey's Medusa is strangely disembodied, for a prominent feature of this performance is her floating head. She asks, 'Is a woman without a body in fact a woman?', and remarks that the bodiless Medusa is 'not very ninetiessssssss.' Dempsey's floating head appears with her hair in large curlers to represent the snake, suggesting a comic response to the myth, while poking fun at the cosmetic processes to which women traditionally have subjected their hair. It is also, as Lizbeth Goodman (forthcoming) points out 'a reversal of an obvious way of looking at Medusa' – the mythical heroine decapitated by Perseus – for it is 'not the body without the head, but rather the head without the body.' This image prevents the objectification of the female body, and responds ironically to those who view women as bodies only, with no regard for their minds or voices.

Like Smartt's piece, *Mary Medusa* is concerned with the violence which may ensue from cross-cultural encounters. This is exemplified by the short story part of the sequence. In this tale, Mary Medusa is a Greek girl growing up in Canada in the 1950s. She is brought up to be proud of her heritage – 'I was a Greek. I was a descendant of Zeus.' (Dempsey and Millan, 2000: 249) – but she soon learns to be an outcast, for her family are shunned as immigrants and her parents are interned at the time of the Cuban Missile Crisis. She is disowned by her adopted mother, then raped by her employer's husband and sacked because of it, echoing Medusa's rape by Poseidon (although as Goodman (2000: xxix) points, out there are also shades of Philomela, especially as she is stunned into silence by the act: 'I stopped talking'). Mary Medusa's response is to try to live as a man, but that fails and, once again, she is sacked from her job. She finds peace by rediscovering her ethnic identity (remembering the stories she had learned as a child) and becoming Medusa:

> As I turned to greet my true self in the window's reflection, each snakey lock reached out to me. 'You're invincible,' they said. 'You're horrible. You're safe.' A smile grew up from deep within me, and spread like the mask of a jack-o'-lantern across my face. My eyes bulged and my tongue grew. I laughed as I thought that now, anything was possible. I could go forth into the world simply as me, unquestioned and unassaulted, my resplendent ugliness as my shield.
>
> (Dempsey and Millan, 2000: 254–5)

Like Cixous's Medusa, this protagonist can laugh at the world. She dresses expensively and takes a powerful job, resuming a female identity, but with 'a look that *Cosmopolitan* describes as assertively feminine.' (ibid.: 256) Within a year her boss is dead (in a darkly comic allusion to the Medusa myth, he is frozen in rigor mortis at his desk), and she becomes president of the company. However, the ending hints at the threat of Perseus: 'Realistically, my days are numbered.' (ibid.: 257) Dempsey and Millan deal with this negative story by drawing from it a celebration of female strength – but they also issue a warning of the need for vigilance. While claiming the power of the Medusa, the protagonist negotiates its fearful reputation: 'because I look very much like a woman (with the exception of my snakey hair) it is accepted that I know my place.' (Dempsey and Millan, 2000: 256)

These two pieces demonstrate how the differing cultural backgrounds of the performers contribute to this diversity of responses to myths. Although both performances about Medusa raised issues of alienation, Dorothea Smartt clearly linked this to her experience as a woman of African descent living in London, while Dempsey and Millan depicted the otherness of an European in America. Both pieces recuperated Medusa by claiming her as a powerful role model – Smartt did this assertively, Dempsey and Millan did it with comedy. However, both acknowledged the negative side of the Medusa's story: Smartt by acknowledging but speaking back to the abuse of her neighbours; Dempsey and Millan by chronicling the violence suffered by the protagonist and hinting at the suppression to come.

*

The task of rehabilitating Medea is more difficult than that of reclaiming Medusa, because her story involves the taboo of child murder. Despite this, female performers are drawn to Medea's crime rather than her earlier, more positive, work as a magician. The first three pieces considered here were all presented at the Magdalena Festival of 1994. Of these, two focused solely on the second half of the story; the third piece, which explored the earlier part, was more concerned with Jason than Medea. Siân Thomas's solo performance of part of Heiner Müller's *Medeamaterial* (in a Spanish translation) depicted the scene of Medea's anger and revenge, and Raffaella Battaglini's *Altri Tempi* presented a traumatized Medea looking back on the tragic events in late middle age. Both of these were monologues and so could be seen as giving Medea a voice and a platform to express her feelings. However, this was more obviously the case with *Altri Tempi,* which was written and performed by women and, as we shall see, informed by concerns to develop distinctly female modes of expression. *Medeamaterial* was written by a man and Thomas acknowledged Müller's mediating role for she described the plays as 'based on the Medea and Jason myth, but seen through Heiner Müller's filter.'[5] The question of giving Medea a voice in these particular performances was complicated by the fact that, when they were performed at the Magdalena Festival – an international gathering where participants did not share a common language – a proportion of the audience would only respond to the *sound* of the actor's voice and to her body language. Although Battaglini distributed handouts including translations of her play in a selection of European languages, in general, audience members had to rely upon their knowledge of the myth to appreciate the content of the plays.

Thomas's performance was a powerful piece of verbal and expressive theatre. The piece began in total darkness as she struck chords on a piano in the orchestra pit and sang in a deep voice, aching with sadness. In a dark, expectant theatre, the sequence created tension, even fear. Thomas then took to the stage, which remained in darkness throughout, except for red or green spotlights on her face (the rest of her body was largely confined to the shadows). The monologue came across as a powerful piece of voice-work, with vocal expression creating the mood as the character worked up gradually into greater and greater anger, interspersed with bitter laughter. Facial expressions were also powerful, as Thomas's furious contortions were exaggerated by the play of light and dark shadows across her face. The sonorous power of the presentation meant that attention was concentrated on the naked emotions of anger, bitterness and suffering.

In an interview, Thomas confirmed that her chief interest in the piece resided in its possibilities for stagecraft. She explained that one of the attractions of the piece is that 'it illustrates in a very direct manner the possibilities in my voice.' When asked whether there was anything special about the story of Medea, she responded strongly:

> No, not at all. In a way, I don't give a damn about Medea! The text by Heiner Müller is so powerful in itself that if you start interpreting the character all you do is confuse the issue. When I first approached the text, I didn't speak Spanish very well, so I approached it as a piece of music. If you see my script, it is full of

musical directions, *pianissimo, fortissimo, crescendo* – that was a collaboration between me and the director. We did talk vaguely about Medea, her revenge and her rebellion but I never worked on her as a character in a psychological sense, as in fact I never do for any other performance. (ibid.)

The emphasis on the music of speech over language and understanding in this statement bears out the audience's experience of the performance of *Medeamaterial* at the festival. This might imply that Thomas's performance subverted the male playwright's interpretation of the character by making the female voice and female face central to the performance. However, Thomas did not, in fact, dismiss Müller's text, but admitted that it is 'powerful'. She went on to explain that she took a conscious decision to let Müller's words speak for themselves, and not to engage with the character herself:

After I had been playing Medea for a year, I started interpreting it and got into a disastrous mess. I asked the director for advice and he said, 'Stop "acting", go back to the words. Before you go on stage each night, read over the text as if you had never seen it before.' As soon as I started doing that, all of the pseudo-emotional stuff disappeared. What the words are saying is so powerful that I don't need to put in any more nuances or meanings. It is as outrageously simple as that. That nakedness is where the strength of it lies.

The Medea story – who Medea was and why she was going to kill Jason's new girlfriend and why she was going to kill her sons – is always there in the back of your mind and there are always life experiences which you can fuel that with. I'm sure that any woman who has been through an emotional crisis with her partner would be able to relate to Medea. A few times I have had to be very careful not to fuel the emotion, but my personal option has been not to mix my private emotions with this text. (ibid.)

Thomas approached the text on a sonorous level, rather than concentrating on the emotional or psychological content of the words. Although she suggests that some women spectators might want to relate to Medea, she insists that it is not the performer's job to infuse the text with personal significance. What emerges, then, is an enabling disavowal of Medea, and one which is at the subtlest end of the scale of what Elin Diamond (1996) has described as the feminist concept of mimesis. Heiner Müller's filter does not so much cut the modern performer and her audience off from their 'mythic mother', but it prevents unhelpful identification; in effect resisting the temptation to make Medea an archetype. Müller's text itself resists simplistic accounts of Medea's story as one of female experience or anger, for, as Bernard Turner has pointed out, the Medea of this play wishes to be removed from a gendered, political context: 'I want to break mankind into two parts / And live in the empty middle I / No woman no man.' (Turner, 1999: 213). In Müller's play, Turner argues, 'the Medea who commits the atrocities is already, and paradoxically, disembodied and undead, in her body but no longer the agent of its actions, working through but not for it' (ibid.: 214). Siân Thomas's performance, where her face rather than her body was in the spotlight, helped to bring out this sense of disembodiment, and (like Dempsey and Millan's Medusa) resisted the spectacle of Medea as a demonized female body objectified for the audience.

The story of Medea was re-told for a more straightforwardly feminist purpose in Raffaella Battaglini's *Altri Tempi*. Unlike Siân Thomas, Battaglini admitted that 'the character of Medea has always interested me a good deal'. In *Altri Tempi*, there is an attempt to bring Medea down to earth. Whereas Thomas presented Medea to the audience through the naked emotion of her voice, using staging which set Medea apart from the audience and the everyday world, Battaglini and Telara made Medea accessible by representing her as a contemporary woman. Battaglini describes her Medea in detail in her stage directions: 'Woman around 50, humble, dressed carelessly, traces of former beauty. Seated, her arms crossed.' The actor, Maria Teresa Telara, wore a rather ordinary costume of a white blouse, black skirt, heeled shoes and stockings, contributing to this sense of the everyday. Telara performed the text in a conversational style. Seated throughout the monologue, she used gestures and tones of voice as though conversing with the audience. By presenting Medea as a naturalistic contemporary character, *Altri Tempi* can be seen to follow the approach of Franca Rame and Dario Fo who in the 1970s presented Medea as a contemporary woman-next-door in *A Woman Alone*; or even the later example of Magdalena's *Nominatae Filiae* which involved the creation of contemporary characters based on Medea and Cassandra, among others. The play thus invited comparisons between Medea's anger and her fate and the situation of modern women.

Altri Tempi was also feminist in its attempt to find distinctive female verbal and theatrical languages. In a talk given at the Magdalena Festival, Battaglini explained that she was interested in mythological figures because they enabled her to explore ways of thinking and feeling she saw as 'particularly female':

I am interested in how memory functions, particularly what I call the processes of 'remotion' which I feel are particularly female. These processes concern our ability to transform or forget, or to deceive ourselves in order to remember only the things we can live with.

This is strongly reflected in the writing, which is made up of interruptions and digressions. It is as if there was a very hot point at the centre of her memory which she keeps approaching, only to retreat far away immediately. The writing is very fragmented and made up of continuous repetitions because her mind functions in a circular way – continually coming back to the same point and then going away from it.

The features of female theatre language which Battaglini identifies – interruptions, digressions, fragmentation, repetition and circularity – are all aspects of Hélène Cixous's definition of *écriture féminine*, and these are much in evidence in the script:

WOMAN: (without emphasis) There. It was there. (Doesn't point. Pause.) The kitchen used to be there. You wouldn't think so now, would you? (Pause.) Can

you imagine it? What it was like before, the old house, and all the rest …
(Moved) Blessed walls! As I've always said … (suddenly distracted) What was I
saying (coming to) Ah, yes: as I've always said, there is nothing like …
(interrupts. In a worldly tone) By the way, can I offer you something? I'm afraid
I don't have much, but anyway … (as if she'd had an answer) No? Not even a
coffee? (slightly anxious) Now where was I? (relieved) Oh yes: as I've always
said, there's nothing – absolutely nothing that is like … (interrupts again)[6]

The monologue is fragmentary for it is constantly interrupted, not only by the speaker
changing the subject, but, significantly, by non-verbal elements, including gesture,
facial expression and tone of voice. The text resists signification – not only in its
frequent repetition of the word nothing, but even in the opening when the character
says 'there' but does not point, thus refusing to give deictic meaning to the words. This
resistance is important for Battaglini's treatment of the figure of Medea. On one hand,
the female character in the monologue displays a naturalistic urge not to remember
something painful; on the other, Battaglini's text disrupts and shatters the master
narrative as told by Euripides. Indeed, the entire monologue does not give us much of
the narrative beyond Medea's memories of talking to Jason as he stood by the door
and getting her children ready for bed, and her present-day fears that she can see
ghosts in the ruins of her house. Thus the play does not engage with Medea's crime,
and prevents the audience from identifying with it either.

Battaglini further grapples with Euripides by quoting his words in her text in a way
which renders them problematic:

The work on memory is done on two levels: the level of the subjective memory
(which I have just described) and the theatre memory, our relationship with the
archetypal character. That manifests itself in Medea when the words of Euripides
come up as if from a great distance. The Medea in my play does not remember
these words: it is as if in that moment the contemporary character I have created
goes back and really becomes Medea.

This process is illustrated in the closing lines of the play, when Medea is in dialogue
with the narrator's voice:

Bad thoughts, that's the problem … Oh, but I know how to send them away. Yes,
yes. I always manage … (Long pause. Narrator's voice) It was a beautiful June
morning. While we were leaving the coast, the sparkle of the sea … (interrupts,
ashamed) Old memories … Rubbish. Please forgive me. (Pause. In a softer voice,
trying to remember) Alas … pierce through my head … flame of the sky …
(interrupts. Anguished) But what was I saying? (Pause. Takes up again, with
effort) Oh yes: the kitchen used to be there. (Makes a vague gesture with her
hand.) Can you imagine it? What it was like before, the old house, and all the rest
…
BLACKOUT

There are two main echoes from Euripides here: in the first, the actor takes on the narrator's voice; but in the second 'Alas … pierce through my head … flame of the sky' she recites Medea's own words from Euripides' play. Yet in both cases, she dismisses those words. Euripides' play is quoted in a way which renders it fragmentary too. Note that these closing lines echo the opening lines, quoted earlier – *Altri Tempi* is circular, but it implies that theatre history may be circular too, for plays are repeated time after time. The fissure between theatricality and realism implied here suggests that Battaglini, like Thomas, is interested in Medea as performance. Like Thomas' performance, this play exposes the juxtaposition between real-life analogues to the myths, which often encourage identification, and theatrical figures which may invite identification but which may also be distanced by the alienating effects of the stage. Thus, Battaglini also makes a reflexive treatment of theatre tradition, comparable to Timberlake Wertenbaker's metatheatre in *The Love of the Nightingale,* in order to invite the audience to critically evaluate the myth and the literary tradition which has perpetuated it.

Medea appeared in more of a marginal role in Guandaline Sagliocco and Gerd Christiansen's *Story of the Fallen Hero.* In their performers' notes, Sagliocco and Christiansen wrote that they came to the myth of Jason and the Golden Fleece while working on the theme of 'Hero Facing Dragon'. They admitted that 'while we acknowledged its connection to the Medea tragedy, we were more deeply concerned with Jason, whose story touched us deeply.' Yet, here again, the story was approached through conscious and stylized use of the languages of performance. *Story of the Fallen Hero,* a one-woman show by Sagliocco, placed its greatest emphasis on storytelling, for she appeared as a raconteur presenting the earlier part of Medea's story and her encounter with the Argonauts. Sagliocco tells the story, mainly in French, in the voices of a variety of female narrators, including Hestia, the eldest of the goddesses on Olympus who control events, and Nannie, the servant of the goddesses, who stows away on the Argo. The figure of Nannie thus becomes a comic infiltrator in the heroic world of men. As Hestia, Sagliocco used a shadow box to tell the story of Jason, working puppets to suggest Hestia's control over the fate of the Argonauts. Using a white curtain, she created a variety of scenes in shadow-play in what was generally a comic and entertaining performance. While the play in general was a comic challenge to the male tradition, her presentation of Medea contrasted with the rest of the play: it was physical and used powerful voice-work to create a sad picture of a tragic heroine. Exiting as Medea, Sagliocco drew across a red curtain, rather than the white curtain used for the rest of the production, to suggest a bloody crime. If the tradition was critiqued, Medea still remained, in some senses, the villain of the piece: although clearly more a theatre villain than a realistic female character.

The three performances discussed here all employed very different styles and techniques, and gave Medea different attributes: in the first, anger; in the second, sadness; in the third, the character was both angry and sad, but her chief interest was from a narrative point of view as one of the villains of the piece. The diversity in approach means that although, as Susan Bassnett noted, Medea was a popular figure in the theatre in the early 1990s, there may be no simple answer to Bassnett's question of 'why … Medea now?', other than to say that Medea is an intriguing figure, and that the problem of how to present her in theatre is one which continues to perplex theatre workers. Indeed, the contemporary relevance of the three pieces discussed here is debatable: *Medeamaterial* was first performed in 1982 and *Altri Tempi* arose out of Battaglini's long-standing interest in the character. *Story of the Fallen Hero* had a contemporary relevance, but this concerned Jason rather than Medea. As Sagliocco and Christiansen noted in their performers' notes:

> When we began work on the piece, the Gulf War had just ended and we found a number of parallels with Jason's story – history was repeating itself. The image of the ship from far away, full of the most ambitious heroes of our civilization with the mission of saving the treasure (the oil) from the monster. The war reminded us of the image of the hero throwing a magic stone into the middle of the dragon-men, to make them cruelly destroy each other. Finally the heroes left the Gulf with their treasure safe – but the war continued.

Although all three performances treated Medea differently in physical terms, all could be seen to challenge the objectification of women in performance. In the piece by Thomas, only the face was fully visible, avoiding the objectification of the woman's body on stage; also, her barrage of words directed at the audience created an element of confrontation. In Battaglini's play, Medea was represented as a modern woman, but her direct address to the audience avoided objectification by implicating the audience by addressing them directly in conversational terms. *Story of the Fallen Hero* presented Medea as part of a tableau: although she was played by the performer, her appearance in robes acted as a disguise.

As Helen Paris suggests in chapter eight of this volume, a more satisfactory solution to the problem of the objectification of female performers could be found through exploiting the possibilities of new media. This possibility arises in a very different response to Medea: Susan Kozel's *Multi-Medea*, a cycle of works-in-progress which form the performance strand of *Electromythologies,* a research project on dance, technology and philosophy which Kozel is conducting at the University of Surrey. Kozel's project gets around some of the problems of dealing with Medea by not confronting the myth directly: the project is 'not a direct evocation of the Medea myth', but instead explores issues of myth-making (Kozel, 1998: 300). Like Dorothea Smartt's adoption of Medusa, Kozel takes one aspect of the Medea figure: in this case, she is seen to represent 'an alternate ontology, ethics and set of physical abilities' (ibid.: 300–1). Kozel also envisages the Multi-Medea as a hacker: a transgressor determined to infiltrate and scramble the codes of those on the inside (ibid.: 301). Kozel counters ideology by translating the myth radically, deconstructing the myth as narrative, for she sees Medea as an 'alien or a cyborg', a term she defines in Donna Haraway's terms as 'a condensed image of both imagination and material reality' (Haraway, 1991: 150; quoted Kozel, 1998: 300). Since this multi-media project uses images of the performer's body, but also uses digital technology to change that body and its performance, it could be said to mediate the way in which the viewer sees the performer, thus mitigating the disempowering effects of the 'male gaze'.

The pieces discussed here offer examples of a variety of strategies for presenting villains. The first, found in the pieces on Medusa, is to turn her negative attributes around, by making her fearful and dangerous image a source of strength – although both performances acknowledged, to an extent, that the negative side of the character was difficult to overcome. Medea proved more difficult to handle: Raffaella Battaglini sought to handle her sympathetically by depicting her as traumatized; but all three of the 'live' performances on Medea sought, in some way, to evoke the figure without fully engaging with her crime. Susan Kozel comes closest to recuperating the myth of Medea, but only by taking her image and 'morphing' it into something else. If Medusa has been at least partly rehabilitated as a heroic figure, Medea remains a villain, but an intriguing one offering possibilities for powerful theatre.

Visionaries: Cassandra and the Sibyls

Although the figures of the visionaries may appear to offer more positive roles for women, such figures have often been feared as villains or pitied as victims. Thus, in one legend, Cassandra is given prophetic powers by Apollo, but fails to pay him, and is punished with the curse that she will not be believed (Graves, 1960: vol. 2, 263–64). The story of Cassandra's victimization is told in Aeschylus's play *Agamemnon*. Cassandra is the princess of Troy who is captured and taken to Greece as a concubine by Agamemnon, who has destroyed her country. Agamemnon's wife Clytemnestra has plotted to murder him and Cassandra. When Cassandra arrives outside the Palace, she is caught in a prophetic trance in which she speaks out against Agamemnon's crimes and predicts that they will both be murdered. Agamemnon is murdered inside the palace by Clytemnestra, who then rushes out and kills Cassandra with the same weapon. Any performance which seeks to recover Cassandra as a positive figure needs to contend with suspicions about women prophets, and needs to uncover her dignity as a princess from her eventual fate as the victim of another woman's wrath.

The Sibyls are among the figures who guarded the Oracles and issued obscure interpretations to those who sought advice. The Oracles were traditionally associated with the worship of Mother-Goddesses before Greece was overtaken by patriarchal Athenians (Graves 1960: vol. 1, 178). Celebration of the 'visionaries' may thus involve an attempt to delve back in pre-history to recover figures of a superseded, female religion. Alternatively (and this is more true of recent responses), their stories and characters may be dismantled to be hailed for some attributes and disavowed for others.

The figure of Cassandra was dramatized by Raffaella Battaglini in *La Nozze* ('The Wedding'), which was performed at the Magdalena Festival of 1994 as a companion piece to her play about Medea discussed above. The play was a monologue based on the moment in Aeschylus where Cassandra stands in front of the palace and prophesies. Thus, Battaglini attempts to disengage Cassandra's story from its tragic ending, by isolating a moment when the protagonist takes centre stage and is in a position of potential power:

31

In *Le Nozze* Cassandra is taken at the crucial moment, immediately in front of the door of the Atrides, as we find her in Aeschylus. The character feels as though she is in the middle of a whirlwind of time and space: she does not know whether the door which is in front of her is that of Argo, or of her town which has been destroyed. The door of the Atrides has a double meaning for her: on the one side, she knows it is the door which will take her to be butchered and on the other side she transforms all of this into an occasion of happiness which is the wedding with Agamemnon. The whole text is constructed on this ambivalence between the mourning and the rejoicing.[7]

By taking one moment, Battaglini resists the sense of inevitability implicit in an extended narrative, in other words seeking to separate the figure of Cassandra from her fate. Unlike Battaglini's piece on Medea, *La Nozze* did not aim for a modern setting or naturalistic performance. Instead, the performance drew attention to its own theatricality: for example, the actor, Maria Teresa Telara, began the piece by straightening a white sheet spread on the floor to mark the performance space. Her costume was minimal, for she wore only a white shift and her hair was loose and her bodily gestures were pronounced. Battaglini explained that she related to Cassandra less as 'woman' and more as 'artist':

The thing which interested me about Cassandra's character is her relationship with her prophetic destiny which in some ways is the same as the relationship between the artist and her/his vocation. On the one hand she finds this destiny a heavy burden and wants to get away from it and return to a kind of normality – although in this case she only has a dream of normality, in the shape of the wedding. On the other hand, she is not able to do without her prophetic powers, because she seeks Apollo desperately at the times when he does not show himself.

(ibid.)

The emphasis on theatricality thus drew attention to the relationship between Cassandra's creativity – her performance as a prophet – and the work of playwrights and actors. The tension between power and powerlessness, hope and despair, generated by this particular moment of Cassandra's story is exploited to show a similar tension for theatre-makers as they practise their craft. In doing so, it releases a sense of potentiality which counters the eventual negative outcome of the story.

Myths played a very different role in the creative process of *Crow Station: A Semi-Divine Side Show* by Toad Lilies, [8] although this performance similarly worked with tensions between power and powerlessness. Whereas Battaglini focused on the story of Cassandra, and was particularly interested in dismantling Aeschylus's version of it, the Toad Lilies introduced the legend of the Sibyls as an analogue to the situation of contemporary homeless women. Sally Rodwell described this layering in a talk at the Magdalena Festival:

Crow Station was inspired by a combination of social concerns and theatrical images. Madeline and I lived in the United States in the 1980s and found it incredible that so many women lived on the street in the wealthiest country in the world. You would see them on the subways, in the bus stations, in doorways. They had incredible power and did not care about the State, the Government or rules.

Madeline worked with these women in Boston and she found many of them had a lot of wise things to say. From these reflections we went back to early Greece, to the Sibyls, the women who guarded the Oracles and prophesied. It seems that the Sibyls made a living by answering questions and we began to fantasize that they ran a kind of circus. People would come down into a cave to ask questions, and there were shadow-plays, sounds, puppets. We worked with the idea that women can become very marginalized, far outside dominant society and from this position they can see clearly what is going on.

So, like Cassandra in Battaglini's play, the Sibyls here are powerful but also associated with the underdog.

As a result of this layering of ideas, the characters the Toad Lilies created – Roberta and Sisterloo (figure 1.3) – were not directly based on the Sibyls but displayed some Sibylline attributes, including skills at predicting the future (by reading tea-leaves) and performing rituals, which in this case also featured traditional Maori dances. Roberta and Sisterloo were two comic and slightly grotesque figures. They wore heavy, multi-layered costumes of combinations, crinoline skirts, hooped petticoats, fur coats and hats. They added and removed layers of clothing as they went about different activities, such as sleeping, dancing and travelling. The set for *Crow Station* was a junk-yard, with unrecognizable objects strewn around, which the performers 'recycled' for different sequences, such as when they used their crinoline skirts to make bivouacs to sleep in. The performance was a constant flow of activity, as the two women quarrelled and forgave one another, sang, chanted, danced and performed circus tricks.

Figure 1.3. Sally Rodwell and Madeline McNamara (Toad Lilies) as Roberta and Sisterloo in 'Crow Station'.

Crow Station has a very loose plot, which may be seen to rework another myth: that of *The Odyssey*. Sisterloo predicts that Roberta will go on a journey and the next morning a letter arrives for Roberta – in the form of a large envelope lowered on wires from the ceiling. The sequence may be seen as the invitation to go on a quest which features in many Greek myths – except that here a woman takes the role usually played by a male protagonist. Roberta's travels take up most of the performance time, but both characters remain on stage throughout, keeping up a verbal dialogue as though by telepathy. Roberta's journey takes her through strange, war-torn countries – for example, she arrives at a railway station which has been taken over by rebels and she visits a field hospital – but in each of these situations human suffering is emphasized, for Roberta does not intervene heroically. The ending is ambivalent as to whether she actually returns home or whether Sisterloo dreams of her return. The sequence takes place as Sisterloo recites lines by Sappho about the reunion of close friends:

> You will say
> See, I have come
> back to the soft arms I turned from
> in the old days ... [9]

Crow Station thus rewrites Odysseus' return to Penelope in a way which affirms female intimacy. The different layers of classical allusion in this piece create a collage effect which open up different perspectives on the myths, resisting any unified, simplistic interpretation.

As in many of the performances discussed here, theatricality was foregrounded in *Crow Station*. All changes of scene were carried out onstage, and the performance ended with the two women tidying the stage and (still in costume and still in character) discussing the show and bickering as they accused one another of muffing their lines and mis-timing their actions.

These performances about 'visionaries' may be seen to recover positive images of the heroines they depict, but they do so in ways which resist a simplistic celebration of 'female' qualities. Firstly, both pieces uncouple the protagonists from the stories with which they are associated: in *Le Nozze* in particular, the protagonist is depicted at a moment in time when she is at centre-stage, although it is recognized that she faces impending doom; *Crow Station* presents a collage of fragments of different stories and female figures from mythology. Secondly, both works deal with protagonists who face danger in a male-dominated world: both depict women who are, or stand to become, victims of a system, but whose prophetic skills enable them to remain morally outside that system and in a position of power for a time and within their own sphere. Thirdly, both pieces interrogate myths by emphasizing theatricality: both performances took a self-conscious approach to staging, and the ending of *Crow Station* was metatheatrical. Thus, both pieces offered a variety of different levels on which to engage with the myth: one of these levels was to present the 'visionaries' of classical mythology as comparable to performers and playwrights today.

The languages of theatre and the question of empowerment

Although not all the performers considered here worked with the avowed feminist purpose of rewriting or subverting patriarchal mythologies, all their work displayed a concern to grapple with the negative aspects of mythology. Broadly, the pieces dealing with mythological 'victims' sought to represent the subjective experience of these victims, even if the pieces were not equally successful in raising questions about how such victimization is brought about. The pieces on the 'villains' sought either to turn the idea of villainy on its head and celebrate figures as a source of strength (as in the case of Medusa) or subtly to disavow villainous figures (as in the case of Medea). The 'visionaries' are hailed for their positive qualities, although both pieces discussed here acknowledge the obstacles and oppression faced by those figures.

Shaping the languages of theatre was an important and complex element influencing the capacity of these performances to rewrite myths. The use of text, body-language, staging, costuming and multimedia in a performance piece all played a part in the process of responding to and reworking mythological material. Text-based pieces were able to reshape the stories consciously and to ask direct questions about the representation of women in them. *The Love of the Nightingale, Mary Medusa, Altri Tempi, Le Nozze* and *Crow Station* (and even, to a certain extent *Story of the Fallen Hero*) sought in different ways, to re-present stories originally told by men. These pieces tended to emphasize the perspective of the female protagonists, and many questioned aspects of the original version, sometimes in witty allusions to the original stories, sometimes simply by disregarding parts of the original story to seize the protagonist in a positive moment. Many of these pieces sought to bring out the relevance of aspects of these stories for the modern world: *The Love of the Nightingale* achieved this most directly by making pointed comments about contemporary politics, while *Altri Tempi* used a modern idiom to cast the story of Medea in the present day.

Many pieces sought to foreground performance: sometimes in order to probe the theatrical history of the myth and sometimes to disown mythological heroines as role-models by reminding us that myths are simply fictitious and that theatre is not life. For example, *The Love of the Nightingale* used metatheatre to encourage the audience to question the myth and its role in theatre and *Altri Tempi*, with its costume and setting and its marked allusions to Euripides, probed the relationship between the traditional theatrical figure of Medea, the modern stage and modern life. Occasionally, as in Wertenbaker's play, but also in Siân Thomas's rendition of *Medeamaterial*, tensions were set up between the performer's physical presence and what the words were saying, thus inviting a reconsideration of the text's meaning or even a questioning of the importance of text itself.

Many of the pieces found ways of structuring the audience's response to the physical presence of the female body in performance, questioning the 'male gaze' to create levels of identification or disidentification with the characters portrayed. In some performances, this was achieved by refusing to show the female body in its entirety: thus in *Mary Medusa* and *Medeamaterial*, the focus was on the face only; in *Multi-Medea* the body was presented through the medium of digital technology. Some pieces, like

Altri Tempi and *Medeamaterial*, sought to break the traditional relationship between spectator and actor by addressing the audience in direct, even confrontational, ways.

What the great majority of these performances have in common is their attempt to open up multiple perspectives on the myths. Thus, many of the performances combined a degree of psychological realism with an element of metatheatre, thus offering different levels of engagement with the myths. This effect was achieved most fully in pieces which combined a variety of theatrical techniques or which drew on multimedia resources – such as the two Medusa pieces, *Multi-Medea* and *Crow Station* – where the spectator was offered several foci of interest, various images which opened up different ways of viewing the story. This process of opening up multiple perspectives on mythological material has become a more prevalent and more powerful feature of performances than either embracing female mythological figures as archetypes or rejecting them outright as products of patriarchal literary and theatrical traditions.

References

1 The performance discussed here is that given at the Magdalena Festival, Chapter Arts Centre, Cardiff, September 1994.

2 *The Love of the Nightingale* was first performed in October 1988 by the Royal Shakespeare Company, the Other Place, Stratford.

3 *Medusa* was first performed at Sauda: An Event for Black Women, at London Women's Centre in October 1991.

4 *Mary Medusa* was first presented in its entirety April 1993 at the Western Front, Vancouver.

5 In an interview with Jane de Gay at the Magdalena Festival, Cardiff, September 1994.

6 English translation of the Italian play-text, supplied by the playwright with the programme notes.

7 From a talk given at the Magdalena Festival, 1994.

8 The performance discussed here is that given at the Magdalena Festival in September 1994. The Toad Lilies went on tour with a later version of the piece in Wellington, Coventry, Amsterdam and Berlin, from May to July 1996.

9 From the play-text.

2 *Lear's Daughters* on Stage and in Multimedia and Fiona Shaw's *King Lear* Workshops as Case Studies in Breaking the Frame

Lizbeth Goodman

This chapter looks behind the scenes at a number of specialized productions of excerpts from *King Lear* and a play about Shakespeare's female characters. It aims to set the scene for subsequent arguments about the voicing of the 'feminine' and 'female' by first demonstrating some of the many ways in which female characters have been presented and re-presented through the years by female directors and actors willing to experiment with gender roles on stage and on screen. It will then go on to consider how *focus,* a particular tool in the language of video production, may be used to open up questions of gender.

In the late 1960s and throughout the 1970s, feminist critics and theatre-makers concerned with the representation of gender explored a variety of means for bringing women to the centre of the Shakespearean stage. Experiments were undertaken in which women's companies cast women in male parts, and rewrote plays from the women's points of view. However, women had played male Shakespearean roles long before the feminist critical revolution of the late twentieth century. The English actor Sarah Siddons (1755–1831) and the French star Sarah Bernhardt (1844–1923), both played Hamlet, as did the Norwegian film actor Asta Nielsen who starred in a German-language film version of the play directed by Sven Gade in 1920. Each generation has dealt with the largely male legacy of Shakespeare's parts in its own way.

In the early 1990s, I compared and contrasted a number of the female-oriented experiments with Shakespeare which English and Irish women theatre-makers had undertaken up to that point (see Goodman, 1993b). That article focused on the choices which women make when approaching the shadow of the bard: whether to play the parts Shakespeare wrote or to rewrite the plays, or to write new plays altogether. Actors Fiona Shaw and Tilda Swinton helped with that article and with subsequent forays into this terrain, in the search for a legacy of 'false fathers' which women playing Shakespeare encounter. One of the case studies considered there was *Lear's Daughters,* a play co-authored and first produced in 1987 by the Women's Theatre Group, based on an idea by Elaine Feinstein. Much has changed since the early 1990s, and indeed since Women's Theatre Group first wrote *Lear's Daughters* in the late 1980s. But much, also, has stayed the same.

In this chapter, I set out to re-examine *Lear's Daughters* in the wake of its most recent major production: a restaging designed for an audio recording made in 1996–97, which I was fortunate to witness in process and production.[1] I also explore the development of a parallel experiment for video: the workshop of scenes from *King Lear* directed by Fiona Shaw in 1997, following on from the student masterclasses led by Shaw in Canada in 1996.[2] These recordings were released as part of the Open University course, 'Shakespeare: Text and Performance' in 2000. *Lear's Daughters* was released on audio CD (Bardwell, 2000) and CD-Rom (Williams, 2000), and excerpts from the *King Lear* workshops have been released on video (Coe, 2000).

Part One: Women's Theatre Group and *Lear's Daughters*

The Women's Theatre Group (WTG) was one of the first all-women's companies to operate in England and is now the only women's company of that era which is still operating (though now under a new name, The Sphinx). In 1987, WTG members decided to work on a play about Shakespeare's *King Lear*, but found that the female characters in the original play left little scope for creative interpretation by the actors. Although *Lear's Daughters* was first written and performed in 1987, it was not published until the plays of the Women's Theatre Group were collected and made available in 1991 in Griffin and Aston's two-volume collection, *Herstory*. The play has since been republished in *Mythic Women/Real Women* (Goodman, 2000), a collection which brings together other plays discussed in this book, including *Ophelia* by Bryony Lavery.

Lear's Daughters is a feminist play, and very much a play of the late 1980s. *Lear's Daughters* was written at a time when the impact of the feminist movement of the 1960s and 1970s had inspired a wave of writing which set out to tell familiar stories from the women's points of view, to recast myth and history in order to uncover what came to be called 'HERstories'. The play is what feminist critics have termed a 'herstory', and more precisely, it is a 'prestory' or 'prequel' to the story of *King Lear*. It shows the three daughters of Shakespeare's Lear as girls and traces their growth into young womanhood. It sets the scene for the pivotal Act which opens Shakespeare's play, when the words and silences of these three female characters breaks open the world of the play, and of the kingdom.

Unlike Shakespeare's original, there is no single author for *Lear's Daughters*. This is a group-scripted play; that is, the five actors and their director Gwenda Hughes worked together to create the script from an idea provided by the poet Elaine Feinstein. There were a number of complications to that group-devised process, and issues about authorship were debated for some time (see Goodman, 1993a: 97–100). Focus here is not on the process of writing the play, but on the process of reviving it for audio production in the late 1990s.

The style of the play is, in many ways, suggestive of a certain recognisable or 'hallmarked' 1980s feminism. It demonstrates much concern for 'women's experience' and for 'liberation' of the female characters from within a 'patriarchal structure' (the kingdom of Lear and, in a wider sense, the male-oriented story of kingship, fatherhood and power which frames the play). At the same time, the play set out to make a social and cultural intervention: it not only retold the story of Lear from the female characters' points of view, but it also attempted to stake a claim on the territory of theatre by pointing out the dilemma of the strong actor or director wishing to find challenging work in a theatre industry dominated by revivals of Shakespeare's plays. To work in well-funded theatre, female actors too often found themselves in the wings, waiting for their moment to walk on and deliver their few lines. *Lear's Daughters* turned that dynamic on its head and removed the male characters from the frame altogether. In this play, it is always the female characters' turn to be seen and heard. The play also exploded the hierarchy of Shakespeare's original, wherein the 'lead part' is Lear's and the supporting players are mainly men, with three good parts for women. In *Lear's Daughters*, there are effectively five 'leading parts' and no supporting parts. This is a work of collective theatre that seeks to explore the nature of collectivity, of empowerment through a sharing of voices.

Lear's Daughters might, at first glance, appear to be a 'liberal feminist' play in that it demonstrates concern for 'liberation' of women (via their theatrical counterparts and through increased access to real stage presence for the actors themselves). Some of the concerns levelled at 'liberal feminism' over the years might be seen to apply here: there is, perhaps, some sense in this play that there is some common 'women's experience' which unites the female characters, like the actors who play them. Yet this reading is too simplistic. *Lear's Daughters* takes the personal experience of each contributing author and incorporates that into the story of the female characters. In that sense, the 'essentialism' (or view that women are, per se, inherently, genetically different as a group) is complicated and undermined by the insistence of the highly personal, widely differing characters presented for the three daughters.

At the same time, the characters of Fool and Nanny both show themselves to be preoccupied with money and responsibility: they engage with the world of the play and the world outside the theatre by pointing to economic, material and symbolic power structures which entrap women as a group, but also offer a route to liberation for individual women and men who choose to act creatively to sidestep their own oppression. The play could, at this level, be seen to encompass something of a 'materialist feminist' concern, in so far as it considers women's roles in relation to the economic and material, social fabric of their context. It might also be seen to demonstrate a variety of 'radical feminist' concerns in its pitting of the female characters against the wall of power which is symbolised by the absent but often mentioned king/father-figure, Lear. Another potential link to 'radical feminism' might be found in the play's implicit suggestion that revolutionary means might lead to revolutionary ends: the overthrow of the kingdom perhaps (which is, in effect, what we find in Shakespeare's play, though there the agency of the female characters, and their possible motivations for their actions, are not clearly defined).

Shakespeare's *King Lear* is an epic tragedy most often performed for modern audiences with large stage sets, large predominantly male casts and, when possible, large budgets. By contrast, *Lear's Daughters* is drawn, quite deliberately, on a less ambitious scale. Both thematically and in terms of the stage space, this is a small-scale domestic play. Yet the play reaches into the realm of the domestic and shows how many wide social issues are encapsulated in each household, each woman's story. It integrates comedy and serious issue-based ideas common to the Women's Movement of its day (unequal pay, unequal access to power on grounds of gender, sexual harassment and other forms of gender-related abuse of power, sibling rivalry and the nature of 'sisterhood'). It takes the idea of cosy domesticity to the extreme by representing the daughters as:

three daughters, locked in a room
with
two mothers, dead or gone missing
and a
Father, waiting outside
three princesses, sitting in a tower
with
two servants, behind the door
and a
King holding the crown.

In this brief description (taken from the original publicity material for the play), gender and power are highlighted as key concerns, and class privilege is also inscribed as a theme, in the references to servants. Interior and exterior spaces are defined, with the young women locked inside and the older women 'behind a door', while it is only the words Father and King which are privileged with capital letters. The King, we are told quite clearly, holds the crown.

The mood of the play is claustrophobic, and the obsessive levels of competition which develop between the sisters seems to arise in part from their lack of contact with the outside world. All five characters invent stories to explain their relationship with Lear. Memory plays a part, and so do role-play and invention. The characters are all aware that they are playing parts. Like Shakespeare's Cleopatra, the characters in *Lear's Daughters* have given thought to their own power to manipulate men with sex. Unlike Cleopatra, however, the three princesses are too young to be held responsible for this knowledge. These are not 'bad women' but impressionable girls whose every experience of the world has taught them to survive by playing roles to please, or to subvert the desires, of a patriarchy contained in a single male figure: the father/king. Here, then, we find the results of a genealogy of masculinist power abuse in its effects on a young generation, who grow to become the women who bring down Shakespeare's Lear.

Given this serious theme, the tone of the play often strikes readers and audiences as inexplicably comic. Here, humour is employed as a subversive strategy, to bring listeners into the stories of the daughters and to help us to rethink the tragedy from the female point of view. *Lear's Daughters* combines elements of farce and stand-up style humour with the tragic stories of Lear's three daughters. In this, it follows the generic model of Shakespeare's original to some extent: Fool brings a comic edge to Shakespeare's version and is often the wisest character, with the nerve to speak the truth (though in riddles). Fool in *Lear's Daughters* takes the lead: this Fool's poor puns dominate the tone of the play and this Fool's androgynous presence similarly occupies attention in the story. The Fool who acts as stage manager and narrator of *Lear's Daughters* is perhaps part male and part female, but played by a female actor. When the comic voice of the Fool gives way to the more intense exchanges between the sisters, the juxtaposition of moods makes these serious moments all the more effective.

Lear's Daughters also introduces a new character: Nanny, who takes the place of the queen. The queen is entirely absent in Shakespeare's original. She appears in *Lear's Daughters*, but not as a character in her own right. Rather, Fool and Nurse re-create the missing queen through role-play and throwing of the voice. The puppet queen is given puppet masters. Likewise, the dead queen's job of mothering is hired out to the Nurse. Here, the theme of economic valuing of women's work is brought to the fore: another tactic of much feminist theatre of the 1980s. The daughters, too, are described in terms of their economic value to Lear and his kingdom. The most chilling description is that of how the middle daughter, Regan, loses economic value when she falls pregnant. The authors and actors of *Lear's Daughters* do not shy away from making explicit political connections and comments about women's status. Here again, the play serves both the 1980s 'liberal feminist' agenda and also materialist feminist ideas about women's relationship to centres of economic power.

Each of the three princesses is described in terms of a pattern: a favoured art form, a way of expressing herself, a colour and a sense of light. In the audio production, however, the actors were required to make decisions which produced the performance styles of the original stage production and of this audio recording. The decision to reproduce *Lear's Daughters* as an audio production was made partly because there was neither time enough nor

Figure 2.1. Hazel Maycock as Fool, recording the audio version for the OU/BBC in 1997–98. Photo: Trevor White.

adequate financial resources to sponsor a full video production. However, we might have decided to opt for an audio production in any case. The audio production was performed by the original cast – Janys Chambers as Nanny/Nurse, Hazel Maycock as Fool, Sandra Yaw as Goneril, Adjoa Andoh as Regan, and Polly Irvin as Cordelia – and these actors had – in the 12 years since they first got together to create the play – developed in their own lives to the point where it might not be quite so appropriate for them to be playing young girls. Time moves on. Yet we very much wanted to use the original cast as they were also the co-creators of this play, of its language and themes.

While the audio production of *Lear's Daughters* captures the essence of the play remarkably well, there is one important moment which is lost. At the end of the play, Fool throws the crown up into the air and the three princesses all reach up to try to catch it. In the original stage production, the lights black out as the crown begins to fall, so the audience is left with the striking image of the golden crown suspended in mid-air, with three pairs of female hands attempting to grab it. By the time the lights come up, the play is over and the focus is back on the audience, who will (if they know Shakespeare's *King Lear*) realise that this is the moment at which the women's play ends and the original play begins. Without the visual cues which live performance and video performance capture for us in their own distinct ways, the audience for the audio production might lose this vital image. In the audio production, a new line was therefore written in. Fool shouts 'Catch!', leaving us with an audio impression of the physical struggle about to begin.

Part Two: Refocusing the Lens: from Lear to his Daughters

Fiona Shaw's workshops focused on key scenes – the opening scene, the 'storm scene' and the closing scene – looking at the impact of setting, style, action and actors' and directors' choices in creating meaning. Shaw pitted the play's text against the images and actions which emerge from performance, requiring the viewer to consider how these come together to create meaning through interpretation, taking us through a complex process from text-based study to a study of Shakespeare in performance. It is often assumed that in filming or making a video of a play, we simply transfer the action to the medium of film. But each performance is different, and each set of creative decisions made by each distinct cast and production team leads to the staging, and recording, of a new production which shows the play in a new light. These interpretations do not simply show the play in different lights, but effectively offer viewers different plays.

While there is not space to discuss the many and varied creative decisions made in adapting Shakespeare's *King Lear* for video, I want to draw attention to a few examples from Shaw's version of the Declaration scene (*King Lear*, 1. 1. 53–107) which demonstrate the unique effects which can be achieved when a gendered lens is brought into focus on the play in performance. Here, of course, I refer not only to the metaphorical lens of the 'eye of the beholder' but also to the literal lens of the camera, which is in turn held by a camera-operator, instructed by a director and advised by a creative team including actors and academics.

Lear's Daughters *on Stage*

The workshop version of the Declaration scene focused on approaches to the play which bring the central conflict between the daughters and their father to light. Shaw selected the disused psychiatric wing of Ealing General Hospital in South West London as the set: a spartan, white, institutional 'stage' with atmospheric architecture and a suitably enclosed sense of space. This space was used to represent a TV studio, castle and heath, staged interior, domestic interior and imagined exterior all at once. The space signals the interior state of Lear's mind as well, and demands a critical response from the viewer.

The play text of *King Lear* opens in a stately chamber of Lear's castle, with his announcement of his decision to divide his kingdom between his three daughters. When he asks them how much they love him, their answers are a measure of their worth in the father's eyes. The extent to which Lear and his daughters understand the weight of this situation determines the outcome of the rest of the play. The video sequence picks up at line 53, Goneril's response. In this interpretation of the scene, the daughters seem more aware than Lear of the significance, and potential problems, of this division. They know the competition between them, while Lear seems not to understand the full implications of his actions or his questions. His amused manner early in the scene turns to bemusement when Cordelia refuses to speak, and then to real anger precisely because he is surprised by Cordelia's response. She knows the weight of his actions better than he does, even in this scene. In this scene and well into the play, Lear struggles to maintain dignity while his daughters struggle to deal with their new-found power. The family and the kingdom are divided.

The decision to start with Goneril's reply to Lear was made for practical reasons in the first instance. We could not afford to pay enough actors to play all the courtiers in the opening few lines. We cut some of the parts, removing Gloucester, Kent, Cornwall, Albany and Edmund, as well as a number of Attendants. We also cut the end of the scene, removing Lear's full tirade, Kent's defence, Kent's banishment, Burgundy's rejection of Cordelia, France's taking of Cordelia as his wife, Cordelia's departure from the court and parting exchange with her sisters, the sisters' first joint counsel. As a result, the video sequence focuses on the dynamic between the father and his daughters (or the king and the princesses) rather than on the bidding for Cordelia's hand in marriage, or for her 'cut' of the kingdom.

Fiona Shaw and the production team made another related decision: they chose a setting which would allow modern viewers to see the difficult situation of the characters in terms which might be more familiar to us than that of a kingdom and castle. Shaw chose to set the scene in a modern TV studio, with the daughters auditioning for parts in their own lives, and with Lear and his Fool (playing the role of director's assistant) watching the female characters through the TV monitor. This staging decision frames and focuses attention on one major conflict, and on four characters: Lear and his three daughters. Cordelia's body language speaks volumes in this video production, but it is Goneril and Regan's words and manners which set the tone. These characters are often portrayed as cold and callous in staged productions. The camera frames them here as slightly vain and a bit ridiculous, but not as evil. It is possible to see their predicament through the lens of the camera, as they might see it in reflection: clearly less favoured than their younger sister, set up to play roles for their father on command, knowing that they cannot 'win' this game.

Each of the three daughters is seen in close-up through the lens of the camera, via the monitor. Here, the theoretical notion of the 'male gaze' is made literal, via the camera lens and monitor, while the directorial emphasis on the women's struggles with their parts encourages audiences to focus attention on the female dilemma to the extent that the gaze, or the lens, is effectively hijacked and refocused on the female by the end of the scene. Meaning is created by a contrast of the text and original context (in this case the castle which Shakespeare indicates as the setting for this scene) and the images and actions which offer an alternative interpretive context (in this case, the modern TV studio).

As in the audio production of *Lear's Daughters* discussed above, it was necessary to make some changes to the script in transferring the play to a new medium and setting (video, set in the contemporary TV studio). A few extra words were added to the start of the scene for this video. They are not very obvious, both because they are spoken quietly and because they seem to be part of the play: Goneril and Regan's voices are heard whispering in the very first shot; they say 'I don't really love him any more. No, I hate him.' These words completely undercut the meaning in the words of the scene which follows, setting the elder sisters up from the outset as manipulative, uncaring, cold. But as the words are whispered, the listener might need to listen very carefully to know what is being said. The added text is there to create a mood.

The other set of added words is more obviously out of place, and anachronistic (or misplaced in time): these are the words spoken by the camera-operator's assistant at the opening of the sequence: 'Declaration, Slate 55, take 1, going in: … five, four, three …' These new words set the scene for modern audiences: they place us in relation to a TV studio, and help us to recognise the frame as a TV monitor through which we view three female characters auditioning for the roles of the daughters in this production of *King Lear*. Lear is here cast both as King and as Director.

Of course, we made many more cuts to the text than we made additions. In choosing only a few scenes, and editing those down to size, we radically altered the play and directed it to a particular audience (students) at a particular cultural moment (the late 1990s and turn of the twenty-first century, when knowledge about media can be assumed but a focus on issues of gender and power may need to be carefully framed).

Cordelia is positioned as a witness to the game, at first. But when Cordelia speaks, everything changes. The silence before her words speaks volumes too. When it is her turn to speak, Cordelia hesitates, and in the moments of hesitation Lear's facial expression and body language undergo a noticeable shift from happiness and candour to perplexity. Then, she speaks: 'Nothing my Lord' (1.1.86): Lear looks up, surprised. His expression suggests that he thinks (or hopes?) she might just be teasing. He directs her to speak again.

Again, she hesitates. This time Lear's expression is darker, more concerned, imploring her to reconsider. At this point, she could still smile and he could make it a game again. However, she breaks the frame, looks away from the camera, directly at Lear. This breaks all the rules. The illusion of Lear's control over the scene is shattered when she decides to look where she wants. She implores him with her eyes to stop playing, to hear what she says. The direction of her glance is as disempowering for Lear as his words. Lear is startled, upset, then gradually angry. He does not like to play by anyone else's rules. He must react.

The rest of the scene, and indeed the rest of the play, can be seen as a reaction to this point. At the pivotal point, the text's plumb line – 'Nothing, My Lord' – is reinforced by action and image. Cordelia breaks the rules with her body too, by breaking the frame of the camera's lens and repositioning her body and gaze so that she looks directly at her father, into his eyes. The verbal challenge is reinforced with a physical challenge and that is strengthened by the medium itself, for it is possible for viewers to replay that moment of defiance and to view it again and again. The effect of the text and image coming together in this way is to enforce a shift in the action of the play: a shift from the frames set by the TV monitor and the camera's lens to the new framework set by Cordelia's defiance in both word and gesture. From this moment on, there is no going back to the game. This pivotal point leads to the tragedy which follows.

While focus in this video sequence is primarily on Lear and his daughters, there is the fifth character who features as well: another figure who sits silently next to Lear and joins in his reactions. He is Fool: Lear's helpmate and jester, who appears later in the play, but Shaw chose to import him into this scene for strategic reasons. In importing the character of Fool, the short extract from the opening scene which is the focus of the video's attention allows the sequence to better represent the whole play. No other character is so important to Lear's identity as is Fool. Here, he sits silently, supporting his master. In this scene, as in the play as a whole, Fool is often wiser than the King. Even in silence, he seems to convey a certain understanding of the daughters and their plight which Lear does not: an understanding, and humorous reaction, communicated only through his eyes and body language in this sequence.

The choice of setting signals a critical approach to the play. The camera brings us in close to the action, just as a TV camera does. But there is something theatrical about this scene as well. The camera and the TV screen are visible – they don't just allow us to see the action, but we have to see the action through them: front and centre. We are encouraged in this video production to pay attention to who is looking and who is being looked at, who is speaking and who is listening and who is remaining silent. This workshop video production emphasizes the power of looking: the importance of considering images as well as words in studying Shakespeare's plays today. In particular, this production encourages audiences to look at the way the female characters are framed, controlled, manipulated by the camera and the men who direct it. In a sense, the emphasis is similar to that in *Lear's Daughters*, though the critical impetus, cultural moment, and medium of production are very different.

Alternative Cuts/Different (Power) Plays

During the workshop process for this video, Fiona Shaw experimented with a range of alternative 'cuts' which viewed each scene from different angles and perspectives. One cut of the declaration scene, for instance, emphasizes the family relationship and domestic power struggle between the characters. That cut is very much led by the text. For example, visual images are linked to body parts and objects mentioned in the text: at the mention of eyesight the visual image is a pair of spectacles; at the mention of breath, a mouth. When the word 'sisters' appears in the text, a corresponding image of the sisters will tend to appear on screen. In yet another cut of the same scene, the ideas of love and truth are played with. For instance at the end of the scene, when the concept of 'truth' is raised, rather than covering the lens of the camera to cut the scene short here, this cut opens the angle even further, showing a range of reactions from the characters and crew who are surprised and engaged. All these witnesses to the scene are silent: their presence is of interest, but there are no literalizing links to precise words or 'synch' points in the text. This cut is led by image rather than text. Whereas the first of these alternative cuts emphasised family connections and used mainly close-ups, this second alternative cut works with images, representing concepts, rather than words, and it uses mainly wide shots to set the scene.

In each of these cuts, and indeed in any cut of a performance mediated by a camera to an audience not physically present in a shared space with the performers, the impact of the actors' work is communicated as much by the conscious framing of the camera, and by the directorial and design concepts of the production team, as by the words of the play. The performance process involves the enactment of text, or of ideas, using gesture, body language, sound, voice, and image to create moments of communication to audiences. Each such communicative 'act' is influenced by and 'readable' in its own cultural moment, and with regard to its medium of expression.

Wrapping Up

The Women's Theatre Group created a piece of 1980s feminist theatre, yet one which speaks to audiences today in its link to experiences of women and men engaging in all manner of power struggles and domestic situations. The production teams working with Fiona Shaw in England and in Canada created work together which translates some of Shakespeare's ideas but also frames them in ways with which contemporary media-literate audiences might better identify.

While it is all too easy to recognise the traces of rather simplistic, essentialist thinking about gender differences in a range of early feminist work, it is most useful to recognise such tendencies without underestimating the value of such work (which was, after all, radical and innovative its own day). Current feminist criticism, in all its varied manifestations, would emphasise the importance of the recognition of differences between women. These differences, of course, influence the approaches which many different women theatre-makers take to Shakespeare and to adaptations of Shakespeare in contemporary practice. So, it is important to frame any study of Shakespeare adapted for video in ways which allow the female characters to make an impact, while recognising the power of the production team and audience to alter Shakespeare's work in re-producing it.

The few examples of mediated Shakespeare discussed in this chapter can only begin to suggest how very rich and varied the field is today. Theatre-makers and media producers alike will continue, no doubt, to value the rich tradition of Shakespeare Studies and also the variously rich and challenging opportunities which Shakespeare's texts offer for (and pose to) contemporary theatre-makers, regardless of gender, class, race or nationality. However, we can also see that by refocusing the lens on gender in relation to performance, there is much to be gained in our understanding of the plays, and of the strategies and choices which women make in approaching them today.

In staging the languages of women, in and through the voices of Lear's daughters in these and many other stage and screen versions as well, we begin to challenge the textual representation of women as characters and to breathe life into these characters as identifiable and transmutable speakers of language, and players of women's roles in time and space.

References

1   *Lear's Daughters* audio CD full production was produced by Jenny Bardwell, with academic advisors: Katherine Armstrong and Lizbeth Goodman. It was produced for the OU BBC in association with University College Chester, and with the cooperation of the Women's Theatre Group/The Sphinx, Elaine Feinstein, Gwenda Hughes, and Faber and Faber.

2   Masterclasses led by Fiona Shaw, with student and professional actors on staff at the University of Alberta in Edmonton, Canada. Academic consultants: Lizbeth Goodman with Stephen Regan. Canadian academic consultants: Beau Coleman, Sandy Nichols, Carl Hare, David Lovett, Lee Livingstone. BBC intern/assistant: Teresa Dobson. Produced for the OU BBC in association with the University of Alberta, Dale Phillips, and RADA.

3 Playing (with) Shakespeare: Bryony Lavery's *Ophelia* and Jane Prendergast's *I, Hamlet*

Jane de Gay

In 'The Weyward Sisters: Towards a Feminist Staging of *Macbeth*', Lorraine Helms offered suggestions for reclaiming positive female characters from Shakespeare's plays. Helms proposed recuperating the witches from *Macbeth* by casting them as travelling players, 'acrobats, jugglers, musicians, mimes, clowns, puppeteers, magicians, singers, and dancers. They will not only play the roles of witches, they will play *with* the roles of witches' (Helms, 1992: 169). She suggests that such a production would celebrate 'liminality', the state of being at the first stage in a process, or in transition (from *limen*, Latin for threshold). It would seek to theatricalize the witches by showing them as players; their dances, cooking, and prophecies would become performances staged for Macbeth. Such a combination of playing and playing *with* roles is potentially a powerful one for feminist theatre-makers: it sets in train a process of exploring traditional interpretations of certain female roles, while taking pleasure in resisting and ridiculing those interpretations. It also suggests how the non-verbal languages of theatre might both question and inform the textual element of a production. In this chapter, I will explore these issues by examining two case-studies of feminist theatre-makers who, in the late 1990s, sought to play and play *with* Shakespeare: *Ophelia*, an original play by Bryony Lavery and *I, Hamlet*, an adaptation of *Hamlet* by Jane Prendergast.[1]

Bryony Lavery's *Ophelia* is structured around the narrative of *Hamlet* but also seeks to recuperate female roles from other Shakespeare plays. *I, Hamlet* took an edited version of Shakespeare's text and staged it in ways that explored gender issues and sought to reclaim or re-view the figure of Ophelia. I will pay close attention to the production histories of the two pieces in order to respond to the proviso Helms made at the end of her article: that a sketch for a feminist staging 'cannot anticipate the risks a fully realized production may run or the discoveries it may make' (1992: 176). I aim to examine the pitfalls facing these productions and to indicate some of the discoveries they made.

Bryony Lavery's play was intended as a feminist project, both in its subject matter and in its creation of opportunities for female characters. The idea for *Ophelia* originated among a group of experienced female actors in the Stantonbury Campus and Collage Theatre Companies, who were interested in putting on a Shakespearean production, but were frustrated by the scarcity of good female parts within any given play. The idea emerged of the two companies doing a production, tentatively named 'Shakespeare's Women', which would bring together a number of female characters from different plays. The director, Rosemary Hill, asked Bryony Lavery to write a script for them.

Given that many members of the team shared feminist views and an interest in women's role in theatre, one might have expected the production to give priority to the female characters, placing them centre-stage and empowering them in ways which would not be possible in the original plays. Collage Theatre Company has a track record of producing challenging plays by women (such as *Masterpieces* by Sarah Daniels, *Vinegar Tom* by Caryl Churchill, *Tissue* by Louise Page, *Find Me* by Olwen Wymark, and *Letters Home* by Rose Leiman Goldemberg), whilst Hill and Lavery are both committed feminist theatre-makers. However, the kind of play which emerged was more complex than might have been expected. This was largely due to the size and mixed nature of the cast – which included women and men, amateurs and professionals, students and experienced actors – who did not share a common political or feminist agenda. In particular, many of the younger members were less aware of gender issues than were the older actors. Although questions of gender were discussed during some of the rehearsals and workshops, this discussion was limited by constraints of time and by the director's need to maintain discipline over a large and partly inexperienced cast. The mixed nature of the cast also imposed certain conditions on the kind of play that was required: besides providing good parts for women, it also had to include smaller roles for the less experienced women and good parts for the strong male actors in the company. As a result, although there were more women than men in the cast, the women characters did not necessarily have any greater importance or prominence than the male characters.

Bryony Lavery's response to Shakespeare is feminist in a more nuanced way. Lavery had in the past expressed an interest in creating opportunities for women and in challenging the canonical male playwrights. As she once put it: 'There are too many Dead Writers being taken out of their glass cases. / There are far too many good women actors for the amount of space in those glass cases' (1984: 30–1), but by the time she wrote *Ophelia,* she had come to see Shakespeare less as a 'Dead Writer' than as 'an old friend with an old friend's strengths … he writes beautifully … and faults … he *never* puts in enough women!' (personal letter, 9 May 1997, ellipses in original). Lavery's play can thus be seen less as a rejection of Shakespeare than as an attempt to rescue him for feminists by interpreting his female characters in ways which raised gender issues, and by viewing the characters sympathetically and offering explanations for some of the actions they are given in the original plays.

Besides the two key female roles of Ophelia and Gertrude, Lavery's play incorporated five major Shakespearean female characters: Katherina (from *The Taming of the Shrew*), Lady Macbeth, Goneril (from *King Lear*), Portia (from *The Merchant of Venice*), and Lady Capulet (from *Romeo and Juliet*). Although these five parts were

Figure 3.1. Shakespearean heroines at the funeral of Old King Hamlet, in Bryony Lavery's Ophelia. *Photo: David Walker.*

generally smaller than those in the original plays, Lavery used them to raise gender questions and to provide a feminist gloss on the characters found in Shakespeare. The five figures are written into the play on the pretext of attending the funeral of Old Hamlet (figure 3.1.), and Lavery uses this setting to raise questions about women's relationship to patriarchy. Each of the women is attending the funeral on behalf of her husband or father, an arrangement which is greeted by the court of Elsinore as a breach of decorum. The ladies try to justify themselves, and the tension is eventually resolved by Lady Capulet, who tells her story of learning to survive after the death of Juliet. She concludes that her greatest claim for attending the funeral is not her social status but because she, too has been bereaved: 'To mourn you need no high-thought name / In grief, all living creatures are the same' (Scene 8). In this speech, Lavery gives Lady Capulet the chance to speak which is limited in *Romeo and Juliet* where she is given just two lines after hearing of her daughter's death: 'O me! This sight of death is as a bell / That warns my old age to a sepulchre.' (5.3. 205–6) Although Lavery's Lady Capulet is old and dying, she is also a survivor, and her speeches testify to the fact that she has learned to live on through grief. This scenario proposes a radical view of power: where one might expect a feminist view of Shakespeare's female characters to give them

51

greater political strength and status, this production celebrates moral courage and strength as worth more than wealth or social and political status.

Lavery plays and plays with Shakespeare in her presentation of these characters. Her process of developing the roles of these Shakespearean characters may be compared to that of an actor preparing to play one of these roles in a production. She explores the characters she draws from Shakespeare and offers explanations for some of the actions they are given in the original plays. For example, she adds a gloss to Katherina's apparent transformation from a 'shrew' into an obedient wife at the end of *The Taming of the Shrew*. Ophelia asks advice for dealing with her father and her brother (who are abusive in different ways), and Katherina replies, 'Love them above yourself, / For so the world does run … / Cherish … , worship, obey' (Scene 9). So far, this resembles the speech made by Katherina in Shakespeare's play, at Petruchio's instigation and in his presence, to the two 'froward wives', Bianca and the Widow, where she says that 'Thy husband is thy lord, thy life, thy keeper / Thy head, thy sovereign', and that women are 'bound to serve, love, and obey' (*The Taming of the Shrew*, 5.2. 147–8). However in Lavery's play Katherina is speaking in private and she adds a comic and pragmatic reason for obedience: 'You have a prick keeps other pricks from shafting you!'

Behind her placatory words, Lavery's Katherina is as angry as the untamed shrew of Shakespeare's play. She describes Elsinore as a place where violence is inflicted on women, where 'invisible fists bruise women's breasts … kisses hurt, glances black the eyes.' (Scene 8). In a vignette we see her pummelling her pillows in sleep, and the most powerful visual image associated with her is a pair of boxing gloves. This version of Katherina as a boxer is not unlike the strongly physical performances of Katherina by Sinead Cusack, who prepared for the role by 'pumping iron' and Fiona Shaw, who contemplated weightlifting for hers (Rutter, 1988: xvii). Lavery's character may thus be seen to provide a commentary on Shakespeare comparable to the interpretations of feminist actors; her quest for a more rounded view of these characters may be compared with the process summed up by Harriet Walter (1993) as finding the 'human being' behind the 'harpy' and the 'heroine' in Shakespeare's texts.

Since she is writing an original play, Lavery can go further and play with Shakespeare by adding background information on the characters which would skew a production of a Shakespeare play. This is particularly true of Lavery's version of Lady Macbeth, who appears as a sympathetic, motherly figure, a vision of what she might have been before her ambition for her husband drove her to pray to the spirits to 'unsex me here', and make her 'unwomanly' and cruel enough to kill Duncan so that her husband would be king. The Lady Macbeth who arrives in Lavery's Elsinore is heavily pregnant, and later suffers a miscarriage. This contrasts with the villain in Shakespeare's play who swears that she would kill her baby if she had committed herself to doing so:

I would, while it was smiling in my face,
Have pluck'd my nipple from its boneless gums
And dash'd the brains out, had I so sworn
As you have done to this.

(Macbeth, 1.7. 56–9)

Lavery's invention comments on Shakespeare's play by leading us to speculate as to whether an experience such as a miscarriage could have led someone like Lady Macbeth to hold life so cheaply as to consider murder. Yet even this elaboration of Lady Macbeth is congruent with recent stage attempts to reclaim the character: for example, Lady Macbeth's childless state was made into a major part of her tragedy in Adrian Noble's RSC production of *Macbeth* in 1986. Noble made frequent use of the image of a bloody child (Rutter, 1988: 56), and the same image appears in *Ophelia* at the opening of the miscarriage scene, where one of the cast is seen painting a baby doll with stage blood.

The five Shakespearean female characters are not empowered in *Ophelia:* although they support one another, they are unable to change the course of events. Goneril and Portia help Gertrude deal with Hamlet by arranging his voyage to England but they cannot prevent his return and his fatal duel with Laertes. And even Portia's diplomacy – which in *The Merchant of Venice* saves Antonio from certain death at the hands of Shylock – is used in *Ophelia* only to settle a quarrel over sleeping arrangements. Some of the less noble characters are able to take advantage of others, but they too are carried along by events. Lavery introduces the character of Ophelia's nurse, who makes extra money for herself by taking bribes, but she is only working a system in which she has no power. Iras and Charmian, Cleopatra's ladies-in-waiting in *Antony and Cleopatra*, appear in *Ophelia* as servants who enter into the main plot. Iras is murdered by Gertrude and her sister Charmian is determined to seek revenge (unlike Shakespeare's Charmian who commits suicide after Iras's death). Lavery thus displaces Hamlet's attempts to take revenge, which are not found at all in her play, onto a woman character. However, Charmian cannot enact revenge herself, and is used as a pawn in a wider game. Gertrude – who takes advantage of Charmian's desire for revenge in order to orchestrate a murder attempt on Ophelia – is the only one of all the female characters in *Ophelia* with any power – and the play did not attempt to deconstruct Gertrude's traditional villainous position. (Bryony Lavery found Gertrude the most difficult character in her play, and she revised the character slightly for subsequent productions.)

In her development of the central character, Lavery was concerned to challenge the interpretation of Ophelia with which she had been presented in literature classes in school, as 'a depressed, obedient, rejected young female lover who pursued governmental edict and familial duty to her own destruction' (programme notes). Rather than inventing a new, more strident character for Ophelia, Lavery sought new ways to understand the character in Shakespeare's play by exploring the pressures which led her to apparent madness and suicide. Lavery focuses on Ophelia's family life, highlighting the domineering, uncaring attitude of her father Polonius but also adding a story-line in which she is sexually abused by her brother, Laertes. Whereas Shakespeare's Hamlet accuses his mother of 'luxury and damned incest', hinting that she is responsible and guilty, Lavery portrays incest as a weapon used against women in an oppressive, patriarchal family. Ophelia is trapped in familial duty because she cannot tell anyone about her brother's behaviour – and the characters who know about it are either powerless to help (such as the servants) or are paid to be quiet (her nurse).

She is torn between seeking help for herself and remaining a 'good', obedient and silent, daughter and sister: 'should I … love myself, / if in the doing I love not others near to me?' (Scene 9). The play thus suggests that Ophelia's 'madness' is genuine distress, and that she is probably not so much mad as angry: with her brother for his oppression, with Elsinore for confining her, with Hamlet for killing her father. She is also pregnant, probably by Laertes. She is therefore given more solid causes for distress than the 'love sickness' which theatre tradition has attributed to her.

Besides interpreting and elaborating on Ophelia's character, Lavery also points to ways in which her story might be rewritten, and here we can see evidence of liminality. Most of the performance time is taken up by a play-within-a-play which, it is revealed at the end, was written by Ophelia herself. *Ophelia* opens, where *Hamlet* ends, with Fortinbras arriving in Elsinore and ordering the removal of the dead bodies of the Danish courtiers. His guards search the palace and find a troupe of travelling players in the basement rehearsing a play written by 'a young lady of the court' called 'The Tragedy of Ophelia, lady of Denmark' (an allusion to Shakespeare's full title, *The Tragedy of Hamlet Prince of Denmark*). Fortinbras commands them to perform it, and a play-within-a-play ensues, re-telling the story of *Hamlet* from Ophelia's perspective. Lavery's play culminates in the revelation that Ophelia did not commit suicide, but was the victim of an attempted murder by Gertrude, who held her underwater until she stopped breathing. At the end of the play-within-a-play, as the travelling players pack up, they reveal that Ophelia is alive and working with them – having held her breath and escaped death – and that she was the actor playing the part of Ophelia in the play we have just seen.

This ending is 'liminal' because Ophelia stands on the threshold of a new life rather than returning to her old one. The happy denouement is characteristic of Lavery's interest in writing plays in which women do not end up as 'losers' (Lavery, 1984: 28); and it invokes but unsettles comic conventions. Penny Gay (1994: 2) has commented that festive comedy traditionally allows subversion and disturbance to occur before normal life is resumed, often with disguises being removed or characters returning home. However, Lavery's play suggests that subversion does not have to give way to 'normal' life: Ophelia retains her disguise as a travelling player, or rather, that disguise becomes a reality; rather than going home, she leaves 'home' (such as it was) to travel with the players. Liminal comedy is a revolutionary form, for it points towards radical change. As Lavery has commented, the structure of the travelling players 'provides a revolutionary model whereby Ophelia is saved … by people who play at rank and gender, but are equal in their roles' (personal letter, 9 May 1997; ellipsis in original). Lavery's decision to turn Ophelia into a travelling player may thus be compared with Lorraine Helms' sketch for playing the witches in *Macbeth*: Lavery questions the authenticity of the traditional view of Ophelia as a mad, weak, obedient girl by turning it into one of many possible roles which Ophelia as actor-writer may assume.

The themes of adopting and rejecting roles were emphasized in Rosemary Hill's production of the play. All the actors were onstage throughout the performance and stepped in and out of the dual roles of Shakespearean characters and travelling players in full view of the audience. The set, designed by Carla Eve Amie, also celebrated liminality (see figure 3.1.). It was predominantly black, with no backdrop but the unadorned dark bricks of the theatre wall, and potting compost or bark on the floor. Although suggesting depression and confinement at Elsinore, this set was also full of potential: a space which could be transformed to represent different scenes with the introduction of props. These transformations (which were announced by two clowns, Props and Player King, who called out the title of each scene) drew attention to the element of performance in the play. The metatheatrical element was further accentuated by the presence of Fortinbras, who sat on stage in a russet-coloured chair throughout the production. Attention was thus constantly directed to the fact that this was a play, and thus to the liminal potential of the props, which did not have inherent meanings but were invested with meaning when used in certain ways.

The play suggested that non-verbal elements do not convey stable truths but contain within themselves the possibility for rewriting and remaking meanings. This is illustrated in a scene in which Ophelia's Nurse prepares to wash sheets used by various female Shakespearean characters who have visited Elsinore in this play (figure 3.2.). Each character has marked her sheet in her own non-verbal way. Katherina and Goneril, both of whom are portrayed as warriors, have ripped theirs. The sheet of Lady Macbeth is stained with blood as a result of her miscarriage. The bookish Portia's sheet is stained with ink. The sheets of Lady Capulet and Ophelia, both of which are white, tell their own stories. The dying Lady Capulet's shows little sign of life; Ophelia's sheet (from a night she had slept with Hamlet) reveals that she was not a virgin that night.

However, Nurse takes the blood-stained sheet to Gertrude, and uses it to extort a bribe by suggesting that this is Ophelia's sheet, and that she has lost her virginity to Hamlet and is now carrying his child. The scene suggests that visual signs do not have inherent meanings, but that those meanings may be made and unmade: in other words, controlled.

The emphasis on the performative in *Ophelia* went hand-in-hand with a questioning of conventional associations and interpretations. Lavery uses this disruption for subversive purposes. Her Ophelia, with comic irony, is a good swimmer: Hamlet has even given her the nickname of 'fish'. As Elaine Showalter (1985: 81) has pointed

Figure 3.2. Barbara Mayor as Nurse in Bryony Lavery's Ophelia. *Photo: Carla Eve Amie.*

out, the association between women and water-based creatures traditionally has sinister connotations: water suggests amniotic fluidity and is considered to be the 'natural' medium of women, an association which has led to a traditional interpretation of Ophelia's death by drowning as an inevitable consequence of her womanhood. Lavery subverts this notion by suggesting that water is Ophelia's medium and that, as a consequence, she is mistress of it and can *escape* drowning – saving herself and her unborn child. The sea is a maternal image in the play: for example, Ophelia's first lines, 'Mother Sea … let your waters break / and bear me!' (Scene 1), highlight the positive and creative, rather than the destructive, implications of the female/water equation. This invocation and subversion of traditional associations is an important element of the play's feminist project.

This is an instance of the play's intertextuality: *Ophelia* needs to interact with Shakespeare's *Hamlet* for its subversive elements to be effective, for the audience needs to know the original story in order to experience what Susan Bennett has described as 'the pleasure in recognition of connection to, yet difference from, the Shakespeare text' (1996: 56). Lavery's play leaves gaps which need to be filled by the audience's knowledge of Shakespeare. It is significant that the play-within-a-play breaks off abruptly: it ends just after Gertrude has reported Ophelia's 'suicide' to Laertes and Claudius, who are plotting to kill Hamlet. The Player King (a female character) reports that the manuscript ends here, and that the deaths of the Elsinore courtiers happened shortly after this scene: she does not narrate the story from *Hamlet* about how the pact between Laertes and Claudius backfired and led to the multiple deaths. While an unsympathetic viewer might refer back to Shakespeare's original play to fill in this gap and will find the new version lacking, a feminist reading will take pleasure in this rupturing of the narrative, and celebrate the play as an example of what the players describe in the Prologue as 'women's work … the ending's not yet fixed…'.

Thus, instead of rejecting Shakespeare as a 'Dead Writer', Lavery endorses a feminine writing which exists, as it were, in the margins of a male tradition and comments on and critiques that tradition. Lavery offers an account of such a feminist tradition in Ophelia's closing speech:

> then 'Tragedy of Ophelia' it is not
> and she must rewrite
> and bend her pen to scrawl its ink
> upon the next page blank and white …

(Scene 23; ellipsis in original)

These lines suggest that Ophelia's task is not complete: that she must now rewrite the play we have just seen, for its title 'Tragedy' has proved false. The 'next page' is a tabula rasa ready to be filled: instead of being fixed in '*black* and white', this page has all the liminal potential of being '*blank* and white' (the first term also alluding to the French word for white). Her account of women's writing is comparable with descriptions of *écriture féminine*: for example, her suggestion that the 'blank and white' page is the female writer's domain is comparable with Cixous's suggestion that a woman 'writes in white ink' (Marks and de Courtivron, 1981: 251), while her emphasis on the need to re-write and the importance of an ending which is 'not yet fixed' may be compared with Irigaray's argument that women are constantly re-making meanings and resisting fixity, that a woman's speech contains 'an *"other meaning"* which is constantly in the process of weaving itself, at the same time ceaselessly embracing words and yet casting them off to avoid becoming fixed, immobilized.' (Marks and de Courtivron, 1981: 103) Thus the play explores a form of rewriting which does not replace 'father' texts, so much as take place in the gaps and spaces left when the written record is ruptured. It can therefore be seen as subversive for exploring particularly 'feminine' ways of making meaning in text and performance.

Jane Prendergast's *I, Hamlet* was similarly concerned with the making and re-making of meaning, working in gaps and spaces in Shakespeare's text, and with giving weight to visual images. Like Lavery, Prendergast did not seek to replace the 'father' text, but in this case sought to adapt it to suit the female actor. Prendergast drew on techniques from visual, experimental, and Noh theatre to stage a highly innovative production of Shakespeare's *Hamlet*. Like *Ophelia*, the play was conceived as a feminist project, albeit with greater emphasis on feminist theory: it formed the practical part of Jane Prendergast's doctoral research on 'Feminisms: Towards "New Theatre"', at Murdoch University. Prendergast presents the results of this project and considers its theoretical implications in the next chapter; the current chapter acts as an introduction to that analysis by documenting the performance and discussing it as a case-study of playing (with) Shakespeare.

Like Bryony Lavery, Jane Prendergast was interested in the under-representation of women in Shakespeare, but where *Ophelia* sought to address the lack of good roles for women in the plays, *I, Hamlet* set out to explore the issues which arise when women spectators are expected to identify with a male hero. Prendergast chose to work with Hamlet because he is not just a character from Shakespeare, but has now acquired symbolic status within western culture. As Prendergast put it in the programme notes: 'The character is closest to a post-modern consciousness in his pursuit to understand and be part of the order of existence: "To be or not to be?"' Prendergast sought to investigate Hamlet's iconic status by performing the role in a production of her own edited version of the play.

Having initiated the project, Jane Prendergast enlisted a small, select team to help her, consisting of Daniel Skinner, a fellow actor from the Rose Theatre Company, and Joe Carey, an actor and musician. She also brought in film-maker Carli Leimbach, who compiled a video documentation of the project as a further stage in the research process. The size of the core group meant that *I, Hamlet* was a more focused project than was *Ophelia*, with fewer contingencies and compromises, and it evolved organically from the collaborators' interests rather than being written, like *Ophelia*, to accommodate the needs of a divergent group of performers.

That said, the production of *I, Hamlet* was not without its constraints. Jane Prendergast discovered during the rehearsal process that there were logistic problems which prevented her from playing Hamlet throughout the performance. For example, she was unable to find anyone else to play Ophelia opposite her Hamlet (the group felt that a cross-cast Ophelia would be too close to pantomime), and so it was decided that Daniel Skinner would play Hamlet opposite Prendergast's Ophelia in the relevant scenes. Also, since the staging of the play placed a great emphasis on the physical aspect of performance, it proved difficult for Prendergast to play opposite Skinner or Carey in the fight scene because of a mismatch in physical strengths, so the scene was performed by Skinner as Hamlet and Carey as Laertes.

These compromises aside, the production sought to question ways in which gender is constructed, whether in Shakespeare's text or in physical performance. In rehearsal, Prendergast and Skinner explored the physicality and energies of their characters by concentrating on the gestures and body language suggested by the text. Prendergast's programme note on the development of the character of Ophelia is a case in point:

> We worked for hours building up the psychic reality of the character of Ophelia. First we moved her to find her bodily movements and tensions; then we worked specifically with her face, how she would move her mouth, her eyes, her eyebrows; then we focused on how the text was to be spoken, using the sounds to guide the meaning – for instance: 'Where is the beauteous majesty of Denmark?' [*Hamlet*, 4.5.21]

By this method, Prendergast attempted to grant interiority to the character of Ophelia by inventing an expressive body language for her, one which emerged from the verbal language assigned to her in Shakespeare's text. This led to an exploration of how occupying a certain body and using certain language might determine a person's mental landscape: in other words, how the psychological experience of gender might be influenced by gendered verbal and physical languages.

The process may perhaps be criticized for taking an essentialist approach to gender by suggesting a causative relationship between physical, mental, and verbal experience. The approach certainly plays down the methods which have become important to feminist actors such as Harriet Walter and Frances Barber (see Walter, 1993 and Barber, 1988), or the cast of Lavery's *Ophelia:* that is, empathizing with characters and carefully explaining and justifying their actions in the play. However, the method also has enormous potential, for it leads the actor to an intimate encounter with the character at a physical level. It enabled Prendergast and her colleagues to explore what it means to become a character, what it means to use one's body to embody a character.

Prendergast explored what Hamlet might mean to her as a woman (and to women more generally) by exploring his character from within her own embodiment as a female actor. The casting is interesting in the light of the theatre history of Shakespeare's play. Prendergast played Hamlet in order to challenge his position as a male icon, but there is a tradition of women playing the role. As Marjorie Garber has suggested, this is because Hamlet is often though of as possessing stereotypically 'feminine' characteristics, particularly insecurity and procrastination: 'Recall the voice-over of Olivier's *Hamlet*: "This is the tragedy of a man who could not make up his mind." To which gender was this dilemma – in 1948, when the film was made – traditionally ascribed?' (1992: 38)

While Prendergast presented the 'feminine' side of Hamlet, she also explored the ways in which masculine identity might be constructed in performance by inventing a body language for him and by reciting his speeches. In an interview with this author in January 1997, she said that she had discovered that some lines – for example, 'the King, my father' – were problematic for her to say. Perhaps this was because the father-daughter relationship called upon when a woman says these lines invokes a different power balance from the father-son relationship which might be suggested by a male actor. Her performance thus dramatized an encounter between masculine and feminine identities within one character, thus problematizing the binary opposition of male or female to deconstruct the status of Hamlet as a 'male' icon.

The encounter between male and female energies in Hamlet was further dramatized when Skinner took over the part of Hamlet from the 'nunnery' speech onwards. This switching of roles part-way through suggested that Hamlet is both male and female, and maybe neither. The casting also resisted an interpretation of Hamlet's madness as 'feminine', in that Skinner played the scenes in which Hamlet is often considered to be genuinely mad, while Prendergast performed in the more playful scenes in which Hamlet feigns madness as a front for speaking his mind.

By performing both Hamlet and Ophelia, Jane Prendergast drew attention to parallels between the two characters. Thus, Ophelia is often treated as a female foil for Hamlet, but Prendergast's performance suggested that, rather than being overshadowed by Hamlet, Ophelia can share his heroic status. That the character is given special prominence in *I, Hamlet* is partly due to Prendergast's near-omission of the part of Laertes from her version of the text, for he appears only as Hamlet's adversary in the final scene. The excision had an important impact on the relationship between characters within the play. Laertes traditionally is seen as a male counterpart to Hamlet: both are sons seeking revenge for the death of a father. The absence of Laertes from most of the play helps to suppress the themes of paternity and vengeance in *I, Hamlet*.

By contrast, all of Ophelia's scenes and speeches are kept in the play, but the period of time she spends on stage is increased by the addition of movement pieces which serve to give visual prominence to her character. In the earlier scenes, where Ophelia is seen talking to Polonius and Hamlet, Prendergast's hair was tightly plaited and her physical movement was restricted – her steps were short and her arm movements kept close to the body – thus emphasizing the restrictions placed upon Ophelia by her family and the court. For her 'mad scene', she is seen with loose hair, her shawl swung rakishly over her shoulders, and she dances a tarantella as she distributes her flowers. The dynamic energy of this performance resisted the tendency to objectify Ophelia as a passive victim.

The expansiveness of physical gestures complements her use of bawdy language and song in Shakespeare's text, suggesting a terrifying freedom from constraint which can only be achieved at the expense of her sanity. In this scene, she is allowed truly to take the stage, for her presence is emphasized by the lighting, which throws her

Figure 3.3. Daniel Skinner as Claudius manipulates a puppet of Gertrude in I, Hamlet. *Photo: Carli Leimbach.*

attenuated shadow over the backdrop. In her final appearance in the grave-digging scene, Ophelia is a silent but prominent presence as she lies, centre-stage, between six candles marking the position of her grave. Thus, even after her death, she remains a powerful visual presence in the play, emphasizing her centrality to the story of Hamlet.

Prendergast interrogates traditional interpretations of Gertrude's character through the strategy of multiple casting. Gertrude is represented by a puppet in her first appearance in the play, as the new wife of Claudius, and her lines are spoken by Daniel Skinner as Claudius (figure 3.3.). This reflects one interpretation of Gertrude's character, which suggests that she is not malicious but merely weak – effectively, Claudius's puppet. In later scenes, Gertrude appears as a chess-piece, again suggesting that she is only a pawn in a larger game she cannot control. The puppet and the pawn suggest that Gertrude as a woman is merely a symbol, only given value by the patriarchal sign-system: but this is counteracted by the fact that Gertrude is also played by Jane Prendergast, as an authoritative and potentially malicious figure. As with Hamlet, the split characterization resists simple interpretations and psychologizing of characters, by emphasizing that there are different ways in which a character might be constructed and understood in the theatre. The use of puppets and props in particular draws attention to the theatricality or performative element in the portrayal or perception of a character, and thus creates a liminal space in which possibilities for different interpretations are opened up.

Thus, *I, Hamlet*, like *Ophelia*, celebrated the process by which meanings are made and re-made in the theatre. As in *Ophelia*, scene changes were done in front of the audience, and were an integral part of the performance. The space was entirely black, only illuminated by candles, and each change of scene was facilitated by the manipulation of lighting and a few props. The edited text of *Hamlet* had been divided into seven movements or moods, and each mood was built up in a collage of visual and musical elements, including physical movement, light and darkness, noise and silence, music and sculpture. The movements were marked off by a pause for a saxophone solo. These pauses created time within the performance in which the audience could reflect upon what was happening as they watched the set in a liminal

Figure 3.4. Daniel Skinner as Hamlet and Joe Carey as Laertes in I, Hamlet. *Photo: Carli Leimbach.*

'state of becoming', being prepared for the next scene. (The reflective moments are also appropriate for a play in which the protagonist frequently criticizes himself for thinking rather than acting.)

Performance, metatheatre and liminality were emphasized in the use of props, which tended to be suggestive and symbolic rather than literal and mimetic. For example, Skinner and Carey used cymbals rather than swords in the fight scene (figure 3.4.). Here, the choreography emphasized the engagement of two bodies in combat, while the clanging of the cymbals mimicked the clashing of swords found in a typical swashbuckling fight scene. At the close of the play, the deaths of Hamlet and the courtiers were subsumed into one final image of death and stasis: a wire sculpture of a skill, lit by a candle, as the music – a one-note rhythm played on a didgeridoo – slowed down and ceased. Thus, the visual images were not used as signs pointing to definitive meanings, but to engage and stimulate the imagination of the audience.

In the simplicity of its stage setting and its emphasis on the process of making and remaking of scenery and mood, *I, Hamlet* is comparable to *Ophelia*, and also to Lorraine Helm's sketch for a feminist *Macbeth*, 'The Weyward Sisters Go on Tour', for it foregrounds the performative element in Shakespeare, and refuses to endorse any single meaning or set of meanings. *I, Hamlet* punctuates Shakespeare's text – verbally, in the excision of certain speeches and scenes and the insertion of periods of silence;

performatively though the insertion of movement, music, and visual images into the spaces between the speeches; and in its characterization by creating multiple perspectives from which a single character may be viewed.

However, like *Ophelia, I, Hamlet* has an intertextual dimension in that it relies upon Shakespeare's text for its subversive elements to become effective and here the audience were called upon to play a part. In *Ophelia* the audience needed to be aware of the original story in order to appreciate that the new play is different. In particular, as we have seen, Lavery's story leaves gaps which need to be filled by the audience's existing knowledge of Shakespeare. In *I, Hamlet* there is one slight break in the continuity of the narrative at a similar juncture, which the audience need to fill by drawing on their knowledge of Shakespeare. Laertes is absent from any scene other than the fight at the end: his complicity with Claudius in arranging the fight has not been depicted and so, as in *Ophelia*, there is no clear explanation as to how all the characters are killed.

As with *Ophelia, I, Hamlet* offers a solution to the danger of appearing faulty for its omissions, in that the references back to Shakespeare are made to work in a positive and dynamic way. *I, Hamlet* is a performance of *Hamlet* which constantly rewrites the play – not simply through the rearrangement of the text, but by opening up gaps and offering multiple perspectives which belie fixed or received interpretations. Since it is a performance of *Hamlet*, it also tempts us as an audience to make comparisons with our own idea of 'the standard version' of the play. Part of the enjoyment of watching *I, Hamlet* is seeing the shift of focus between the two versions, letting the new version inform and literally play with the old. The changes in perspective which result challenge us to question our assumptions, leading us back to Shakespeare's play in new ways.

Although *Ophelia* and *I, Hamlet* are different projects – one a new play, one a version of Shakespeare's play – they demonstrate in similar ways the problems and benefits of performing feminist responses to Shakespeare in the contemporary theatre. As we have seen, the effectiveness of any feminist attempt to respond to Shakespeare is determined by a wide variety of factors in the production process, including the nature and composition of the company or team producing the play, logistic considerations in casting, and the audience's knowledge of Shakespeare.

These two case-studies show women theatre-makers manipulating the languages of theatre in a dual strategy of interpreting and representing Shakespeare's text on the one hand, while also interrogating Shakespeare's texts and even questioning the value of text itself on the other. The comic element in *Ophelia* helped to unsettle conventions, and the strong visual elements of the production ironically unsettled the supremacy of text. In *I, Hamlet*, the split casting and the use of varied and provocative visual images denied the audience the chance to settle on any fixed definition of the play or its characters. Both productions drew attention to the liminal element of theatre and to the fluidity of meaning, often through visual images and metatheatre. In the playful oscillation between looking back at Shakespeare and celebrating the need for constant rewriting, *Ophelia* and *I, Hamlet* played and played *with* Shakespeare to powerful effect.

Reference

1   *Ophelia* was premièred at the Stantonbury Campus Theatre in Milton Keynes in 1996, directed by Rosemary Hill. A second production was presented by students from De Montfort University, at the Bowen West Theatre, Bedford, in May 1997. *I, Hamlet* was performed by the Rose Theatre Company on tour throughout the UK, Central and Eastern Europe, and Scandinavia in 1996–97. My thanks are due to Bryony Lavery and Jane Prendergast for taking the time to discuss these productions with me, and to Rosemary Hill for inviting me to watch the rehearsals for *Ophelia*. A version of this article appeared in *New Theatre Quarterly* 54 (1998).

4   Theorizing Practice-Based Research: Performing and Analysing Self in Role as '*I, Hamlet*'

Jane Prendergast

A feminist performance praxis that is 'lived' is a fertile ground for dramaturgical, and thereby social, experimentation. Holding up a mirror to canonical performances of gender and identity, feminism as an evolving movement with its commitment to social change, has the possibility to revision social practice, or resignify, what Elin Diamond calls the constrictive social script (Diamond, 1997: iii). Building upon structures of traditional Shakespearean theatre practice, the feminist interrogating Shakespeare can extend traditional performance boundaries by performing male roles as well as female roles, in order to explore new performance practices and languages that can best describe these processes.

Challenging the canon with its entrenched historicity from a feminist perspective within the Academy of Shakespearean criticism is no easy task. To be a feminist 'performer' of a Shakespearean text is to position oneself at the front line of a debate that literally challenges the fabric of Western literary culture, and to do so *is* a political process. Not only what you are criticizing comes under scrutiny, but by becoming the centre of focus and inquiry, you challenge your own social and cultural positioning. The predicament of the feminist Shakespearean performer is therefore overtly political because it is avowedly personal: seeking change is a 'living' and 'lived' process. My performance project '*I, Hamlet*' is overtly political because I seek to expose *Hamlet* as a hegemonic landmark of classical Western literature and patriarchal culture. Throughout my project, I worked with the premise that it is the business of Hamlet to subjugate the 'feminine' to his own cause – for 'male' enlightenment, in order to nurture and perpetuate a social system that privileges the male.

The performance of '*I, Hamlet*' was toured in 1996 and 1997 under the auspices of The Rose Theatre Company, a touring Shakespearean company, that I worked with as a core company member for over six years, based in East Sussex, England. '*I, Hamlet*' toured throughout the United Kingdom, Central and Eastern Europe, and Scandinavia, taking nine months from the beginning of the rehearsal period to the completion of the tour. The project grew out of my desire to contest the canon – to make a space in the play *Hamlet* for the life of a 'real' woman: to interrogate how I might construct a performance of Hamlet as a woman and as a feminist.

I employed an eclectic cross-section of feminism in my praxis to assist me in re-defining fe/male subjectivities, and to construct languages that can offer alternative perspectives to masculinist figures of women. As a starting point, to shift the old text away from the linear system of acts and scenes, I (re)constructed the text into a performance of Seven Movements to imitate a musical scale. I did this as a strategy in 'deterritorialization', a term used by the philosopher Gilles Deleuze and psychoanalyst Felix Guattari, to describe the process of shattering the linear (patriarchal) unity of knowledge (Deleuze and Guattari, 1996: 6). Because the activity of deterritorialization encourages 'lines of flight', or multiplicities of meaning, this re-structuring of Shakespeare's text had the effect of emulating what Deleuze and Guattari term a 'continuous variation' or 'continuum' – terms that they use to portray a shift away from a linear mode of language to a more variable or 'rhizomatic' state which is 'superlinear', that is, a 'plane whose elements no longer have a fixed linear order", this they stress is the 'rhizome model' (Deleuze and Guattari, 1996: 9). [i]

Because music sends out lines of flight, like so many 'transformational multiplicities' by working with Movements instead of acts and scenes, the text became more of a musical score; a model of working that seemed to me to have the potential to map the multiple pathways of my performance (ibid.: 11). Deleuze and Guattari suggest that by placing all the components in continuous variation, music itself (in this case the text) becomes a superlinear system, a rhizome instead of a tree, and enters the service of a virtual cosmic continuum of which even holes, silences, ruptures, and breaks are a part (ibid.: 95).

By leaving out the eighth note (Movement) of the octave in the reconstructed text, I set out to create a free space in the performance where audience and actors could meet, after the performance, continuing the performance in a shared forum; a 'plateau' moment, where pathways of the performance met (assembled) in moments of 'becoming' (ibid.: 21). Reconfiguring the narrative of *Hamlet* into Movements was also an attempt at magnifying and distilling, or, slowing down and speeding up, the timing of the fictive world of the 'straight' text, so that the audience was directly confronted with the struggles and issues between the characters. Working with the text in this way also enabled me to play with the flow of action as it was unleashed from the restraints of its original form, that is, a deliberate shifting away from its hierarchical phallocentric social system of meanings.

Working with the model of the rhizome, itself a 'non-system', I set out to explore in '*I, Hamlet*' where the holes, silences, ruptures, and breaks of the original text, occurring as an integral part of the staging of a new 'feminist' text, might exist. I questioned whether the interstices were potential sites for 'new' performances of the text; spaces that were undefined, and therefore, places of 'becoming'. In order to find languages that could 'map' this inquiry, I referred to Deleuze and Guattari's discussion of secret or continuous language (the language of the performer?) that places the 'public language's system of variables in a state of variation', to embody what Deleuze and Guattari suggest is 'a generalised chromaticism', to create language close to musical notation (ibid.: 97). Because this is a language that is both structured and free-flowing, it seemed to me that it could offer the possibility to come close to the notion of a feminist language.

Foregrounding the performativity of the body engaging with canonical text in performance, I positioned myself to be at the centre of my interrogation as the subject of my own inquiry – a feminist woman performer, performing Hamlet in *Hamlet*. The performance of my body therefore became the chief 'cartographic' tool to my envisioning and creating of a new form of 'subjectivity' not displayed by the characters of the 'old' text. Employing several voices to reconstruct the text in performance – an autobiographical narrative writing, a theory based analysis, and video – I set out to examine how these multiple voices could intersect to produce new praxis.

Working with Hélène Cixous's notion 'writing the body' (*l'écriture féminine*) as a strategy in uncovering my experiences in rehearsal, I found that writing in narrative about my experiences during the project, I was able to make sense of them. In a process much like that described by Anna Cutler in her article 'Abstract Body Language: Documenting Women's Bodies in Theatre' (1998), my written landscape also became a performance landscape 'I, *Hamlet*' became therefore, a written map of what was performed subjectively on and off the stage. This process became a 'therapeutic' undertaking because I was then able to recognize 'dysfunctional' historicizations in the 'old' text. The (re)constructed 'new' text ('I, *Hamlet*'), assumed a different performance priority by retaining its narrative sense, but because it was fragmented, defamiliarised the story line enough so that 'I, *Hamlet*' told an alternative story. As Diamond, speaking about gender in performance points out, when gender is 'alienated' or foregrounded, the spectator is able to see what s/he can't see: a sign system *as* a sign system (Diamond, 1997: 47). Moreover, identifying with the 'I, *Hamlet*' text as a composite (re)construction of Shakespeare's *Hamlet,* I discovered in the later stages of the project, was to retrieve myself from the type of death suggested by the canonical text for women. This was because my reading of the text does not discount the binary structure of the play, but rather, I am removed from the dialectical exchange between myself as the subject, and the text as the object of my interrogation.

> As I write, I find that I meet monstrous dark barriers, gaps in myself that reveal blockages of pain, regret and frustration when I examine them. This is the shadow-side of my process with Hamlet that is now becoming more real than the performance of the text. I think that process has to do with two things: the patriarchal and 'mythic' structure of the play, and my feminist interrogation of the play. One clashes against the other – the unconscious of the text and my own unconscious as it interfaces with the text; it is all now in disarray.
>
> (Jane Prendergast, 'I, *Hamlet*' Production Journal, 1996)

As a philosophy, feminism served my 'lived' process by becoming a magnifying glass through which to locate places (sites in the dramatical text), and spaces (potential acts), or as Gillian Rose proposes: 'collisions between discourse, fantasy and corporeality' (1999: 247). By seeing the play as a 'map' of inside and outside spaces (binaries and collisions), I contrasted the two texts – Shakespeare's *Hamlet* and '*I, Hamlet*' exploring potential new meanings. To locate spaces in the text, not to harness them, but rather perform them imaginatively and release them into different forms, I also endeavoured through words and figures, or figurations, to map my performance of *Hamlet*. My mapping aspired to be both an imaginative, personal/subjective, and physical (performed) mapping of the text(s). Basing my interrogation of *Hamlet* on the assumption that the play is a meta-theatrical text about masculinist theatre, a play within a play, a mirroring of the patriarchal world as a stage, and therefore an historical document, in my mapping I have also drawn parallels between Renaissance geographic sea and land explorations with '*I, Hamlet*' as a touring production: travelling with the text inwardly (subjectively) and outwardly (on tour). In a similar way to the Renaissance explorers who produced pictorial mappings of their explorations of spaces and places, I navigated my way through the text of *Hamlet* to produce mappings that attempt to locate new spaces and places.

The philosopher Rosi Braidotti has had a significant impact upon my devising a language to describe my critical process because she has extended the work of Gilles Deleuze into feminist discourse. Braidotti describes a multi-voice style of speaking based on the notion of 'figurations' (Braidotti, 1994: 1).[2] Her indications were easily applied in my project because they enabled a fluidity in speaking feminist concerns that facilitated a crossing of linear boundaries. She states

> … I deliberately try to mix the theoretical with the poetic or lyrical (musical) mode. These shifts in my voice are a way of resisting the pull toward cut-and-dried, formal ugly, academic language.
>
> (ibid., 37)

To sum up: the question of what sort of languages could map the experience(s) of my performing Hamlet/*Hamlet* differently was an overall concern in this project. Therefore, as an act of feminist intervention in canonical text, in order to 'deterritorize' the 'academic' mode, I ventured on a 'line of flight' by including in the theorization of my praxis, multiple 'voices'. Working with the notion 'Writing-the-Body' I experimented with a narrative writing, interspersed with my theoretical writing as a stylistic procedure. This multiple way of working then became a way of 'voicing' the gaps in which my performed mappings occurred. To find a language that could tell the stories of the gaps, I was compelled to become both the geographer and the map. I became the body mapped; actively recording my own 'lived' attempt at a feminist praxis where theory and practice could meet.

An 'Other' Language

> Could the map of this language be imagined as: A turnaround the margins drawing close to the centre? A double textual vision, the performed enactment of the inside-outside; activity and analysis working against the character and yet with the character, against the constitution and yet in the development of it? The

silent body a site of exploration and inscription, speaking a new map with its
own integrated visual geography and autobiography, a nomadic text, imagined
and silent?

('*I, Hamlet*' Production Journal, 1996)

A language that could articulate the creative processes of women has been imagined by
a number of theorists and practitioners, including Christiane Makward who suggests a
language that is:

open, nonlinear, unfinished, fluid, exploded, fragmented, polysemic, attempting
to speak the body i.e. the unconscious, involving silence, incorporating the
simultaneity of life as opposed to or clearly different from pre-conceived,
orientated, masterly or 'didactic' language.

(1980: 96)[3]

Makward's idea of a free-flowing language that can open up the gaps in a text so that
they can become re-visioned spaces has become a task in feminist, and women-centred
projects. Discovering new languages to document women's bodies in performance is
also the project of Cutler, as I mentioned previously, who has explored the possibility
of voicing a third or potential body as a way to find a language for women's 'hidden'
or censored bodies on the stage (Cutler, 1998: 115-16). The relevance of Cixous's
l'écriture féminine, as Cutler points out, is that it is a conscious creation, which is why its
effects are so far reaching, and crosses genres in the feminist movement:

The process of writing the feminine for performance and for the performing
female body can therefore be seen to represent the live and potential nature of
performance itself ... The written landscape becomes the performance landscape
– conscious creation to represent the performance, not just through description
and denotation as though it were a verbatim transcription of events, but through
suggestion and feeling as though it were responded to in a way which reflects
the sense of the event and, indeed, a sense of the performed body.

(ibid.: 117)

Even though the foundational structure of '*I, Hamlet*' is dependent upon the words and
meanings of Shakespeare's *Hamlet*, where it takes its own 'line of flight' is in emulating
a musical score. In this regard, '*I, Hamlet*' is a mobile text; it is musical because it thirsts
for dislocation, and because of this, facilitates the construction of new languages that
appear through the gaps – between the 'old' and 'new' text, to include the languages of
'real' women and women's-ways-of-knowing.

Gaps and Spaces

Finding ways to navigate gaps between texts was to begin with a daunting task. I
began my reading of *Hamlet* as a 'historical' document by imagining myself performing
in a 'straight' reading of the play. To contrast this reading, I then visualized how the

text it might look if I inserted myself into it with 'difference'. I did this by questioning and imagining the revisions that I would make in performance. To do this I had to find middle ground between the historical text and this new text – to occupy a viable position between these two textual worlds. This process became a difficult transposition of personal spaces as my own unconscious interfaced in the gaps between the two texts.

It was through an exploration and experimentation with the gaps between texts, and the dislocations of time and space between the 'old' and the 'new' text, that I have come to consider the effectiveness of what Susan Bennett describes as a possible method for challenging and subverting imageries in Shakespeare, that also contemporize them. Bennett (1996: 2) suggests that the 'gaps and the excesses' of the Shakespeare corpus become the foundation for a performance of the present, using the word *excess* to describe what I consider to be potential spaces between texts. Bennett states that the

> gaps and excesses are always inherent, even in a 'straight' production/reading of a Shakespeare play, [...] it is when they become the text that their inclination to disrupt the notion of the linearity of progress is made manifest.

> (ibid.)

Reflecting upon my explorations during rehearsal time, I found that Bennett's words suggested a way of describing the substance of subversion, that is, that the 'gaps and

Figure 4.1. Jane Prendergast holding papier-mâché skull in rehearsals for I, Hamlet. *Photo: Carli Leimbach.*

excesses' had the power to contemporize the text. Furthermore, I discovered that once these gaps were explored and made conscious in performance, new texts emerged that could disrupt the master narrative. That Bennett has indicated a way to approach the disruption of social ideologies perpetuated and reinforced in straight readings and performances of the play, is further affirmation to me in my praxis that I may have contributed to the revision of the cultural apparatus that has produced Shakespeare. Experimenting in this way through a 'lived' practice, what emerged for me as an actor were figures of new/old characters that could be built up from out of the one-sidedness of the original characters. For example, I began 'performing' set or known classical Hamlet gestures, such as the figure of Hamlet holding Yorick's skull at a spectatorial distance:

While exploring this gesture however, I observed that the holding of the skull away from myself at a spectatorial distance did not feel right. Through experimenting with the holding of the skull in a variety of positions I discovered my need to cradle and nurture the skull, an image of death, and take the skull to myself, to hold it, as I would a child.

Observing gaps in the performance also facilitated a change in the intensity of the action to give the audience time to reflect. These became active moments (spaces) where my practice of feminism could be staged. For example, when I was playing Hamlet, so that I could gain more physical control over Hamlet's male inscribed bodily movements, at circumscribed times in the performance, I slowed my bodily movement to a bare minimum so that my hand gestures, and/or facial gestures, became the main focus for the audience rather than the spoken text. Focusing the action on my hands or face had the effect of highlighting the difference of my female physical structure and thereby my performance of the character as a woman.

Constructing mappings of performance that emerged out of this exploration of 'new languages' also included mapping the unconscious gaps of a text, rendering them as conscious spaces, in order to live in-between (limen), or third/potential: a position where re-visionings of Shakespeare's characters could take place. Feminist/women-centred performance needs to be seen as spatially sited theatre which makes re-visionings of women possible through its capacity to focus on the physical body and its intention to look beyond the physical body to something 'other'. This, perhaps, is the reason why feminist theatre has a conscious and compelling need to find languages that can best describe these processes. 'I, Hamlet' is one attempt.

References

1   A 'line of flight' is the term used by Deleuze and Guattari to describe how the multiplicity of the rhizome works. They state: 'Multiplicities are defined by the outside: by the abstract line, the line of flight or deterritorialization according to which they change in nature and connect with other multiplicities. [...] The line of flight marks: the reality of a finite number of dimensions that the multiplicity effectively fills; the impossibility of a supplementary dimension, unless multiplicity is transformed by the line of flight ...' (1996: 9).

2   Braidotti describes the term 'figuration' in the following way: 'figuration refers to a style of thought that evokes or expresses ways out of the phallocentric vision of the subject. A figuration is a politically informed account of an alternative subjectivity.' (1994: 1)

3   See Baym, 1991 for an excellent discussion on the notion of women's languages.

Part 2 – Speaking for Themselves: Women Theatre-Makers at Work

5   Transmitting the Voices, Voyages and Visions: Adapting Virginia Woolf's *To the Lighthouse* for Radio

Lindsay Bell

What began as a commission to adapt *To the Lighthouse* for a live radio performance, evolved into a journey of questions about the adaptation process, the nature of radio as a performance space, and the performative aspects of both radio and theatre.[1] The critical inquiry that surrounds this discussion of the adaptation was developed post-production, and has expanded into an inquiry not only into the development process itself, but into the interaction between Woolf's own performance theory, radio art, and the final production draft of the adaptation. The language of Woolf's novel and narrative structure, and the language of radio as a performative medium, established the aesthetic for the language of the adaptation. Radio, as a body-less entity, offers a unique performance space that is neither governed by the male gaze, nor fettered by the physical presence of spectacle and, as such, is particularly amenable to Woolf's stream-of-consciousness narrative structure. Realizing that Woolf, in many respects, anticipated feminist discourse, it is interesting to isolate a through-line from her essays on theatre which rejected the body in performance, to the nature of radio as a feminist performance space, to the performance of the adaptation that brings the two together – bringing Woolf's novel from a private reader's experience to a public performance of transmitted voices giving a new shape to the voyage and the vision of Woolf's poignant novel.

In several essays, Virginia Woolf discusses the act of reading, the theatre, and the anticipation of a literary form that would blend prose, poetry and drama.[2] What is most discernible from these essays is her scepticism of the 'performing body' and the communal nature of theatre that is pitted against her penchant for the quiet solitary reader's experience. Her persuasive arguments make it a challenge to justify a theatrical adaptation of her work – an adaptation which makes her prose performative, and makes her cherished private reader's experience public. However, with her thoughts on theatre in mind, I would like to pose the notion of theatricalizing her prose for radio as a hybrid solution to her scepticism – for radio is both public and private, and the performing body which she found greatly disconcerting, is absent. Her position on reading, theatre, and form all speak directly to, and intersect with, our understanding of radio art today. To illustrate the intersection of her performance theory and the advantages of radio, this essay will examine Woolf's opinions on the body in performance (the body as text), the Greek chorus tradition, and the power of the imagination. This line of inquiry provides a theoretical framework for a discussion of the strategies of adapting *To the Lighthouse* for radio.

Although Woolf wrote for radio, and read various essays on the air, her essays and reviews on theatre and performance issues are the most beneficial to this discussion. What is of primary interest is the recurring dialectic between reading a dramatic text and the text in performance. Since radio is often closely aligned with the experience of the reader, this dialectic invites the argument for radio as a medium that encompasses all the imaginative power of reading and excludes the distracting physical elements of performance. Martin Esslin, in his essay 'The Mind as a Stage' discusses the power of the wireless imagination:

> The dialogue can carry the scenery and the costume within it and the human voice can powerfully suggest human experience … imagined pictures may be more beautiful and powerful than actual ones … In radio, each listener will automatically see his [or her] ideal before his [or her] mind's eye and thus be satisfied.
>
> (1971: 5)

Almost in direct response to several statements in her essays, this quotation is intrinsically linked to Woolf's attitudes towards performance and reading that will be discussed here.

In his article, 'Virginia Woolf and "The Distance of the Stage"', Steven Putzel provides a comprehensive examination of Woolf's performance theory (as expressed in her essays and in *Between the Acts* (1941)), and applies it to recent American and British stage adaptations of her novels *To the Lighthouse* (1927), *Orlando* (1928), and *The Waves* (1931) – most of which faced severe criticism from the public and the press.[3] The discussion initiated by Putzel will be used in this essay as a springboard into considering radio as an appropriate medium for adaptations of Woolf's work. Inherently, radio reduces the distance between the audience and the stage, changes the nature of performance, and is perhaps a more suitable medium for stream-of-consciousness narrative than what can be physically realized on the stage. Putzel isolates the practical and theoretical challenges to the adaptation process, several of which intersect with my own experience in adapting *To the Lighthouse* for radio. He concludes his article with some strategic advice for dramatizing Woolf:

Adapters who rely on the realism, naïve symbolism, or the traditional musical still fail in their attempts to bring Woolf to the stage. It takes the post-modern stage – with its use of mime, dance, opera, contrapuntal music, minimalist sets, and, most of all, its demand of complicity from the audience – to produce a successful performance of Virginia Woolf.

(1999: 466)

The primary criticisms of these stage productions can at once be solved if we consider radio as the target medium for the adaptation. By relying solely upon an absent presence (the voice), radio drama is a performance in the mind that engages the listener's emotions and intellect, and transcends the traps of 'literal' adaptations. Radio is a medium in which the imagination is not fettered, nor earthbound, by the performing body and the scenery. It offers a freedom within the listening experience, within the wireless imagination – a freedom that Woolf herself found in reading the dramatic text in her garden.

Woolf's responses towards theatre, or more specifically, towards performance, oscillated between attraction and repulsion. Her attraction to the theatre often relied on how closely her own reader's version of the play resembled the play as performed upon the stage. The version created in her mind when reading the dramatic text was regarded as a standard of how theatre *should* be performed – and any deviation from this 'ideal' was disturbing and often critically dismissed by Woolf. The dialectic between text as read and text as performed evolves into a polemic between the mind's 'ideal' stage and the 'real' stage – between Woolf's acute imagination and the performance of *The Cherry Orchard*, or *Twelfth Night* at the Old Vic, for example:

> Although every member of the audience at the Art [sic] Theatre last week had probably read Tchekhov's *The Cherry Orchard* several times, a large number of them had, perhaps, never seen it acted before. It was no doubt on this account that as the first act proceeded, the readers, now transformed into seers, felt themselves shocked and outraged. The beautiful, mad drama which I had staged often enough in the dim recesses of my mind, was now hung within a few feet of me, hard, crude, and overemphatic, like a cheap coloured print of the real thing. But what right did I have to call it the real thing? What did I mean by that?
>
> ('*The Cherry Orchard*': 246)

The solitary reader's experience allows her 'time ... to make a note in the margin, time to wonder' (Woolf '*Twelfth Night*' at the Old Vic': 28), whereas the experience in the theatre, with its bodies as text is distracting and 'the body is almost as upsetting as the scenery' (ibid.: 29). These comments, as well as the excerpt below, suggest a spectatorship that reads the performance against the printed text in the mind:

> The actual persons of Malvolio, Sir Toby, Olivia, and the rest expand our vision-ary characters out of all recognition. At first we are inclined to resent it. You are

not Malvolio; or Sir Toby either, we want to tell them; but merely imposters. We sit gaping at the ruins of the play, at the travesty of the play. And then by degrees this same body or rather all these bodies together, take our play and remodel it between them.

(ibid.: 29)

The body in performance, as noted by Woolf above, generates a multiplicity of texts, far beyond that which was intended by the dramatist. Woolf's response to theatre in this regard, anticipates a primary tenet of late-twentieth century theatre discourse, namely, the significance of the multiplicity of meanings inferred by the body as text in various modes of representation.

Martin Esslin also discusses the difference between reading and performance, but unlike Woolf, he does not appear to be reluctant to engage in the theatrical experience:

Reading a play is not the same thing as witnessing it – there is no immediacy, the experience is without involvement, the illusion of being present and identified with the action; for, as Aristotle has it, the narrative form – and hence all that is read – takes place in the epic past; the drama is an eternal present.

(1971: 5)

Woolf, in comparison, holds the two versions of the text within the same dimension, and therefore, in a more direct line of conflict and more susceptible to comparison. She makes explicit reference to the reader's and the performance texts: 'let us compare the two versions … compare [the actors'] version with our own … wherever the fault may lie, they have very little in common' ('*Twelfth Night*': 29). The implication here is that the two versions *should* be a perfect match, they *should* have everything in common. She continues:

The printed word is changed out of all recognition when it is heard by other people … The word is given a body as well as a soul … the flatness of the print is broken up as by crevasses or precipices; all the proportions are changed … we are … reminded that Shakespeare wrote for the body and for the mind simultaneously.

(ibid.)

Woolf questions the purpose of exchanging her idyllic reader's experience for the whims of the theatre profession when her own 'mind's stage' is perfectly capable of rendering the 'ideal' *Twelfth Night* performance. For Woolf, 'imprisoning [the characters] within the bodies of real men and women' (ibid.) becomes absurd. 'Why exchange this garden for the theatre?' (ibid.), she asks. Why exchange the 'ideal' for the 'real'?

It is as if these two texts collide – the play text as read and the performance text as seen. The nature of performance inscribes an additional text upon the body which, for Woolf, is distracting and inevitably conflicts with the pre-existing text in her mind. The result of this collision of the two texts is that the bodies as text 'overpower' the printed text. She expresses this aspect of her performance theory in a later essay, 'Congreve's Comedies' (1937): 'The bodily presence of actors and actresses must, it would seem, often overpower the words they had to speak' (82). This overpowering relates to her recognition of the multiplicity of texts conjured by performance. As a reader she is free to imagine without boundaries, but as a spectator, where elements of theatre are made concrete, there are too many extraneous associations from every word and gesture to be contained within the architectural space of the theatre. The inevitability of multiple meanings is discussed in an earlier essay, 'On Not Knowing Greek' (1925): '[T]he later plays of Shakespeare, where there is more of poetry than of action, are better read than seen, better understood by leaving out the actual body than by having the body, with all its associations and movements visible to the eye' (5). Her imagination as a spectator is confined within the walls of the theatre, and this feeling is just as disconcerting as the actors, the 'imposters', embodying characters. At the theatre, Woolf experiences an overwhelming distortion of the play she knows intimately, and is greatly offended by the infinite associations and multiple meanings.

And yet, despite this recognition of the collision of texts and the disillusionment of seeing the body in performance, she also acknowledges the responsibility of the audience: 'It is we [the audience] who fumble, make irrelevant observations, notice the chocolate or the cinnamon, the sword or the muslin' ('Congreve's Comedies': 78). This distraction in the audience, this distance from the stage, leads her a few years later, near the end of her life, to acknowledge the difference between the reader and the spectator in an unpublished manuscript, 'The Reader':

> As time goes on the reader becomes distinct from the spectator. His sense of words and their associations develops ... there is the specialized reader, who attaches himself to certain aspects of the printed words ... the curious faculty – the power to make places and houses, men and women and their thoughts and emotions visible on the printed page is always changing. The Cinema is now developing his eyes; the Broadcast is developing his ear ...
>
> (Silver, 1979: 428)

Here, we catch a glimpse of what seems to be a broadening acceptance of spectatorship for technologized art in the form of cinema and radio, beyond newsreels and war reports. In the 'C Version' of 'The Reader' manuscript, Woolf sums up the central principles of her performance theory, tying in the performing body, the audience and the struggle of the reader as spectator:

> We have lost the sound of the spoken word; all that the sight of the actors bodies suggests to the mind through the eye. We have lost the sense of being part of the audience. We miss a thousand suggestions that the dramatist conveyed by the inflection of voice, by gesture, by the placing of the actor's bodies. This can still be proved by comparing our impressions after seeing the play acted with our impression after reading the play alone.
>
> (Silver, 1979: 430)

The last word of the excerpt above is of key importance to Woolf's debate between reading and theatre-going – this notion of solitude, privacy, of being alone with the text. Her relationship to society often waxed and waned from exuberance to misanthropy, and her theatre writings express this dichotomy, this attraction and repulsion. The following excerpt from 'Notes on an Elizabethan Play' (1925), offers both reverence of the sublimity of theatre and the contrasting want for solitude:

> Wandering in the maze of the impossible and tedious story suddenly some passionate intensity seizes us; some sublimity exalts … It is a world full of tedium and delight, pleasure and curiosity, of extravagant laughter, poetry, and splendour. But gradually it comes over us, what then are we being denied? What is it that we are coming to want so persistently, that unless we get it instantly we must seek elsewhere? It is solitude. There is no privacy here. Always the door opens and someone comes in. All is shared, made visible, audible, dramatic. Meanwhile, as if tired with company, the mind steals off to muse in solitude; to think, not act; to comment, not share; to explore its own darkness, not the bright-lit-up surfaces of others.

(61)

For all her trepidation she expresses towards the theatre, she does, however, champion the capacity of theatre to elicit physical sensations. In 'Congreve's Comedies', she writes: '[T]he illusion takes hold of us … and what with the rhythm of the speech and the indescribable air of tension … the world of the stage becomes the real world and the other, outside the play, but the husk and cast-off clothing' (78), and the experience expands and allows for 'a lightning swiftness of apprehension that snatches a dozen meanings and compacts them into one' (78). Here she catches a glimpse of her 'ideal' transformed into the 'real.' In another essay on William Congreve, she very briefly allows for the subtly of performance to capture moments which would inevitably elude the reader: 'It was natural to expect that the same words spoken by living men and women would warm and blossom, and that there would be drawn to the surface other subtleties of character which scarcely come to the top in reading' ('Congreve': 296). Intuitively, she realizes the power of the body in performance, the silence in a crowded theatre, and the significance of a pause that the reader would simply skim over and miss completely. Her reaction to the first act of *The Cherry Orchard* turns to appreciation as the play progresses, and the following excerpt touches on several key elements of the inner conflict between reading and attending theatre:

> … before the second act was over some sort of compromise had been reached between my reader's version and the actor's one. Perhaps in reading one had got the whole too vague, too mad, too mystical … I felt less and less desire to cavil at the acting in general and more and more appreciation … With every word … spoke[n], one's own conception of that part plumped itself out like a shrivelled skin miraculously revived … the atmosphere of the play wrapped us round and shut out everything alien to itself … Long before the play was over

we seemed to have sunk below the surface of things and to be feeling our way among submerged but recognizable emotions … it sends one into the street feeling like a piano played upon at last, not in the middle only but all over the keyboard and with the lid left open so that the sound goes on.

('*The Cherry Orchard*': 248)

This oscillation between rejection and attraction to the theatre can be traced back to earlier writings that speculated upon the future of fiction. In her essay, 'The Narrow Bridge of Art' (1927), she describes a new literary form that would embrace prose, poetry and drama – one that would be 'dramatic, and yet not a play. It will be read, not acted' (224). This essay looks at the role of poetry versus prose in modern literature and she posits the questions of whether prose can be dramatic, and if in the near future, prose will envelop poetry. These anticipations of form intersect with Putzel's advice to adapters of Woolf's prose and with my own experience of adapting *To the Lighthouse* for radio. Dramatizing stream-of-consciousness seems most amenable to poetic abstractions and contrapuntal structures in a form that 'envelops poetry'.

In her earlier essay, 'On Not Knowing Greek', Woolf idealizes the combination of poetry, drama and fiction that exists in ancient Greek drama. She sees several elements of the Greek dramatic tradition as an alternative, and even perhaps as a solution, to the 'real' theatre of her time: 'The intolerable restrictions of the drama could be loosened … if a means could be found by which what was general and poetic, comment, not action, could be freed without interrupting the movement of the whole' (5). This 'means' was the new art form she envisioned. Radio, it seems, answers this prescription in its malleability of form, meaning and content, and its ability to shift effortlessly in time and space, and from the objective to the subjective realm.

For Woolf, the Greek chorus provides the necessary link between the performance and its audience and, as a result, achieves her ideal. The Greek chorus as narrators, 'loosen' the 'intolerable [dialogic] restrictions' of traditional dramatic conventions by offering 'undifferentiated voices who sing like birds in the pauses of the wind; who can comment, or sum up, or allow the poet to speak himself, or supply, by contrast, another side to his conception' ('On Not Knowing Greek': 5). Is it possible that Woolf sees the chorus as a potential remedy to her reservations about theatre, in that they displace the performing body? The chorus takes on the text that is inscribed upon the bodies of the actors, comments upon it, and ensures that the performance-audience relationship is given and received in a specific manner. Again, this argument lends support for radio, as there is no interfering performing body, and no text can be inscribed upon the voice that is an absent presence. Taking this concept a step further, Frances Gray points out in her article 'Carry on Echo: The Dissident Sound Body', that a 'voice may not always signify the presence of a human body' (3.1).

Woolf's theoretical position on theatre is reflected in the narrative strategies of her novels. Stream-of-consciousness narratives privilege the mind over the body, and therefore, privilege the mind over action. Conversely, theatre brings bodily presence to the characters which privileges the body over mind – characters are action-driven and their thoughts are externalized. Steven Putzel discusses this point and suggests that 'Woolf makes it clear that the problem with theatrical "drama" lies in its very "essence", that it is played out in external action and plot, what is "done as opposed to thought"' (1999: 440).

What is striking about Woolf's theory of performance discussed here, are the undeniable points of intersection with radio art today, and with the adaptation of *To the Lighthouse*. My adaptation was written for a staged public reading at the Shaw Festival, and was recorded and edited for a later radio broadcast. These conditions demanded a hybridized cross-pollinated form – a play that isn't a play, a play that is read *and* acted. It is also 'dramatic,' according to Woolf's definition, since the inward thoughts and emotions are dramatized and externalized through 'narrative in performance' and through a chorus and narrators. The adaptation is poetry, drama, and fiction, and the medium is live performance *and* radio – spontaneous *and* technologically manipulated. It was written 'for the body and for the mind simultaneously' ('*Twelfth Night*': 29).

Listening to radio drama is closely related to the reader's experience in its privacy and its ability to project a sound environment that mirrors the inner mind of the listener. Canadian novelist and playwright, Timothy Findley aligns the listening experience with that of the reader in his brief article 'Voices in the Dark': '[R]adio is for people who read … [it] not only invites the listener's participation – but demands it. Just the way a book does … It uses all the same facets of the imagination. Radio, like books, is provocative, not passive – stimulating, not stultifying' (1980: 7). The creation of a multidimensional reality that is absent from the visual field gives radio the ability to transmit visual images. But what does it mean to listen in a continuum in which presence is characterized by its absence? Gregory Whitehead addresses this question by suggesting that 'the investigation of radio has disappeared into the investigation of sound, the wireless body stripped and redressed to provide a broadcast identity for the nebulous permutations of diverse *ars acoustica*.' This element of artistry is discussed in Esslin's essay and, inadvertently, provides support for the viability of adapting Woolf for the radio: 'The radio play can deal with the same subject-matter [as theatre] without disillusioning heavy materiality of flesh-and-blood actors and paint-and-canvas sets. Radio is indeed an ideal medium for the most highly subjective poetic drama' (1971: 8). Woolf's theory of performance, her preference for reading, and dramatizing her prose for an aural medium come together in a mutual respect for the spoken word, the written word, and the power of the imagination to take both forms to transpose and elucidate images within the mind.

Virginia Woolf rejected the performance presence and privileged the visual absence by privileging the act of reading over the act of theatre, as previously mentioned. With radio, however, there is both presence and absence in the paradoxical intangibility of sound. There is both privacy and community. Radio is 'intimate but untouchable, sensually charged but technically remote' (Whitehead). Woolf's reticence towards theatre in performance primarily resides at the site/sight of the body, where the body becomes both text and icon. Her essays and theatre reviews continually return to the collision of two texts – the dramatic text inscribed within her reader's mind, and the text of the actor's body on stage. The presence of these bodies on stage come to embody her inner dramatic text – the 'real' collides with the 'ideal' and she becomes sceptical and resistant rather than a complicit audience member. But for the purposes of this discussion, the performance space, in this case, is returned back into the mind and the imagination – radio offers no body as text, merely the breath and the voice of the body signified – 'a voice is not a site. You cannot inscribe anything upon it' (Gray: 2.2). In radio, physical presence is characterized by its absence. Frances Gray asserts that 'the sound body, clearly, is a different thing from the body on stage; it has no necessary limits or boundaries; while to stand on the stage is to be confined both by the integrity of the actor's body and by the nature of the gaze directed at it' (6.1). In recognizing the body as text, its physical presence in radio becomes a site of resistance against the male gaze. 'Feminist theatre,' Gray continues, 'has sought strategies to resist the male gaze. But a body which is voice alone, which reforms and metamorphoses itself entirely through the sounds it can slip past the censor, is already engaged in the process of resistance' (2.1). This line of inquiry leads me to ask whether Woolf was resisting the gaze, or more specifically, resisting compliance with the ideologically dominant male gaze in her scepticism of theatre in performance. And does this suggest that she anticipated current feminist theatre discourse?

My adaptation of *To the Lighthouse* is not a transliteration between genres in the sense that I searched for and found expressions that correspond in both general meaning and specific feeling. Rather, it is an adaptation by distillation – maintaining adherence to Woolf's aesthetic and the 'spirit' of the original through processes of selecting and reconfiguring the stream-of-consciousness narrative to distribute amongst a chorus of voices. The third and final section of the novel best suited the fifty-two minute radio format, both in action and characterization. In this section, two teenagers, Cam and James, go to the lighthouse with their father, Mr Ramsay, while Lily Briscoe paints on the lawn. It also provided several opportunities to revisit the past (the two previous sections of the novel), and more importantly, reconnect Mrs Ramsay, whose death had been announced in the second section. The narrative was then distributed across six voices: Lily, Cam, James, Mr Ramsay, and two principal narrators, (F1 and M1), who, together, comprise a chorus-like body of voices. Cam and James double as minor narrators, and F1 doubled as Mrs Ramsay. The adaptation is also one of reception – presenting it publicly shifts the source text from a private reader's experience to a communal experience for the live theatre audience, and a private listening experience for the radio audience.

The rhythm of the adaptation became an interpretation of the stream-of-consciousness narrative. The rhythm and patterning of images invited great shifts in speed and time – where the act of painting and Lily's associated thoughts as she paints become a torrent of images and words simulating the movement of the brush flickering over the canvas and the movement of her gaze from the canvas to the house, the hedge, the jacmanna bright violet. This musical structure was realized through verbal collages, with choral qualities, and repetitive wave-like patterns of speech – gathering momentum, then receding. The placing of the words on the page became significant rhythmic indicators for the actors and helped to sculpt the narrative into a multi-voiced aural experience of stream-of-consciousness. Below is an excerpt from the first sequence (which was preceded by a prologue) that introduces the characters, the setting, and establishes the free-flowing use of 'undifferentiated voices.' The spaces between the dialogue signify a break in the flow of images, a technique I found useful rather than inserting 'pause' throughout the script, and in this way it became as much a musical score as it was a script. By employing contrapuntal, and choral structures as dramatic equivalents of stream-of-consciousness, the rhythm of the spoken word was just as important to the meaning.

Sequence I: The House & The Expedition

F2:	In the house –
F1:	all was silence.
LILY:	To come back after all these years.
F1:	Lily looked at the house, sleeping in the early sunlight.

(*A torrent of images*)

MR RAMSAY:	The terrace
LILY:	The horizon
JAMES:	The Lighthouse
MRS RAMSAY:	The Hebrides
CAM:	The Isle of Skye
M1:	Waves mountains high
CAM:	A house where there was no privacy to debate anything
M1:	The dining-room
JAMES:	The drawing-room window
MR RAMSAY:	The terrace
CAM:	The tennis lawn
M1:	The road to the fishing village
MRS RAMSAY:	The garden
LILY & M1:	She sat in the window
CAM:	Children playing cricket
MR RAMSAY:	The men happily talking
MRS RAMSAY:	The fall of the waves on the beach
M1:	Eight children!
CAM:	Cam,
MRS RAMSAY:	the youngest girl;
LILY:	picking Sweet Alice on the bank
JAMES:	James,
MR RAMSAY:	the youngest boy
MRS RAMSAY:	and most cherished
CAM:	Rose, Nancy,
LILY:	and Prue.
CAM:	She died though.

MR RAMSAY:	Last summer.
JAMES:	Roger and Jasper
MRS RAMSAY:	routing a flock of starlings
CAM:	and Andrew.
M1:	He died too?
MR RAMSAY:	Yes, in the war.
CAM:	Sea-birds and butterflies,
JAMES:	bats,
MRS RAMSAY:	flannels,
M1:	strawhats,
MR RAMSAY:	ink-pots,
LILY:	paint-pots,
CAM:	beetles,
JAMES:	skulls of small birds.
LILY:	Long frilled strips of seaweed pinned to the wall,
MRS RAMSAY:	a smell of salt and weeds,
CAM:	towels gritty with sand from bathing.
MRS RAMSAY:	Wipe your feet and try not to bring the beach in with you!
JAMES:	Crabs, she had to allow,
CAM:	if Andrew really wished to dissect them.
JAMES:	Or if Jasper believed one could make soup from seaweed
CAM:	Rose's objects –
MRS RAMSAY:	shells, reeds, stones.
JAMES:	The girl standing on the edge of the lawn painting.
M1:	Painting?
CAM:	Painting what?
LILY:	Mrs Ramsay sitting in the window with James.
MRS RAMSAY:	Lily's picture!
CAM:	She was supposed to be keeping her head as much as possible in the same position for Lily's picture.
MRS RAMSAY:	Lily's picture
LILY:	of the house –
JAMES:	the jacmanna bright violet,
M1:	the wall staring white
LILY:	of the hedge,
JAMES:	the house,
M1:	the children.
MRS RAMSAY:	The house, the room, the chairs,
MR RAMSAY:	shabby
MRS RAMSAY:	What was the point of buying good chairs to let them spoil up here all through the winter.
CAM:	Things got shabbier and shabbier
MRS RAMSAY:	summer after summer.
JAMES:	The mat was fading.

LILY:	The wallpaper was flapping.
Mrs Ramsay:	Never mind.
CAM:	The children loved it.
MR RAMSAY:	Three hundred miles from my library
MRS RAMSAY:	and his lectures
CAM:	and his disciples.
MRS RAMSAY:	It did him good.
LILY:	And there was room for visitors.
CAM:	Mats
JAMES:	camp beds
MRS RAMSAY:	crazy ghosts of chairs
M1:	and tables
JAMES:	A photograph or two –
MR RAMSAY:	and books.

Choosing the third section of the novel as the structural framework for the adaptation becomes problematic with respect to Mrs Ramsay, since it takes place at a time after she has died. It was imperative, however, to incorporate her presence as much as possible – for what is *To the Lighthouse* without Mrs Ramsay? The third section of the text can be read as a process of mourning the loss of a mother, a wife, and idealized role model in that the characters attempt to resuscitate her through memory, flashback sequences, and echoes from the past. She only exists in memory in the adaptation, and because of her absent presence, the mythic dimension of her character is augmented. She is conjured by the memories of Lily, Cam, James and Mr Ramsay, and as such, the focus of the adaptation becomes the memory of, the myth that is, Mrs Ramsay – the resonance, the residue, the force, and the strength of her that lingers.

The mode of expression of the adaptation becomes a memory play – capturing the journey of the 'remembering mind' – the flashes, the imprinting, the haziness, the sensuality – and these impressions are interwoven with the 'present mind' – the minds of Lily, Cam, James and Mr Ramsay – all of whom progress further and further towards some philosophical goal with each visitation into the past, mining deeper and deeper for some resolution, some vision.

The adaptation is essentially a reflection of my personal reading of the book, my interpretation, privileging certain images over others, isolating sights, smells, sounds, textures and colours. It is my interaction with the text, my comment upon it. Merely by exerting the choice to select or disregard a section of the original novel, I am foregrounding the process of adaptation. Parallels of this process can be drawn with interpretation theory, and consequently, there is the possibility of misinterpretation.

Respect and reverence of the original text led to the discovery of the playfulness of language inherent in Woolf's writing. The dramatization of the stream-of-consciousness narrative was made manifest by paying particular attention to the inherent rhythm of the language – the word selection, imagery, and narrative patterning – which sets the scene, the atmosphere, and defines the internal characterization. This explicit interior landscape of the characters is effortlessly expressed in radio performance where the corporeal physicalization is not part of the performativity of the medium. I would like to point out that every word in the adaptation is directly from *To the Lighthouse*, with the only slight changes made in verb tense. The salient feature of the adaptation, in this case, becomes the selection of phrases and images, and the assigning of specific voices to these selections. The specific aesthetic of the adaptation developed from following Woolf's punctuation, where each sentence, each comma, signalled the start of a new line. Then looking at this vertical column of sentences and fragments on the page, I was able to break it up further – lists of things, or a series of adjectives were isolated, and I began to play and react to the individual words. The multiplicity of voices, the lightness of perspective and perception, the agility, the flightiness which characterizes her narrative demanded that the vocalization of it must be as agile, as unfettered – lighting from impressions to thoughts, to sights, to sounds. I found that distributing these sentences, fragments and single words amongst the characters achieved this lightness, this flight of the mind – where sentences are initiated by one voice, and another takes over, and another and another – each contributing to the completion of the thoughts and images. The section of the script included below, in which Lily is painting, helps to illustrate this concept.

F1:	Lily stood screwing up her eyes.
LILY:	There is something,
F1:	something she remembered
LILY:	from before
F1:	in the relations of those lines cutting across,
LILY:	slicing down,
M1:	and in the mass of the hedge
LILY:	its green cave of blues and browns,
M1:	there was something,
F1:	which had stayed in her mind,
M1:	which had tied a knot in her mind
F1:	so that at odds and ends of time
LILY:	as I walk along Brompton Road,
M1:	as she brushed her hair,
F1:	she found herself painting that picture.
M1:	She took her hand and raised her brush.
LILY:	Where to begin?
F1:	One line placed on the canvas committed her to innumerable risks
LILY:	and irrevocable decisions.
M1:	As if she were urged forward
LILY:	and at the same time must hold myself back,
F1:	she made her first quick decisive stroke.

M1:	The brush descended.
F1:	It flickered brown over the white canvas;
M1:	it left a running mark.
F1:	A second time she did it – a third time.
M1:	Pausing and flickering,
F1:	lightly and swiftly pausing,
M1:	striking,
F1:	she scored her canvas with brown running nervous lines.
M1:	She looked at the canvas.
LILY:	It will be hung in the servants' bedrooms.
M1:	She began precariously dipping among the
M1 & LILY:	blues and umbers,
LILY:	It will be rolled up and stuffed under a sofa.
F1:	Moving her brush hither and thither.
LILY:	What was the good of doing it then?
M1:	She kept looking at
M1 & LILY:	the hedge,
F1:	at the canvas.
F1:	She was losing consciousness of outer things;
M1:	her name,
F1:	her personality,
M1:	her appearance,
F1:	her mind kept throwing up from its depths
M1:	scenes
LILY:	names
F1:	sayings
LILY:	memories
M1:	ideas,
F1:	like a fountain spurting over that
F1 & LILY:	glaring,
M1:	hideously difficult
F1:	white space,
M1:	while she modelled it with
M1 & LILY:	greens
F1 & LILY:	and blues.
LILY:	Mrs Ramsay,
M1:	she thought,
F1:	stepping back and screwing up her eyes.
LILY:	It must have altered the design a good deal when Mrs Ramsay was sitting on the steps with James. There must have been a shadow.
M1:	This moment which survived after all these years,
F1:	Lily dipped into it to re-fashion her memory of it

M1:   and it stayed in her mind
M1 & LILY: like a work of art.

It then became a matter of discerning who would say what. As I mentioned earlier, the cast was narrowed down to the primary characters of The Lighthouse section: Lily, Cam, James and Mr Ramsay, with two chorus-like narrators. It became clear by reading the text over and over gain, with these characters in mind, who would say what – some lines strongly suggested a male voice ('Miserable sinner that she was' and 'A woman, she should have known how to deal with it' (Bell, 2000: 13)) or a female voice ('He had gone and she had been so sorry for him and she had said nothing' (Bell, 2000: 8)), or others suggested Cam ('Seabirds and butterflies' (Bell, 2000: 4)), rather than Lily or Mrs Ramsay. Slowly the rhythm of the piece and the characterization soon became tangible.

The primary difficulty I faced was in selecting which sections to include and which to disregard, as the more I worked on the script, the more precious each word became. As each word had acquired such significant weight, I was reminded of Shakespeare – you cannot drop one word for fear of losing the full meaning – dropping a stitch and having it all come undone, unravelled – it is so tightly knit, it is a daunting task to find anything that seems remotely unconnected.

The adaptation developed into a form that subscribes to some of Virginia Woolf's theories on reading, theatre, and her anticipated hybrid form of art. It incorporates 'narrative in performance' with a chorus-like collage of voices commenting and questioning the telling of the story. Sentences melt into each other as they move from one voice to another, from one character's perspective to another's. Throughout the writing, the rehearsing, and the performing of the adaptation, I had hoped to achieve a distinct Woolfian aesthetic. Since I did not come to the adaptation of *To the Lighthouse* as a Woolf scholar, it was not until afterwards, when reading her essays, that I recognised how the finished adaptation intersected with her thoughts on theatre. She writes in 'Congreve's Comedies' of the futility of describing a specific experience of theatre in words, but she offers up the notion that the essence of the experience is 'conveyed in the curl of the phrase in the ear; by speed; by stillness' (78). My own interaction with her writing during the adaptation process can be described in exactly the same way, for the selection process, the assigning certain voices to certain phrases was, in essence, governed by 'the curl of the phrase on the ear, the speed, and the stillness.' This is what I found most salient and at the heart of her writing: the musicality, the phrasing, the pace, the moments of being, the moments of the 'flight of the mind', and the moments of profound stillness – 'Mrs Ramsay saying "Life stand still here"' (*To the Lighthouse*: 218; Bell, 2000: 17). The adaptation echoes Woolf's call in 'On Not Knowing Greek' for a form that is 'general and poetic, comment, not action' (5), such that the theatricalization of the novel resides in the transmission of images, in the shapes and movement of individual thoughts, character relationships, voices, voyages, and visions.

To conclude then, it appears that there is an intersection between Woolf's cherished reader's experience and radio – in its privacy and its ability to project a sound environment that emulates the inner mind of the listener. Arguably, radio has an acute ability to transmit visual images, engage the imagination and the intellect through the creation of a multi-dimensional reality that relies solely on the aural field – where the body resides solely in the imagination, and we are free to make notes in the margin while we listen alone in the garden.

References

1   The adaptation of *To the Lighthouse* was commissioned by the Shaw Festival Theatre, (Niagara-on-the-Lake, Canada) and performed at Royal George Theatre, Shaw Festival, on August 3, 2000, as part of the Bell Canada Reading Series. This production was directed by Ann Hodges with the following cast: Severn Thompson (*Lily Briscoe*), Sharry Flett (*Mrs Ramsay / Female Voice 1*), Bernard Behrans (*Mr Ramsay*), Catherine McGregor (*Cam Ramsay / Female Voice 2*), Jeff Meadows (*James Ramsay / Male Voice 2*), and Guy Bannerman (*Male Voice 1*). It was recorded live by Canadian Broadcasting Corporation and broadcast nationally on CBC Radio One and CBC Radio Two, April 22 & 23, 2001. The CBC producer for the Bell Canada Reading Series was Barbara Worthy.

2   These essays include: 'The Cherry Orchard' (1920), 'Congreve' (1921), 'Notes on an Elizabethan Play' (1925), 'On Not Knowing Greek' (1925), 'Twelfth Night at the Old Vic' (1925), 'Congreve's Comedies' (1937), 'Ellen Terry' (1941), and two draft essays published by Brenda R. Silver: 'Anon' and 'The Reader' (1940).

3   The stage adaptations discussed in Putzel's article include: *To the Lighthouse* (Empty Space Theatre Company, Lyric Studio, London, 1995); *Orlando* (musical version by Guildhall School of Music and Drama, London, 1988; semi-musical version by Red Shift Theatre Company, Edinburgh Festival, 1992; Robert Wilson's version with music and dance, *Le Festival d'Automne*, Théâtre Odéon, Paris, 1993, English version performed at Edinburgh Festival, 1996; Fevered Sleep Company, Tabard Theatre, 1997); *The Waves* (musical adaptation, New York Theatre Workshop, 1990).

Acknowledgements

Canada Council for the Arts, Canadian Broadcasting Corporation, Milija Gluhovic, Ann Hodges, Stephen Johnson, Damiano Pietropaolo, the staff at the Shaw Festival and the cast of the production, Robin Sutherland, Barbara Worthy, and Roxy.

6 Voicing Identities, Reframing Difference(s): The Case of *Fo(u)r Women*

A Brief Commentary on the Text of *Fo(u)r Women*

Adeola Agbebiyi

'Struggles around difference and the appearance of new identities in political and artistic arenas have provoked powerful challenges to the dominant narratives of modern world. Live art's very resistance to categorization and containment and its ability to surprise and unnerve makes its impact far reaching …'

(Ugwu: 1995, 54)

'Conceptual in nature the work is driven more by the expression of ideas.'

(ibid.)

My Skin is Black

Fo(u)r Women was conceived as an idea by Patience Agbabi and myself, put together in a remarkably short time for a performance piece and successfully staged to a packed house at the ICA in May 1996. Inspired by the Dr Nina Simone song 'Four Women' – a superbly cogent expiation of the power imbalances reflected in life paths experienced by four African-American women of differing skin shades – it explores the intersection of skin tone and gender in the construction of power and identity. Simone remains a true intellectual singer-composer: one of the strong voices whose work and whose expression of her work continues to inform and (in a phrase borrowed from Black performance poetry of the period) 'edutain'.

Patience and I conceived the central idea behind *Fo(u)r Women* in just one evening. We discussed dramatizing Nina Simone's 'Four Women', being inspired by the song to create a new structure, a new piece which would explore the lives of Black British women with a particular focus on women who love and respect other women. We wanted to use the particular voices of British women of African descent. At the time it was, and to an extent still is, far too easy to derive a definition of UK Black experience from the US and the Caribbean. The UK Black Experience is a perfect example of hybridity, with diaspora stories coming from all over the globe mixing with the local hybrid culture, creating exciting new forms of art content and practice. Hybridity offers dynamic possibilities, as Kobena Mercer notes: 'In a world in which everyone's identity has been thrown into question, the mixing and fusion of disparate elements to create new hybridized identities point to ways of surviving and thriving, in conditions of crisis and transition.' (1994: 259) And, indeed, since we wrote and performed *Fo(u)r Women*, there has been a series of publishing explosions of definitive, dynamic, powerful writing particularly by Black and mixed-race women located in Britain. Our criteria at inception were that the piece should deal with Black British female voices and include the voices of women who love women, and that we should get paid. So often the cultural economy deprives artists of the rights to their own work or due payment for it. In this case, it was essential that proper recompense and reward be made. Patience and I parted company at the end of a good evening and I went home to mull over *Fo(u)r Women*.

We met, always with food, at different houses to work through and share our ideas and stories, to stand around microphones improvising chants, to write, chat and rewrite, eschewing theory in favour of our individual narratives in order to create an alternative discourse of the style bell hooks has posited, controversially reframed by Suleri as 'the unmediated quality of a local voice serves as a substitute for any theoretical agenda that can be made more than a causary connection between the condition of postmodernism and the questions of gendered race.' (Suleri, 1995: 141) The weakness of using unmediated local first person voices is precisely the lack of engagement with theory. However, given that most of us live without theoretical approval, it is for theory to attempt to explain what is or seems to be, not the role of the individual to bow to theory. Postmodernism (for what it's worth) may be a condition or a symptom of the same response to crisis spoken about by Kobena Mercer: namely a move toward hybridity, or the attempt to label and fix the fluidity of creative collaboration embodied by the creative impulse, which can be viewed as the coming together of creatives as if it were the coming together of lovers.

We collectively agreed, after much discussion, to avoid labelling sexuality because: a) some Black women who love women don't identify with words like dyke, zami or lesbian; and b) we are writers regardless of who we sleep with; and c) sexual expression is gloriously fluid.

Process, Text and Performance

Fo(u)r Women was essentially a work in progress. We set deadlines for work to be completed and brought back in, brought in existing work and found areas to create new pieces. Collective pieces were created in up-beat energetic spaces, using sequenced beats and basslines as rhythm for the raps. For example, the opener 'Fo(u)r Women' – a rhythmic rollicking call and response between lead and backing vocals, a Diana Ross and the Supremes style jog through a litany of practical problems, feisty sexual expression and spiritual desire – was written in part all together, then taken away by individuals to add solo voices. Simone's 'Four Women' is a 12-bar tune in D minor with congas, bongos and a hypnotic bass line that holds the whole song together. I sequenced a percussion and blues bass track which played as we circled like demented backing singers round a mic in the middle of the room saying whatever came up and taping it. We would all take a copy of the tape away and then write our bits, bringing them back later to slot together. During these sessions, we'd find ourselves borrowing strong rhythms from that immortal 1970s Pepsi ad, chipping in short fill lines, cross rhythms and all. 'My Skin Is' – a chanted, half-sung hymn to our own skins – was a collective chant with solos reflecting a key aspect of each performer-writer's agenda or substitute form of expression.

We supported each other through difficult meetings, got to know each other more deeply as people and performers, hugged and cajoled one another through performance nerves and line-loss fright. We created a safe energised performance space with clear role boundaries and definitions, while allowing for fluidity and flexibility. At the time problems were encountered by my spitting out ideas like a chaotic Catherine Wheel, and natural reticence from the other two about writing the press release and publicity before writing the show.

Jillian Tipene, a mixed Maori performance poet and actress joined us as director. In many ways, she was our real fourth woman. Jillian co-ordinated our movement and staging and was a wonderfully invaluable support, source of beautiful energy and a clear directional eye.

Mother lover sister other

Early in the writing process, we made the choice to use 'Mother, Sister, Lover, Other' as our starting point. We felt these were the main limiting labels/states that were traditionally accorded to Black women: Hattie McDaniel mammy stereotypes; the use of sister in the community – especially church communities; the 'exotic' love interest for a politician or newspaper editor in film and TV drama. The fact that these themes related to some of our existing work was of no concern, but very convenient! Incidentally, the Holy virgin/whore split that occupied the minds of 1970s and 1980s feminist literary critics doesn't ever seem to have been applied to Black women: it is more like mother/maid or queen/whore, a theme which has subsequently also been explored by Valerie Mason John.

In choosing 'Mother, Sister, Lover, Other', we were also choosing to challenge audiences to reframe these stereotypical roles by creating our 'real' text in those names. Defining ourselves internally was central to the piece: putting ourselves into the world; a birthing of a vision of a strong independent self-defined, active, empowered Black women, a sharing of collected individual histories. Moreover the content expressed woman-loving sexuality, but accepted the duality of male and female which is at the heart of the lovers' meeting and also played out in the performativity of staging, if one is to add a gender label to audience or performer. *Fo(u)r Women* is a coming together in points of similarity to explore difference.

The use of quartets and the concept of reframing stereotypes led to the choice of set: four old gold frames.

Framing

> '{On Framing} the voyeuristic fantasy of unmediated and unilateral control over the other.'
>
> (Mercer, 1994)

We used four empty old gold frames like those found around plantation photos, in four graduated sizes. (These were successful enough in execution to have the Cable Street Police stop me as I was loading them into the back of my car – an event which speaks for itself.) They were placed as though appearing from the past and moving to the future, getting larger: above which was suspended a glitter ball – colonial meets with disco camp.

For 'Ufo Woman', the chorus in 'Ident' and 'Faultlines' we were fixed, static in the frames. The colonial style framed the action: disfigured golliwog gestures, minstrel turns, laments to the pain that splitting a family along skin shade lines causes, the first part of the cosmic twenty-first century voyage of Ufo woman …

Hello Heathrow.

This way, we could capture and fix the perverted twisted positions adopted by Black people under force of white supremacist thinking, by women under patriarchal gaze. Fix like fetish objects in a voodoo ritual, trap and discard as novelty souvenirs no longer needed.

The entire stage formed a frame: the black box space, set up with side fresnels moving in sequence as though we were all in a car on a night time road trip, but with the glitter ball suggesting a night club, and the frames an antebellum southern US stately home.

Finding expression in polyvocality and movement between the constricting boundaries of the frames, we gave personal, poetic accounts of different perspectives of Black British Womanness, using the four label states. In our version, there is fluidity between these labels: they are not necessarily exclusive or single. The set had the visual impact of allowing the show to frame all the problem issues arising from a colonial mindset. With hindsight, it is clear that the issues we were working with – concerning identity, belonging and the past leaking into the present – have theoretical relevance and may be seen in their rightful place in the evolutionary chain of Black female performance expression.

The following looks at the text from the perspectives of mother, lover and other:

Mother, the Creator, Earth, grounding

> 'Indeed mother of her son and his daughter as well, Mary is also and besides his wife.'
>
> (Kristeva, 1986: 160)

The role of the mother in raising and nurturing her offspring. The way fractured and fragmented or jarring and dissonant relationships poison a child. The tension between mother and woman summed up above, motherhood risks unsexing the woman who is the 'mother'. The strains in between of two unbalanced cultures with a history of one colonising the other and the other returning the favour in the personal narratives and electric excitement of new forms (as seen in Bernadine Evaristo's *Lara* or Zadie Smith's *White Teeth*); the meeting of the Old deep power of Nigeria and the Old school tie, cool divide-and-rule power of England. All these are explored in Agbebiyi's 'Ident' and Agbabi's 'My Mother' tracing a course from a beginning which was less than ideal to a point where love, somewhat painfully, transcends into peace.

Lovers – creativity, coincidence, creation,

Lovers come together – maybe briefly, maybe for longer – to share mind body and soul, to synergize energies, to share pleasures, and reveal true identity to each other. They share joys and creation, like Adam and Eve giving birth to a new world, a family. Even as two women, two men, two creatives, they/we are anima/animus, each embodying the Orisha tradition (Yoruba cosmology) of duality within a spirit body striving for elevation, working for the light via self mastery and/or collaboration with spirits similarly minded. Lovers emit a light vibration which enlightens and lifts the world around them: twin halves of the same creative soul. These are themes of my song 'Wrap You Up':

> You hold a mirror to my soul
> You know that you've got the key
> You reflect the truth that we both know …
> I want to wrap you up in rainbow colours

Other

However, this most beautiful and poetic coming together is disrupted in *Fo(u)r Women* by the presence on the stage of the third woman, who is always there but always changing her identity:

> The other woman finds time to manicure her nails.
>
> (Jesse Mae Robinson 'The Other Woman')

> I'm awfully bitter these days.
>
> (Nina Simone, 'Four Women')[1]

She is at once part of, yet apart from, the perfect union. Her jealousy and confusion about inclusion/exclusion alienates, sparks bitterness, spews bile (see 'For You' and 'Snow Queen'). She brings about the pain of separation, sorrow for the fleetingness of the contact so longingly sought, so perfect, so ephemeral. 'Snow Queen' describes the bitterness of lovers caught tightly in a binding of opposites (red blood/white snow) that attract, yet cannot find a way to come together without bloodshed on virgin snow, without the pain of misunderstanding and confusion jarring like the jagged fragments of glass from broken mirrors/splintered egos, personalities unrevealed. They are transfixed, incomplete in the fragmentation of light from the glitter-ball as it reflects many surfaces, all glittering but broken, yet creates an entire rainbow as it spins. The cause of the fragmentation is left unexplained: Is it in the blood, the root or the snow? In sugar? Cocaine? Cold heartedness? Lack of sun?

> Traditionally, historically, The Other has been viewed from the position of a solipsistic (i.e. solely self-referencing) self. The Other is that which may or may not be colonized by the self but is viewed from the position of the self.
>
> (Ronnell, 1991: 128)

The 'Other' was the audience who, while mirroring the performance, also became its collective shifting fourth woman. The 'Other' was also part of the content of the show, as we looked at alienation, difference and belonging in social, national and family contexts. The 'Other' is where the projection falls of anything unwilling to be owned by the self or the group, where the possibility of revolution/revelation is greatest. Other people, other countries, other wise (other wisdom).

Hair

Hair is also a frame. We discussed hair as a signifier of so much to/for Black women. At the time our position was generally quite essentialist (natural good, processed bad), which was perhaps completely missing the point of the rich tapestry of expression/aspiration and identification Black women's hair has:

> Hair issues are among us. We must tease them out, hold them up to the light, and coax them into art.
>
> (Jones, 1994: 303)

In *Fo(u)r Women* we cheerfully poke fun at the processing industry ('Hot combs Relaxer Curly Perm Keep Still' ('Ident')), rather from the point of view of a grumpy child forced to sit still, while torturous processes are applied to her in the name of beauty or possibly conformity. The self-erasing: What will the neighbours/Pastor/other girls/women in the typing pool/my boyfriend/that fine man/woman over there think? The reverse, the self-referential and emotional: How will this make **me** feel before the eyes of the world? Hair has a time-honoured role in sex as a weapon of war and in this arena two styles classically win out for straight hair: the pile it up Dolly Parton trashy easy 'fuck me' ho hair look and the long natural flicky *Charlie's Angels* look (for 'ho' read 'whore', as in 'bitches and hos'). The traditional lament of Black women in the 1970s and 1980s was that these styles of hair, which were most successful for securing great genes, were out of the reach of Black women without significant trauma and financial outlay, and furthermore, completely dependent upon good weather. This is hilariously demonstrated in Julie Dash's animated cartoon *HAIR!* (a film which explained to me, a loosely nappy headed mixed race kid, in three seconds why there are no shower scenes in movies with Black people).

However, since we all became Postmodern and Ethnicity became 'nothing more than a market niche, a field of products and the hair trade is leading the way to the mountain top' (Jones, 1994: 302), Black women's hair products have mushroomed and are becoming easy and affordable. The total women's hair care product market in the UK is worth £1.2 billion. Black women's hair products include wigs, weaves, etc. as well as shampoos and chemicals and Black women in the UK and US can easily spend up to 20–30 % of their income on hair care. Interestingly, the majority of Black hair care products are manufactured by non-Black owned businesses.

UFO?

The text largely speaks for itself, though some readers may find problems with sections of the piece Patience's wonderful 'Ufo Woman' being one. Patience explains:

> There may be an African word 'ufo' but I've never come across it. Ufo was simply wordplay, quite common in my work. I play with a word and extract all possible levels of meaning as in my first book R.A.W. (rhythm and word etc). So Ufo is 'unidentified flying object' and 'you fuck off' and a newly-coined African term. It served my purpose admirably.

The poem is a humorous and light-heartedly triumphant exploration of identity issues, as Patience notes:

> In my piece, which charts my own history (and in the beginning that of my parents) from a futuristic and somewhat humorous perspective rather than remaining in the claggy past, I'm also named 'those sticks and stones may break my bones but names' and 'Ufo woman, oyinbo/from the old days …'. But I leave the poem triumphant. 'I rename myself/Ufo woman …' unlike Simone's original. (Oyinbo is a Yoruba derisory word for a white person. The term is used in pidgin English all over Nigeria irrespective of 'ethnic group').

Ident/identify

There were two light-hearted physical sections. One was an interlude (costume change) before 'Ufo Woman' involving making a head tie out of a union jack to a drum and bass with an out-of-tune modified Westminster Chimes sound-track (a similar soundtrack was subsequently used in the BBC *Windrush* show). The other was my 'Ident' piece – in which I concretely establish my own sense of self in my mixed race identity – which was unexpectedly funny. The piece ends with the performer brandishing a white and black marbled dildo in the context of personal agency and self respect – sufficient to play with usurping the phallic/racist signifier white dildo for the purpose of saying 'I told you so'. This was more powerful than labels or the constricting sense of belonging to a community which can lead to self-compromise through fear of losing community support.

As state labels break down as multinationals and corporations run the world, we are part of a fluid alliance of related interests. Roaming freely signifying/identifying as we chose, in pursuit of higher ideals, emancipation, communication and power.

Issues? Bless you!

In common with many live art shows, we had a feedback session after the piece. I will explore here two issues that arose.

My poem 'For You' caused controversy. No one was happy with its vindictive bigoted tone and language, but it was kept in mainly because I felt it represented a voice that does exist, it certainly reflected perhaps more violently, conversations I had experienced with Black women who felt scorned by and despising of Black men or women who chose to have relationships with white women. The doctrine of when two or three are together, they shall diss Black men still holds (many would say with good reason). It is something frequently played out in shows like *Jerry Springer*. I should say that it does not reflect the views of any of the contributors. But just because it neither involved nor attracted us does not make it any less real.

The piece 'My Skin Is' got confused feedback. It is an up-front personal three-point take on 'my' skin which is performed to a background chant of 'MY SKIN IS'. Patience used extracts from an existing piece of hers, 'Pain doesn't hurt'. Dorothea, wrote a hymn of love to her skin, and I explored the question what is skin for and made of, with the help of a couple of dermatology text books. I think that audiences were perplexed by the conjunction of these three points of view: textbook references, SM type references and proud affection.

In general, the quibbles we had among ourselves were largely around presenting unredeemed negatives and less than perfect poetry and from audiences, some discomfort with 'intellectual sounding stuff'. Feedback sessions after the show were in general very positive – for having done it at all, for the use of music and singing, for having jokes, for expressing personal issues so clearly and boldly, for not emotionally dumping and fleeing (a cardinal performance sin).

After *Fo(u)r Women* we had intended to tour the show but other commitments and a degree of post-show shock got in the way and we all moved on. I co-devised The Millennium Hag Project, wrote music for Litpop and explored low-level acting. Dorothea collaborated with Susan Lewis and completed a manuscript. Patience wrote and toured her second book, among other things. Jillian Tipene went on to co-write and perform a four-woman poetry show at Jackson's Lane Theatre, featuring women from different racial/cultural backgrounds, African, Asian, Jewish, Maori. Others, notably Valerie Mason John, wrote and performed pieces: *Surfing the Crone*, superb *Queenie* play, and *Babes in the Wood* at Theatre Royal Stratford East.

Process 101

Have the idea. Define it.
Invite the players. Jam and play,
Laugh and enjoy. Lift each other's spirits
Work hard and fast
Perform, revise, move on.

Next?

Fo(u)r Women is an example of 'non commercial' art (despite the packed full house for every show) being made, performed and funded. I hope to see more novels, plays, performance pieces, films and TV shows which deal directly with the lives of and are written in the voices of those who tend not to be heard in the mainstream. Of course, those of us who own the voices have to write them first. But for starters, the fetishized image of Black women happily brandishing dildoes is being wonderfully developed in the photographic work of Renee Mussai. Watch this space … NO – celebrate yourself in it.

Reference

1   'The Other Woman' by Jesse Mae Robinson, sung by Nina Simone, on *Let It All Out* (US, 1966, Philips PHM 200–2); available on *Nina Simone: The Legend at her Best* (Collectibles, 2000). 'Four Women', written and performed by Nina Simone, on *Wild Is the Wind* (US, 1966, Philips PHM 200–7); available on *The Essential Nina Simone* (Metro Music, 2000).

Fo(u)r Women

Adeola Agbebiyi, Patience Agbabi and Dorothea Smartt

Figure 6.1. Fo(u)r Women logo.
Picture: Florence Fayol.

Fo(u)r Women is a jazz based poetry performance piece. There are solos, solos over music and solos with echoes. The voices marked are those that obtained for the first performance. They are not hard and fast rules. We soloed our own writing. Staging is a good idea as is music. Neither is compulsory, but the ensemble should ideally augment the solo work both physically and vocally.

Written by and for three female performers and first performed in *The Ripple Effect* series at the ICA Theatre 20th May 1996. Some pieces were pre-existing, some written specially for *Fo(u)r Women*. Publisher credits and dates are at the end. All pieces are copyright of the individual authors.

First performance: Voice one: Adeola Agbebiyi
Voice two: Patience Agbabi
Voice three: Dorothea Smartt
Director – Jillian Tipene
Designer – Birgitta Hosea
Lighting – Justin O' Shaughnessy
Music – Adeola Agbebiyi

Thanks to Andy from Babes for the use of Pablo dildo, Catherine Ugwu and Lois Keidan ICA liaison, Lee for sign language.

Programme: **Writer**
1: Fo(u)r women   Group
2: My mother   Patience Agbabi
3: Forget   Dorothea Smartt
4: Crossroads: Junction 17 from 22   Dorothea Smartt
                                              Flag business – an interlude
                                                 (music Adeola Agbebiyi)
5: Ufo Woman   Patience Agbabi
                                                 (music: Adeola Agbebiyi)
6: My skin is   Group
                                                 (music: Adeola Agbebiyi)
7: Faultlines   Dorothea Smartt
                                                 (continue 'My skin is' chant)
8: Ident   Adeola Agbebiyi
9: The Snow Queen   Patience Agbabi
                                              Playing with it: Crystal Visions
                                              Adeola Agbebiyi music and words
10: For you   Adeola Agbebiyi
11: Wrap you up   Adeola Agbebiyi music and words
12: Four Women reprise   Group

1. Fo(u)r women
A chant in 4/4 time

(Three voices speak simultaneously when their words appear on the same line – Eds.)

Voice one	Voice two	Voice three
four women;		
four women		
four women;	lover, mother, sister, other	
four women		
four women;	lover, mother, sister, other	women loving women
four women		women loving women
four women;	lover, mother, sister, other	women loving women
four women		women loving women
four women;		for women – who have something to say
four women		for women – trying to find a way
		for women – trying to make sense of it
		for women – who want to rise above it

for women – working it out
    together
for women – travelling
    different roads
for women troubled by the
    sisters
for women – burdened with
    whispers

clit licking, nipple piercing   … zami … zami   women loving women
sassy walking, ass slapping   women loving women
woman loving, woman fucking
butch. femme. switch

lover, mother, sister, other   women loving women   for women – trapped in a
                                                             snowstorm
                                 women loving women   for women – daring to
                                                             remember
                                                         for women – mothered by
                                                             shame
                                                         for women – humbled by
                                                             change
                                                         for women – on the move
                                                         for women – in the groove
                                                         for women – trying to make
                                                             sense or it
                                                         for women – taking you, to
                                                             the heart of it

clit licking, nipple piercing   … zami … zami
sassy walking, ass slapping
woman loving, woman fucking
butch. femme. switch

                                 four women   lover, mother, sister, other
                                 four women

fo(u)r women is a dream breath
hope wish act.
A prayer to you we reach out
to touch four women – made
flesh in a place of declaration
revelation affirmation

101

For women – like us right
here right now
where our lives have value
and meaning
Fo(u)r women – a dream made
crystal clear in the light
reflected in mirrored eyes
For women who have seen
and lived their lives for
women lived out for women
their lives

for women their lives for women lived	women loving women	lover, mother, sister, other
in for women their lives for women	women loving women	
women lived		
for women for women …	for women for women …	for women for women …

2. My Mother

(First column identifies speakers, lines are read across – Eds.)

Voice two leads:	My mother	has two heads
Sans Serif and **bold**	speak	alien tongue
	their words	***flow in***
Sans Serif Italics: voice three	***one ear***	**in the other**
Times roman: voice one	battle	*in heart*
	head	know better
Roman Italics: Voice 2 with Voice 3	***bolder***	**wiser** older
Bold Roman Italics all:	My mother	***married at 16***
	24	long time ago
	where water	was unsafe
	to drink	frozen solid
	had chilblains	*children*
	sang under ***coconut***	**chestnut**
	save yourself	they say
	for a rainy day	be ***bold***
	chic	rouge on the cheek
	out *out*	you must go
	say	*no*
	Study hard	*you read*
	too much	I never see you

always out
drab clothes
so much
of your *colour*
don't be *different*
find a nice
African man
tomorrow
go out
will notice you
my mother

My mother
thrusts
onto me
cannot quite
cannot quite
then I am
fight against her
she *loves*
my strength
a common
common
painfully
an adult

reading wearing
I miss you
be proud
culture
difficult
Black
no hurry
will do
or no-one
that there is no-one
cannot believe

thrusts
her womanhood
and my nipples
focus
breathe
stronger
battle
hates
we share
resentment
battle
I emerge
The following

day   allies in conflict   *we stride bareheaded*
I am   no   longer   single   she
seeing   in   me   herself   in   her   self   me

3. forget
Voice three

convenient forgetfulness is my guard
against slights and hurts
your vacant this-isn't-happening eyes
your don't care eyes I don't remember
a lot of things quite deliberately
I shove it away someplace inside
to implode later when I least expect it
when someone does the things
I don't remember why should I
walk with it hold it know it
for all its unpleasantness feel it

103

choke me smoke me dope me
I don't remember is my favourite reply
when put on the spot about my feelings then
how did I get broken
I don't remember the sound
the impact of your words shattering
as you chatted on dismissing a quiet plea
said again don't be boring
shuddering as another piece hit the playground tarmac
spreading into a pool of once-me
trampled again and again
by my big sister's silences and refusals
to look me in the eye at least
to share a silent moment of sympathy
I don't remember my wanting her
to do the enid blyton best friend thing
and rescue me from the little girls that bullied me
or her bringing the taunting to our front-room
laughing at my swan-neck and my cowardy-custard ways
only the mirage of my hopeful fantasy
of ever-lasting super-glue love
like the infant fingers of that boy in my class
doing everything together
grown like one like twin plantains
that could never be parted with whole skin
that would not remember itself
always being in half
I don't remember being unwanted
the day I ran out the school gate
away from the isolation everybody's eyes except hers
witnessing another humiliation
out the school gate to get away from – who
I don't remember
Mr Grant with his big six-foot army self
charging after me escorting me
an easy captive in biting April sleet
white like his big hand
leading up to the hair in his nose
and a crowd of schoolkids telling me
I was really in trouble now
and the only eyes I wanted to see me were yours
away over at the other end of the playground
you wouldn't see me there
we'd walk home with me not telling

feeling too shame
convenient forgetfulness stinging
from your mouth
to the soothing front-door
our Yelverton Rd home
where you were all the world I thought I needed

4. Crossroads: Junction 17 from 22

Voice three

the turmoil, disruption and absolute despair
I felt at eighteen
the loss of someone
so much a part of me
I did not feel I could function
sprawled me into chaos

Early mornings
waking up feeling on the verge of tears
desperate for sleep
desperate for someone to be with me
for her presence

And the house would be so quiet!
missing a voice
thrust out of my boundaries
panic-stricken

Tears first thing in the morning
'cause I'm scared to go out on my own
standing in front of the window
looking out
on the largest railway junction in the world
with a train going by every three minutes
wondering
where
to go.

(musical interlude and Ufo music – drum and bass stylee – including something reminiscent of Westminster Chimes in the minor/diminished: well out of key)

5. Ufo Woman

(pronounced oofooe)

Figure 6.2. Patience Agbabi. Photo framing: Florence Fayol.

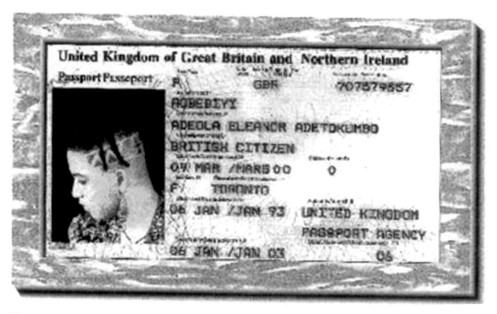

Figure 6.3. Adeola Agbebiyi. Photo: Paloma Etienne; framing: Florence Fayol.

Figure 6.4. Dorothea Smartt. Photo: Shirlee Mitchell; framing: Florence Fayol.

Voice two:
with chorus augmentation
and scene setting
on most quoted parts

Music for Ufo
spaced out drum and bass

First World meets Third World
Third World meets First World

Mother Earth, Heath Row. Terminal 5. Yo!
Do I look hip in my space-hopper-green
slingbacks, iridescent sky-blue-pink skin
pants and hologram hair? Can I have
my clothes back when you've finished with them, please?
Hello! I just got offa the space ship.

I've learnt the language, read the VDU
and watched the video twice. Mother Earth
do *you* read *me*? Why then stamp my passport
ALIEN at Heath Row? Does my iridescent
sky-blue-pink skin embarrass you, mother?

LONDON. Meandering the streets paved with
hopscotch and butterscotch, kids with crystal
cut ice cream cones and tin can eyes ask 'Why
don't U F O back to your own planet?
Streets paved with NF (no fun) graffiti
Nefertiti go home from the old days.

So I take a tram, tube, train, taxi trip
hip-hugged bell-bottomed and thick-lipped, landing
in a crazy crazy cow pat. SUSSEX.
Possibly it's my day-glo afro, rich
as a child paints a tree in full foliage
that makes them stare with flying saucer eyes.

Perhaps my antennae plaits in Winter
naked twigs cocooned in thread for bigger
better hair makes them dare to ask to touch.
'*Can we touch your hair?*' Or not ask at all;
my two tone hand with its translucent palm,
lifeline, heartline, headline, children, journeys,

prompting the '*Why is it white on the inside*
of your hand? Do you wash? Does it wash off?'
Or my core names. Trochaic, Dactylic,
Galactic beats from ancient poetry,
names they make me repeat, make them call me
those sticks-and-stones-may-break-my-bones names.

In times of need I ask the oracle. Withdrawing to my work station I press
HELP. I have just two options. HISTORY:
The screen flashes subliminal visuals
from the old days which I quickly translate:
Slave ship:space ship, racism:spacism.

Resignedly, I select HERSTORY:
the screen displays a symmetrical tree
which has identical roots and branches.
I can no longer reason, only feel
not aloneness but oneness. I decide
to physically process this data.

So I take the train plane to the Equator
the Motherland, travel 5 degrees North
to the GO SLOW quick-talking fast-living

finger-licking city known as LAGOS.
Streets paved with gold-threaded gold-extensioned
women and silk-suited men: market stalls

of red, orange, yellow and indigo.
Perhaps it's not my bold wild skin colour,
well camouflaged in this spectrum of life,
but the way I wear my skin, too uptight,
too did-I-wear-the-right-outfit-today?
too I-just-got-off-the-last-London-flight;

or my shy intergalactic lingo
my monospeak, my verbal vertigo
that makes them stare with flying saucer eyes.
They call me Ufo woman, oyinbo
from the old days which translates as weirdo,
white, outsider, other and I withdraw

into myself, no psychedelic shield,
no chameleonic facade, just raw.
Then I process Ufo and U F O,
realise the former is a blessing;
the latter a curse. I rename myself
Ufo Woman and touch base at Heath Row.

No. Don't bother to strip, drug, bomb search me
I'm not staying this time. Why press rewind?
Why wait for First World homo sapiens
to cease their retroactive spacism?
Their world may be a place worth fighting for
I suggest in the next millennium.

So, smart, casual, I prepare for lift off,
in my fibre optic firefly Levis,
my sci-fi hi-fi playing *Revelations*
and my intergalactic mobile ON.
Call me, I'll be surfing the galaxy
searching for that perfect destination.

6. My Skin Is ...
*(Bassline, a D minor arpeggio with conga / bongo fills, finger clicks and hand claps is
established then the following text is sung as a harmonised chant)*
My skin is, my skin is, my skin is, my skin is. *– also include different pacings, pitches,
non-sung pitches, partial repetitions e.g.* **My My skin** *etc. – Bassline and chant continue*

throughout, with the following text soloed over the top. There are pauses between the verses. It's jazz after all!)

Voice Three: My skin is honeymelon sugarsweet brown
My skin is, my idea of heaven sent

My skin is comfortable
   travels with me wherever I go
My skin is hard work
My skin is dark in England, darker in Barbados
My skin can jangle or ring true

My skin is deep
My skin sprouts my particular hair

My skin rises to your touch
My skin is ecstasy

My skin is a melanin miracle
My skin is not the same colour all over my body

My skin is black – do you know what that means?
My skin is liable to crack
   under the strain of your stare

My skin is a revolution
My skin is not the same I had seven years ago

My skin is the same as yours
My skin is different to yours
My skin is breathing with open pores

(music/chant/moves)

Voice One: My skin is not just my skin.
It's my protection, my defence, my reason for being here.
My skin keeps the outside out and holds me in.
My skin is one organ: including the hair, nails and mucous membranes.
It consists of three components:
the outer epidermis consisting of four cellular layers made of keratinocytes;
the inner dermis, a complex mesh of protein fibres, fibroblasts,
blood vessels, nerve-endings which sense
touch, pressure, pain, movement;
immune cells like macrophages, mast cells
and the appendages: hair follicles and sweat glands

Fo(u)r Women

Scattered throughout the epidermis are melanocytes secreting the pigment melanin.
They are found in only three places:
the brain, the eye and the skin[1]
My skin is a living communicative organism.

(music/chant/moves)

Voice two:

My skin is my
stone-age
space-age
all-in-one
defying
figure-hugging
fig-leaf

My skin is the
damson
plum-brown
sloe-black
silk zone
where my
thighs meet

Don't leave my
mind on the rack
I want your smack
I want you to carve a love heart
into my black bark back

My skin is the
flower in bloom
butterfly in June
sweet earth
after monsoon

My skin is the
pleasure zone
for my heart's
bass
slap
open tone

Don't leave my
mind on the rack

111

I want your smack
I want you to carve a love heart
into my black bark back

My skin is my
sloe-black
plum-black
full bloom
very own
silk zone

7. faultines
voice three solo

black? brownskin? highbrown? red? yellow?
some nights I am awake
wide-eyed as d'full moon
though not as yellow
as gran'mudder Estelle
a property owning coloured
widda ten poun deposit
ope'nin a Savings Bank account in Barbados
when white women were occupied
wid being ladies
money money to be made tru'
panama canal years making silver men
war years I do not know
mother tells me of
mischief out on d'Man O'War
sunken treasure
calling up tru' the sea
in the wite lite of a moon
awake in a sky teeming wid stars
that abandon me in Englan'
d'glare from
streets paved with gole
making it too light for stars
only the large but distant winter moon
remaining wide-eyed
and just as rich and yellow
set in a black sky
the two inseparable like
mother and child
daughter, to be exact

a mother troublesome
with her dark darkness
all wrong in a climate
where for the lite almost wite
the occupation of 'lady'
is almost within reach
and the pity of misfortune
with the judgement and expectation
of wrong-she-all-wrong
an'baad-she-too-baad
but whuyuh could x-spec'?
from a literal black sheep
that when she rear up she own flock
the light yellow red skin will have to pay
(they have it too easy)
she will shut a few doors
for the many that were slammed
in her way some nights
I lie awake in the shadow and light
of a moonlit night
wondering
at how the sins of mothers & fathers
meet the unknowing child
and lie in wait
to slither between sisters
cocktailing with english days and ways
to break them up along colour lines
and continue in spite of itself
a silent contract down generations
to breed out the unseemly dark
the get-you-nowhere stumbling darkness
and bestow the freedom of
highbrown skin
yellow skin
red skin
lite skin
high brown
yellow skin
red skin
lite

8. Ident

Figure 6.5. Adeola Agbebiyi in 'Ident' from Fo(u)r Women. *Photo: David Glew. Finishing: Adeola Agbebiyi.*

Fo(u)r Women

<table>
<tr><td>voice one</td><td>Voices two and three: echo (with actions):</td></tr>
</table>

	skin, hair, lips, nose

It's like 'I'm Black' you know, it's obvious.
I have the skin, hair, lips, nose and all. It's clear.
Growing up in Burnley, Lancashire, I always knew. Whether I   skin, hair, lips, nose
was called Paki or Sambo I knew I was black, that it was hard:
people were colour prejudiced - and I had to fight for my right
to everything they, in their white 'snowflake' stupidity claimed
for themselves alone. Things like Blackpool Tower, Jazz,   skin, hair, lips, nose
Culture, Civilisation. But I always knew.

Sometimes, when I thought I was my mother, when I wasn't
sure where she stopped and I started, the sharp contrast
between her milky skin and my brown sugar was enuff. I knew   (silence)
I was black: the skin, hair, lips and nose and everything. I was
black.

     skin, hair, lips, nose
     etc.
     (silence)

But I had to open my eyes to see it … and for a long time, she
and I would pretend my colour didn't mean anything, didn't
need anything different, like we were the same. But I found
ghettos in me that she would never willingly visit. And I found
places of such richness, it was hard to believe in them.

But I knew, I was black.

I didn't always like it or want it. I sucked in my lips, wished for   skin, hair, lips, nose
a Roman nose, freckles and mousy high bunches. No one told
me 'be careful what you wish for because it might happen'.
Fortunately some prayers are not answered.   skin, hair, lips, nose

I coveted things I could never have that I saw brought power   skin, hair, lips, nose
and respect: like white skin, a penis and marrying selected
Royalty.

     (silence)

I worked hard to 'fit in' to a completely uncomprehending,
hostile white environment. I assimilated myself into near
oblivion. Even when I had succeeded, when white friends and
acquaintances behaved as though my skin didn't need anything
different, have a different experience, I knew I was black. I

knew, by the broken promises and lies which are at the heart of
the change from colour prejudice to colour blind to blind.
I knew, I was black.

The more I worked to 'fit in' the more my hair became the
Badge of my Black Pride.

hot comb,
curly perm, relaxer,
KEEP STILL!

The hair that my mother used metal toothed combs to subdue,
tugging and pulling at my scalp while I squirmed in agony. The
hair that was the talk of my grandmother's bridge circle for its
incredible properties at the swimming pool. Apparently, it was
waterproof for 15 whole minutes, then became so waterlogged, I
was in danger of drowning. The hair that no hairdresser in town
had a style for. The hair that automatically sprang back into
shape when patted by complete strangers.

hot comb,
curly perm, relaxer,
KEEP STILL!

etc. (in a measured
way)

I never wanted to straighten my hair. If god had meant me to
have straight hair, I would have been born with it.

I could desire white power, but my hair was sacred.

This splendid attitude born of my Isolation; unbeaten, free of
the hot comb, ignorant of cornrows and extensions, even of
Angela Davis, made me a one-woman campaign in support of
negro hair and its fantastic natural potential. I knew nothing,
except that I was black.

hot comb,
curly perm, relaxer,
KEEP STILL!

(silence)

So I was surprised when dark women whose skin promised a
sweeter juice within cut their eyes at me and called me coconut.
These sisters with perms or weaves in their heads and a budget
for hair products I could have lived on for a year cut their eyes
at me.

It's like I was back there in a school yard, surrounded by people
who saw me as 'other' and as 'other': a legitimate target, and all
the natural hair pride in the world wasn't going to save me.

I needed a new badge while I recovered my old heart.
But would my badge be the one that celebrated my Black identity by trying to look as not African as possible or the one that
celebrated my Black identity by trying to look as not African as

possible? I mean how many Nigerians do you see with locks wrapped in kente?[2]

I had to open my eyes to see it … I might wish, but there is no pretending that my colour doesn't mean anything, doesn't need anything different, like we are the same.

I'm Black. I have the skin, hair, lips, nose and everything. And that's great.

I have power and I can have respect.

skin, hair, lips, nose
(silence)

So, I dress for success by wearing my heart warm on the inside and my skin – as it is – on the outside but, for old time's sake, I can always wear a white penis.
(brandishes and appropriately holds white dildo)

9. The Snow Queen
voice two
with chorus on 'white as snow' etc. background and 'down home'
music electro style 'crystal visions', instrumental, plus lyric … see end of 'The Snow Queen').
Techno club atmosphere.

white as snow
black as ebony
red as blood

white as snow
black as ebony
red as blood

white as snow she melted on my tongue
black as ebony I tell the tale with ink
as red as the ebb and flow of my pain

snow white
crystal powder
winter
wonder
queen
let the black cat pass

snow white
crystal powder

117

winter wonder queen
let the black cat pass
let the black cat lick the looking glass

snow white crystal powder winter wonder queen
let the black cat pass thru the looking glass
let the black cat catch your six six six fingered hand
let me lick scratch smell taste touch wonderland
let me lick scratch smell taste touch wonderland

snow white
crystal powder
winter wonder queen
let me touch
taste
your cut glass lips
let me taste fish
smell fish
let me hear you scream let me
suck
lick
like a sex kitten

touch me with your
six six six
wicked witch of the west
rich bitch on heat
dancing melting on my tongue
turn to sleet
frozen tidal wave
I'm the midnight sun
touch me with you sixth sense
sex
I'm in ecstasy
crystallise this night
(freeze)

Take me to the ice age
our love is flowing rivers
but my tears
drawn like daggers
stalactite
white

Let me skate on your hand
ski down your back
let the ice not crack
seven years bad luck

wicked witch drown
burn in hell
with your seven month itch
scratch
I'm cracking up

Can't crack my face to a smile
can't touch that dial
bitch
I need your six digit fix
an' well hung tongue
not your frostbite

So I'm spitting out the apple
Snow White
taking off
coming coming coming
down
home

Lyrics for Crystal Visions: ...
(used as required)

Sorrow is my bride sorrow is my lover
takes me down in caves of tears she keeps me
trapped inside the shell of someone's wishing well
hard and fast I know I'm sinking slowly, going

Round round again Round round again
Round round again Round round again

the Winter Wind cuts deep, the Ice Queen blowing kisses
Reflection shatter sin another mirror
I've seen it in her face, her Empire lies in tatters
she no longer knows what really matters
going
Round round again Round round again
Round round again Round round again

119

Crystal visions come without a struggle
the bluest skies are shining thru my window
a stand a beat away from your open doorway
release the beat and take me through to a new adventure

going
Round round again Round round again
Round round again Round round again

10. For You ...

voice one

For you – I would go down on my knees
and crawl across the floor
to beg at your feet like a puppy.
Defying the strictures
of Church ladies in hats
out shopping like, not like, us
in Safeway

I will show you my secret private places
let you into me
in quiet moments,
to witness the stillness and rage.
I would break my silence
let down my barriers, hold my boundaries,
For you.

So, don't turn your face away
to some skinny ass white girl/boychild
unless the sound of a black heart breaking
turns you on

For you I would do-be-do the Black Bottom,
bugalu to your touch
let you do anything, anything at all.
Take you into me deeper
let you push me further
til my rivers over flow and
keep on flowing.

I would top you, tie you, cuff you
deny you release
hold you so still on the knife edge of a

cumming worth waiting for
holding your breath
hanging out for pleasure so long
you might die.

    So, don't turn your face away
    to some crutch, some drug, TV, scratch card addiction
    unless the sound of a black heart breaking
    turns you on

For you I'd move the stars to spell your name,
chant to make the sun
shine in your house all through a London winter
create oases of
calm honesty
and promise to absolutely deal
with my feelings

    So don't turn your face away
    to some always remembered nightmare of despair
    unless the sound of my black heart breaking
    turns you on

See we're in this together,
if you won't love yourself
you're wasting my time,
wasted too much in
years spent turning
the other cheek

    so don't turn your face away to some
    I don't care what it is
    it ain't you or me.
    Don't turn your face away

    If you want my love
    don't turn your face
    don't turn your face

(ptsssssssssth)   *(the sound of teeth being sucked)*

    Next!   *(snaps fingers like a snap diva)*

11. Wrap You Up

All on choruses with harmonies and solo verses and middle 8

Your beating heart touches my mind and I'm
Free falling into your arms
You kiss my mouth, I come alive and
Baby I know this love tastes so sweet
I think we've found heaven between us

I want to wrap you up in rainbow colours – hold you there.
Touch you like a true born lover – so sweetly baby
Wrap you up in rainbow colours – hold you there.
Touch you like a true born lover – like girls do
Baby – you know

Yesterday I was like any girl here til
Your kiss blew that away
Today I find, the world's a strange new place and
Now that I know how it goes I see clearly
My head is turning, my heart is burning

I want to wrap you up in rainbow colours – hold you there.
Touch you like a true born lover – so sweetly baby
Wrap you up in rainbow colours – hold you there.
Touch you like a true born lover – like girls do
Baby – you know
Baby you hold a mirror to my soul.
You know that you've got the key.
You reflect the truth that we both know
Loving you baby,
You make it easy …

I want to wrap you up in rainbow colours – hold you there.
Touch you like a true born lover – so sweetly baby
Wrap you up in rainbow colours – hold you there.
Touch you like a true born lover – like girls do
Baby – you know

Four women reprise

Credits:
Permission to perform *Fo(u)r Women* must be obtained from Adeola Agbebiyi. Please contact: adeola@guildmartin.fsnet.co.uk

Patience Agbabi
'My Mother' in Patience Agbabi, *R.A.W.*, London, Gecko Press, 1995.
'Ufo Woman' in McCarthy, K. (ed), *Bittersweet*, London, Women's Press, 1998.

Dorothea Smartt
'Crossroads : Junction 17 From 22' in *Cutting Teeth* 12 (1998)
'Forget' in *Feed* (1993) and *Kunapipi* (1995)
'Faultlines' in *Writing Women* (1995) and Ross, J. and Anim-Addo, J. (eds), *Voice, Memory, Ashes* (London, Mango Publishing, 1999)

Adeola Agbebiyi
'Ident' in *Journal of Lesbian Studies*, 3/4
'Crystal Visions' on *Crystal Visions* (Shango Music, 1993)
'Wrap You Up' at http//:www.shango.demon.co.uk

References

1   Taken from a textbook in dermatology.
2   Kente is a Ghanaian cloth for special occasions including funerals; commonly seen as trimming on Afrocentric clothing, e.g. choir robes in Black Southern Baptist churches especially for TV specials, vacuum cleaner covers in the shape of rabbits seen in thrift shop Oakland CA, greetings cards, hats etc.)

Part 3 – Practising Theory and Theorizing Practice

7   Scratch in the Record

Leslie Hill

In her solo piece *The Day Don Came With the Fish*, the artist Helen Paris employs the voice and language of the body in concert with the voices and languages of digital and analogue sound and image recording, composing an eloquent, but troubling score. The result is a performance punctuated as much by the silences as the sounds: the rising and falling of the voice; the irregular beat and pause of the performer's heart; the incidental sounds of the body as she speaks in sign language; the noisy whirr of the film projector as it plays silent film; the stirring bittersweet melody of the record and, inevitably, the harsh, irreparable sound of the scratch. Paris's blending of live and mediated moments, of analogue and digital timing, which are presented so seamlessly in much current performance work seem, in this piece, to stutter - to leave each other speechless.

Figure 7.1. Illustrations: a sequence of photos of Helen Paris in The Day Don Came with the Fish. *Photos by Leslie Hill.*

Performer stands opposite Super 8 projector, switches it on, silent film rolls noisily. Small images are caught on delicate circles of rice paper, strung together and hanging from the ceiling on a silver fishhook.

Figures 7.2–3

Performer peels the circles off, layer by layer, each fragile screen catching an image – a ruined castle on a cliff, a man's face, smiling – and slowly eats them one by one until the film reel spends itself and only the stark white light of the bulb remains.

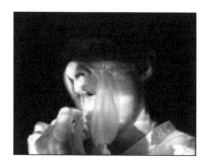

Figures 7.4–5

Performer eats a final translucent disk and moves into the projector light until only her mouth is lit, outside and in. Finally, she speaks:

> *What day of the week was I born on mother?*
> *Wednesday I think dear,*
> *hold on and I'll ask your father.*
> *Tony, what day did Don come with the fish?*
> *Wednesday I think dear.*
> *That's right,*
> *you were born on Wednesday,*
> *The Day Don Came With The Fish.*

A video projector facing the opposite end of the space casts an oscilloscope reading of the performer's dis-rhythmic heartbeat onto a film screen. Performer stands by projector, cupping her hand under the light so the shadow of her hand appears on the film screen, as if holding her beating heart. She speaks the following on a single breath:

When I was a baby I stopped breathing one day.
My mother noticed that I was very quiet
and very blue.
She gave me the kiss of life and then, because we had no phone,
she grabbed me and ran with me clutched to her, to the nearest house.
I often wonder about that run
Just the two of us
Both gasping for breath
bouncing jerkily together
suspended in time and running for my life on her big brown shaky legs.
She wasn't able to speak for weeks after that
And it was my first kiss.

Figures 7.6–7

Heartbeat sound blips dissolve into the image of oscilloscope reading of Edith Piaf's *Je ne regrette rien*. Subtitles to the French song appear on the screen but they are only a faltering, incomplete translation of the words.

Figures 7.8–9

Performer, stepping into the black sea of the screen and the green storm of waves from the oscilloscope, signs the words to the music in American Sign Language (ASL).[i]

 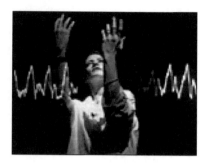

Figures 7.10–11

The sound reading has been digitized from a 78" record with a scratch halfway through the song. The song and concurrent signing 'stick' on the word 'nothing' for 12 scratches, then stop abruptly.

This scratch, this break in the music, this mute moment just before the needle skips and the melody is restored seems the best place to begin to talk about Helen Paris's film/performance, The Day Don Came With the Fish, *a piece that constantly juxtaposes and re-examines the boundaries and the glitches between the body and technology, between live and recorded, between analogue and digital, between the moment and the moment just before the moment that changes everything. In the programme notes, Paris features the following quotation:*

> You can always tell when people are using a digital watch. Ask them the time and they will invariably say something like, 'It's 4:41.' … An analogue watch user will just glance at the time piece and say, 'It's about a quarter to five.' In digital time keeping it's always one time or another. It's never 'about' anything. However, there is an instant when a digital watch is speechless. When the display flashes from one second to the next there is a tiny gap in the information. So, although the watch seems to supply a constant and exact reading of time, it is in fact a discontinuous display sampling individual moments of time and displaying them.
>
> Tony Feldman (1997: 2)

This 'speechless' moment is at the heart of the piece in various manifestations: a scratch in the record; a gap in the information; a scorch in the celluloid; an irrevocable physical action – the split second of eternity between ejaculation and infection. As an artist, Paris scavenges these fragments and uses them as the raw materials to build extensions onto reality, unfolding the remnants and stretching them into canvases upon which to work. For Paris, the scratches seem to occur most frequently in fateful moments of palpable physical contact: razor with skin; heat with film; virus with blood; storm with landscape, whereas the unfolding process, the habitation of these moments takes place in the overlapping of the body with another media – 8mm film reels, oscilloscope sound images, digital editing techniques that can isolate, stretch, slow down, freeze, repeat and reconfigure.

In *The Day Don Came With the Fish*, the crux of the relationship between the visceral and the mediated lies not only in the examination and manipulation of these moments but in the very nature of Paris's simultaneously live and pre-recorded relationship to the audience. Paris's hybrid of live presence, Super 8 film and digital editing techniques serves to foil the mortality of live performance with the 'immortality' of film and in turn the fragile nature of Super 8 film with the gymnastic possibilities of digital editing. The relationship is sexy yet jealous, co-dependant and frustrated, as both the film and the live performance rely on each other for their context and narrative. In contrast to performance, film claims a certain 'immortality' as a medium that can be saved and reproduced, but in this case the film is mortally wounded by its inextricable bond with the performer and the performance. Live performance, while ephemeral in nature, exerts a spontaneous energy, an excitement of the moment, a promise never to be the same twice, yet here it is curiously predestined, directed, circumscribed by the film. Desires to edit the film, to alter the performance, to re-live the moment and to rewrite the past are frustrated. The film and performance aspects of the piece exist as Siamese twins, reliant on each other for their lives. In this way, Paris investigates the ruptures, the cracks, the silences by suturing living flesh with synthetic media.

Language of the Unspoken

Silent film of performer standing in front of Dunluce Castle, Northern Ireland, shouting against a gale. Live performer steps into the picture, tidily layered beneath her projection and lip synchs herself in a normal speaking voice:

Most parts of England and Wales can expect some reasonable spells of sultry warm sunshine, but a few scattered thundery showers may break out in the afternoon, and drizzly rain is lightly to affect the south-west of England and Wales later. Showers and localized thunderstorms are likely over Scotland and Northern Ireland, but some places will escape the downpours and stay dry. The East Coast of Scotland will be plagued by mist and low cloud throughout the day. Tomorrow, most parts of England and Wales will be warm and humid with sunny spells ...

A storm of green vector waves erupts across the coastal filmscape, correlated with the monotonous drone of the BBC shipping forecast which fades in steadily until it drowns the voice of the performer completely.

The 'spoken' and the 'unspoken' in this piece are passed like batons frequently from live performance to film, resulting in a particular fascination with the unspoken, the silences and an unusual attention to Paris's sparse text. At times the baton is dropped completely, always in relation to pivotal or ruptured moments in time. The piece opens with silent 8mm footage of a man revisiting the site, ten years previous, of his HIV infection, the ruins of Dunluce Castle. The silent film sequence is projected onto mothwing-like surfaces and ultimately muted by disappearance into the mouth of the performer. The story of mother and child running for life, told on one breath, is choked as the performer's lungs deflate and she pushes out the final words in a rasping, unfamiliar voice from deep within the body's last resources, 'she wasn't able to speak for weeks after that and it was my first kiss'. The moment the record is damaged, and from which it will never play smoothly again, is recreated and heightened in the broken audio track, the sign language repetition of the same half-gesture twelve times, the looping visual image of the gash in Edith Piaf's voice on the oscilloscope readout. The shipping forecast, a guide for safety, warning against possible peril, presents itself as an abstract indecipherable code of vector waves over the filmscape of two previously catastrophic moments, while the filmed performer valiantly shouts warnings into gale force wind, only to be silenced by the limitations of the silent film. The live performer fills the void, supplying the missing words, but it is too late – the moment has passed, the storm has struck, the skin is broken.

SILENCE = DEATH

He told me as we walked the narrow precipitous pathway that jutted out below the cliff.
It was dark and wet and we walked unsteadily, pushing against the strong wind blowing off the sea.
After he had told me I looked down at the water swirling below us and thought how silent it was
In a deafening sort of way and I thought about the moment just before the moment that changes everything …
the moment when everything is OK …
The moment when everything is going to be all right …
And then I thought about the moment that changes everything

Shot of a man's hand holding a medication beeper containing an assortment of protease inhibitors, which he opens and empties into his cupped hand. The piercing sound of the beeper insistently punctuates the performer's speech:

Dunluce Castle just about stands on the tip of the windswept Northern Irish coastline.

The castle dates from 1300 and is described in the guidebooks as 'one of Northern Ireland's most romantic ruins'.
In 1639 a huge freak storm carried off the kitchens of the castle taking with it all the kitchen staff busily preparing for the evening meal. Only a tinker mending pots in a window embrasure survived.

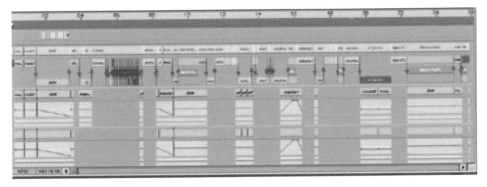

Figure 7.12. Digital program, The Day Don Came with the Fish

Je ne regrette rien fades in. Close-up shots of a man's body dissolve slowly into footage of the tide crashing in over rocks at the foot of the cliff. From within the filmscape, performer signs the words to the song. Again the song plays up until the scratch in the record, then stops short. The familiar, hourly blips of BBC Radio 4 are heard and the film freezes once more on the walkway, at a bend on the path with the waves crashing on the rocks below. The camera moves round the corner to reveal a small figure sitting on a bench in the distance. Performer remains in the filmscape:

Paul will point up to one of the wards, 'that is Kenneth's ward,' he will say 'Let's pop in and see how he is.'
I will sit in a green waiting room and listen to the dull rubbery sound of shoes on the hospital corridor
drink tea from a green cup
gagging
from too much milk.
Kenneth's dead Paul will say.

The moment just before the moment that changes everything is a moment of silence, the intake of breath one would hold for eternity to stop the inevitable. Paris articulates these moments through a language of the body and mediated images, her arms cutting through filmscape, slicing into vector waves, sculpting mute sentences over subtitles, *'Je ne regrette rein … No, I have no regrets.'* In talking about a performer with a physical presence as striking as Paris's, it is interesting to note the deliberate hybrid of the body and technology in these 'speechless moments'. In an interview, Paris identified strongly with an anecdote told by the artist Marina Abramovic about her fascination with videophones in Japan. The aspect which most interested Abramovic was not so much the communication/imaging technology itself as the flaw, the glitch between the human body and the mediation, the time delay wherein one could start a fight with their lover while watching their stuttered image continue to smile lovingly from the tiny screen, the moment before …

Heightened, sometimes violent physicality is a trademark of Paris's work, refreshing in relation to her use of technology and her interaction with and control over these mediated moments. Rather than simply using film as a medium to record and display the body, Paris develops a physical relationship with the media she works with and incorporates it into the performance: threading the film reel, eating projected images, illuminating her mouth with the naked bulb of the projector, declining to edit human errors out of the footage – traces of breathing, the inconsistencies of hand-held camera work. For Paris, film imagery isn't simply a medium, but a physical entity to be grasped, cut, eaten, held. This is the intuitive artistry, in form and content, of her treatment of the fateful instants, the glitches, the scratches, the sears, the moments just before and the moments that change everything. In relation to her intensely corporeal performance sensibility, it seems only fitting that Paris's chosen media for this piece's pre-recorded imagery is Super 8 film. In an interview with Donna Cameron, Super 8 filmmaker Fred Camper observes the body language, which is an unspoken trademark of the small gauge format:

> ... the hand-held 'look' of Super 8 is very different from that of 16mm. Hand-held movements can be jerkier, and the camera is more susceptible to random jiggles. There is a long tradition, from Leacock to Brakhage, of the filmmaker adding his bodily presence to the scene, through the inevitable small random movements of hand-held imagery; in Super 8, those movements tend to be accentuated, and what is often an undercurrent becomes a major aspect of the imagery, another kind of 'scrim', similar to the grain and the dust and the scratches, through which the subject matter is seen. In this, as in other ways, Super 8 films tend to almost necessarily incorporate an acknowledgement of the materials and conditions of their making. Just as in a diary the actual act of writing the diary entries is often as much the subject of the writing as the incidents described, so Super 8 films are partly about their inevitable distance from the world they purport to depict.
>
> Fred Camper (1998: 29)

Other 8mm filmmakers interviewed in conjunction with The Museum of Modern Art and the San Francisco Cinematheque exhibition *Big as Life*, a retrospective of American 8mm works, express insights into 8mm filmmaking which perfectly mirror Paris's performative use of the medium in this piece, pivoting on mortality and isolated moments. Their reflections on Super 8 and the relationship between form and content in their films and in their filmmaking process are so relevant in relation to *The Day Don Came With the Fish* that it seems appropriate to include a few short excerpts from these interviews here:

> What first attracted me to 8mm film in particular was its materiality and the way it produced tangible problematics on all levels: the acquiring and setting up of increasingly scarce quality projection equipment, the physicality of the sound made by the film strip running through the projector gate continuously reminds the viewer of the machine's presence in the room, the attention to projection

132

speed (variable fps), and the frequent act of projecting camera originals (the horror!) instead of film prints. And then there is the film itself – the sensuous texture of the projected image, the subtlety or sumptuousness of gradations in black-and-white or the discriminating use of color, the graininess of the image (as emotionally satisfying and particular as the actual silver nitrate sparkles on 35mm nitrate stock), the unpredictability of the sound stripe and the fragility and fleeting sense of the image's presence on the screen. All these qualities contribute to the intimacy created between the projected films and any group able to give themselves over to the act of actually seeing.

Jytte Jensen (1998: 16)

Since the time we began making Super 8 films there's been this cloud of doom that what we're doing is going to become obsolete or worse, nonexistent in a matter of years ... It's a little like being with someone who is terminally ill and being committed to them ...

silt (in Geritz, 1998: 48)

The 'intimacy' of the Super 8 image lies precisely in the tension between distance and proximity. The spectator is close to the screen, which is the origin of meaning; but it is the nature of the image to repel, or to enforce a distance. Articulating the tension between proximity and distance, Super 8 films implicate makers and viewers alike in a chain of desire; we are invited to the doorstep of a world of meanings, but are never able to enter the dwelling itself.

Nina Fonoroff (1998: 88)

Like all film, small gauge films guarantee the presence of an absence. But they have the heightened charge of often being one-of-a-kinds, outside of mechanical reproduction. They regain an aura, but at the cost of immortality. Each run through the projector has the potential of being the last – what if a splice breaks? the film gets chewed?!

Kathy Geritz (1998: 47)

Super 8 footage has come closer and closer to the ephemerality of performance as the 8mm medium is pushed ever nearer the edge of the obsolescence. The sound strip on Kodak Super 8 film was recently phased out, the elimination of which filmmaker Saul Levine likens to 'someone ripping out my tongue ...' (Cameron, 1998: 62) and 8mm diehards concede that the film stock itself will probably cease to be produced within the next decade. Prints of camera originals are no longer made, making each three-minute roll of film almost as unique and one-of-a-kind as live performance. Film shot now in the post-print age is irreplaceable, decaying and risks partial destruction with each showing. The 8mm reels used in each performance of *The Day Don Came With the Fish* voice the central theme of the work all the more poignantly for this. The film reels Paris worked with were, indeed, camera originals and these originals became shorter

133

and more delicate with each performance as frames were lost to old, temperamental projectors. Each time each frame is projected, then, is potentially the moment just before … the splice breaks, the film is chewed, the memory is severed, the body is wounded, the film is destroyed. In a medium that has been described as 'immortalizing' people, places and events, this is an ironic truth which makes the relationship between the mediated and the live, between the moment and the just moment before the moment, so captivating, so alive, so painfully mortal. Near the end of the piece, Paris pulls a small severed strip of film from her pocket, a gesture that begins the final sequence of the piece:

> *This is the moment when my father points to something in the distance and my mother and I follow his gaze. I especially like this bit.*

Edith Piaf fades in for the third and final time, performer signs the words. This time the audience knows exactly where the scratch is. During the 12 repetitions before the needle jumps, Paris explains:

> *I used to listen this song when I was young.*
> *I would accompany it with actions.*
> *These would be executed with great passion and feeling.*
> *The record belonged to my father and it always had a scratch in it.*
> *I only ever knew that the song sounded like this.*
> *I would always be waiting for that moment.*

The audience, braced for the coitus interruptus of the scratched record, breath a sigh of relief as the needle jumps forward and the performer signs the lyrics to the end of the song, with great passion and feeling. Her final act, as she leaves the performance space, is to hang the severed filmstrip on the silver fishhook.

After Paris leaves the gallery/performance space, the audience are free to examine the miniature filmstrip 'artifact', the severed moment in time: three figures on a beach on a sunny day. The man is pointing to something in the distance, his wife and his daughter follow his gaze. The frames have only about the same surface area as a fingernail, but

Figure 7.13

when viewed up close the images they capture are clearer and sharper than any of the digitally mastered video projected footage than Paris has performed with during the piece. The absence of the performer, and the sudden void of the digital audio-visuals is palpable. This is heightened by the fact that Paris has declined to use any conventional seating for this piece, instead having the audience gather around the Super 8 projector and the small images on the rice paper circles at the beginning of the piece, then follow her to the video projector in the centre of the gallery from where she cups the image of her oscilloscope heartbeat, and then to the far end of the gallery for her performance in front of the film screen. With the video projection concluded, with the performer gone and the only sound that of the end of the last spent reel flapping gently as the Super 8 projector continues to run, the group of people assembled to experience this piece shift out of their roles as 'audience members' at a performance. Those assembled are now a room full of people held together in space and time only by 8 small frames, a severed moment suspended. This piece, which has combined the live presence of the performer with the authentic chemical presence of the one-and-only camera reels and the digital mastering of analogue sequences, ends with the 'immortal' medium of film physicalizing the expression of the mortal, of the past, of the terminally ill, of the isolated moment just before ... Thus it is the language of the 'obsolete' technology, of the ruined filmstrip, of the dying art form that gives final voice to Paris's halting language of time and timelessness, of fleeting and frozen moments, and which remains in the space as a 'lasting' artefact after the inevitable 'death' of the live performance.

The Day Don Came With the Fish was commissioned by the Lux Center
and the London Filmmaker's Co-op, 1997.

References

1 Though her speaking voice is clearly British, in sign language Paris is an 'American', coached by her former student, Cherry Lundquist in ASL.

2 This program was created on Media 100 at the Institute for Studies in the Arts, Arizona State University.

8   One-to-One: Lone Journeys

Helen Paris

Much Western theatre evokes desire based upon and stimulated by the inequality between performer and spectator – and by the (potential) domination of the silent spectator. That this model of desire is apparently so compatible with (traditional accounts) of 'male' desire is no accident. But more centrally this account of desire between speaker/performer and listener/spectator reveals how dependent these positions are upon visibility and a coherent point of view. A visible and easily located point of view provides the spectator with a stable point upon which to turn the machinery of projection, identification, and (inevitable) objectification. Performers and their critics must begin to redesign this stable set of assumptions about the positions of the theatrical exchange.

(Phelan, 1993: 163)

Re-embodied Roles

In live performance the audience/performer relationship is fuelled by the potentials of same time same space interchange, the contact and communication possible in the live moment. Advances in technology not only expand the communication enablers available, they impact on *what* and *how* we communicate. Within this piece I discuss *Vena Amoris (love vein/vain)*[1], a performance which attempted to fully utilize some of the unique communication possibilities of live performance and at the same time explore the communication enabled/disabled by (mediating) technologies. In previous performance work, I had explored optimising the contact possible between audience and performer through focusing on the viscerality of the body. Throughout my practice questions and theories surrounding the representation of the female body on stage, the nature of the gaze – reciprocal, voyeuristic – had infused my performance work, confronting such issues face on. Rebecca Schneider posits that, 'contemporary feminist performance artists present their bodies as dialectical images' (Schneider, 1996: 157) and this awareness, coupled with the challenge to subvert, control and manipulate the image, became a focus of several of my solo performance pieces.

One strategy I employed in performance was to fully inhabit the 'erotic', stereotyped female body on stage, only to subvert those images once they were in place, opening up the flesh to expose what is abject. This construction and subsequent deconstruction of female stereotype was a double-edged sword. In order to convey the duality of images, appropriating an image in order to subvert it oftentimes meant that I

137

placed myself as performer in a position of personal oppression. In reviewing *C'est La Vie*, a solo piece I performed at the Institute of Contemporary Arts, London, 1996 (figure 8.1), Barbra Egervary writes that:

> She gives a sense of biting as expression of the need for a 'true real', as an acknowledgement of pain, as an expression of need and desire to really feel, to feel that emotion is real. Such a reflection of ourselves shows us the marks we each carry – the marks on our psyches reflected and made real within the frame of reference in the marks on the performer's body.

(Egervary, 1998: 41).

Figure 8.1. Helen Paris in 'C'est La Vie'. Photo © Curious.com

As performer, this embodiment of the 'true real' felt at times too intense and debilitating a stance to continually take. In *Vena Amoris* I wanted to find a way to 'be' as fully present as in previous work, maintain the 'stickiness of the organism' (Blau, 1992: 120) and yet not leave a stain, to be physically more 'absent', to find a place where sexuality is transcended, and to mark yet remain unmarked.2 This led to my eventual decision predicated on a looking-at-being-looked-at-ness that as performer I would neither look nor be looked at. The exchange between myself as performer and with the audience would, in Phelan's terms renegotiate 'the (potential) domination of the silent spectator', using a strategy which fully informed the content and which would redesign performer/audience 'assumptions about the positions of the theatrical exchange.' This strategy was that a one-to-one performer/audience interaction would take place and that this interaction would be enabled not by face-to-face communication but by communication relayed to the audience member by the performer via a mobile phone.

The mobile phone enabled a format from which to explore the depth of contact possible between audience and performance, accentuated by a desire to confront *what* and *how* we communicate to one another. Travelling to and from the rehearsal studio I was aware of the almost constant buzz of communication taking place on mobile phones. The cacophonies of conversation around me echoed a basic emptiness and redundancy of information exchanged: 'I'm on the train'; 'I'm on the bus'; 'I'll be there in 5 minutes.' Through observations of the lost and found potentials of communication through technology, the presence/absence simultaneity, and the desire to find an audience/performer intimacy through distance, the mobile phone became the device to both connect and disconnect performer and audience member. To enable and disable communication. The performances of *Vena Amoris* took place over the course of two evenings during which audience members arrived at allotted times at 20-minute intervals. Throughout each performance I remained in situ in a studio on the second floor of the building, whereas the audience members began the piece in the café bar downstairs via cell phone and moved gradually closer and closer to the 'real' presence of the performer. Through this process my aim was to present a performance where the female performer remains unmarked and wherein the gaze of the spectator is redirected through the performer back onto itself, at the same time enabling the audience member to be performer.

Disembodied Voices

From the very beginning of *Vena Amoris* the spectator/performer boundaries are blurred. The audience member is seated in the bar and suddenly their mobile phone rings. It is the performer who says:

> **Performer:** Hello. The performance is about to begin so if you'd just like to make your way to the theatre. It's just through the pink door, follow the signs to the back and should we lose touch – if for some reason we lose contact, please move to somewhere I can find you again and I'll call you back. I promise.

The wording of the instructions seems to follow the usual theatre format, the familiar announcement to the audience in the bar informing them that 'the performance is about to begin', yet the way this message is delivered, via the mobile phone, to one person only, immediately signifies something Other. With the ring of the phone there is an awareness that a performance has in fact *already* started. The pre-show nervousness usually felt only by the performer is now shared by the audience member as they sit in the bar, phone before them, waiting, not knowing exactly when it will ring, but knowing that *at any moment it will ring*. Who is the performer and who the audience? The audience member fulfils their role as audience as they pick up the phone, enabling the interaction with the performer to start, for the performer to literally be audible to them. Conversely, the shrill call of the ringing phone and the ensuing conversation between performer and audience member are witnessed by others present in the bar. Many of those present know that a performance is taking place and so from their perspective the audience member becomes the performer in that moment. Those present in the bar *unaware* that a performance is taking place witness merely a familiar interchange, which *they do not question*. Thus the familiarity of this communication and the technology which enables it is *reinforced*. Performance has become invisible, discreet, hidden by technology. What will those present in the bar, who know that the phone conversation is actually a performance, contemplate when next they see a conversation on a mobile phone. Art? Life? 'I'm on the train'?

The audience member follows the performer's instructions and walks towards the auditorium and in so doing they are *enabling* the performance.[3] The duality of the audience member's role is further signified as they enter the theatre space and are directed, not to the rows of empty, red plush theatre chairs but to the stage itself where, already positioned, set, and waiting for them, is *their* light, an empty spot on the stage which the performer instructs them to enter:

Performer: Can you see your light? Could you possibly step into your light?[4]
   [Audience member steps into the spot. In the centre of the spot-lit area there
is a box of matches and a cigarette.]
Performer: Please feel free to smoke.

Taking their place, spot-lit and silhouetted centre-stage, a coil of cigarette smoke
curling in the shaft of the light, the audience member presents an image that is
instantly recognizable as Theatre. Any audience who now walked into this moody,
atmospheric and quintessentially *theatrical* mise-en-scène could begin to interpret a
scenario, instantly recognizing a Performance in progress.

The performativity of the theatrical set up, the illusionary magic is further
heightened when, by an invisible cue, lights come up downstage, bathing the
'performer' in full light, signifying the start of something. Simultaneously music
fades up and fills the empty auditorium. But the manipulation of the theatrical
mechanisms has not only been subverted, the devices have been switched, they
seem to operate of their own accord. The Theatre plays out its phantasmagorical
nature; its existence as a 'seeing is believing place' as performative elements
mysteriously float into place; lights magically come up, sound is invisibly cued and
with the music that fades up and fills the auditorium the ghosted presence of the
audience is augmented as Doris Day's song, 'Make Someone Happy', resonates
through the emptiness:

   The sound of applause is delicious,
   It's a thrill to have the world at your feet.
   The praise of the crowd is exciting,
   But I've learned that's not what makes life complete.

   There's one thing you can do for the rest of your days
   That's worth more than applause,
   The screaming crowd,
   The bouquets ...[5]

The lyrics confirm the dual roles of audience and performer, which the audience
member appropriates and, at the same time there is a growing awareness that as well
as performer, the audience member is also, in a sense, the *performance* itself.[6]

And what is the answer? According to the words of the song 'Love is the answer',
a love that is firmly embedded within the title of the performance the audience has
come to see/be. It is a love that is completely visceral – a flow, an exchange from the
vein from the finger to the heart. It is the flow from the finger that dialled the number
to contact the audience member in order to lead them inextricably to them, to the
heart of the performer and to be the heart of the performance. The audience as
performer holds the performer as audience on stage with them, they performing
together and they are audience for each other whilst both perform.[7] The disembodied
voice of the performer through the phone both heightens the awareness of the absence

of the performer from the stage and simultaneously affirms the presence of the performer, speaking, intimate, into the ear of the audience, instructing, guiding. Are then the audience member and performer in fact performing *together*? Earlier in this article I stated that one of the aims of *Vena Amoris* was to create an intimacy between performer and audience member, a closeness, despite a physical separation. The use of the phone served to fulfil this desire on several levels. In part this was achieved by the characteristics of the medium. Paul Levinson describes the telephone as a 'highly sexually charged instrument' stating that, 'The whisper in the ear – lips of the speaker literally at the ear of the listener – is permissible in snippets between friends, but is by and large the domain of lovers and loved ones' (Levinson, 1997: 66–7). This notion of intimacy, of sound as caress, as touch, the performer reaching out and touching the audience member with her voice once again works towards fulfilling initial aims for *Vena Amoris* about the depth and closeness of the communication between performer and audience member, engendered despite/because of the fact that the performer cannot be seen.

The music comes to an end and the lights on the audience member on the stage fade slowly to black and then the house lights come up in the theatre – the presumed end of this stage performance being signified by the lights fading slowly fade to black, and the house-lights come up. This pattern is what usually signifies that the show is over and it is time for the audience to leave the theatre. This is the moment when the audience go to the bar, go home, re-enter 'real life' autonomous and, from the outside, seemingly unmarked by what they have experienced. Here, though, the audience member remains in the theatre, and what is more, remains onstage. The onstage world is now altered, the bright, overhead fluorescent lights illuminate the area offstage in the wings: the dusty ladders, forgotten sets from old productions. The music, which previously filled the auditorium, is finished. The magic of theatre has gone and is replaced by the 'real' theatre, the building itself with all its cracks and fissures, its worn carpet and faded velvet seats. And in this space the performer and audience remain in an assignation almost explicit in its flagrant disregard of convention. This rendezvous is in a complete reversal of the usual, acceptable encounter between performer and audience, in the dark, when the performer is onstage and spectator in velvet seated oppositional security. The danger here is not about what happens when the lights go out but rather when they come up. What is the role of the audience member now in the cold stark theatre light, still wondering if someone is watching, feeling themselves more 'seen' without the magical vestments of the theatre giving them their performance role in the warm embrace of the spotlight? The audience rules and established codifications have been overturned; they have no set ways to respond, 'The eruption of the binary scheme question/answer is of incalculable importance … It short-circuits all that was … the dialectic of the signifier and the signified, of a representing and a represented' (Baudrillard, 1983: 122). The visual semiotics are present as in traditional performance, the theatre venue, the proscenium arch, the lighting, the sound and yet the positions have been reversed.

The theatre building itself now becomes an artefact to be viewed, a historical document to be witnessed as the performer's voice on the phone relays a lecture-like description of theatre architecture and design and how both were determined at the end of the nineteenth century by the Victorian fear of fire. As mentioned previously the mobile phone is a communication enabler which usually signifies the communication of everyday instructions/information, 'I'm on the train' etc. It is not therefore perceived as a conveyer of a long, detailed lectures on the processes of 'making' or historical accounts, both more reminiscent of a museum speaker phone, enabling the viewer to wander round various buildings or artefacts and have a simultaneous factual description of what it is that they are seeing. This establishes the performance 'tour' that the audience member is about to take, a sightseeing tour in which they are guided by their own eyes and the performer's voice:

> I don't know whether you are aware of this but a hundred years ago when theatres switched from fire to electricity – from gas lights and lime lights to electric lights just about every aspect of theatre design was influenced by the fear of fire. Brick walls were built to further contain the theatres. So the theatre building became something of an architectural leper, separated out, cordoned off, walled in, and swallowed into the earth. The real danger, and this is the part I particularly like, was perceived as coming directly from the stage. In the event of fire it was stage and audience that had to be separated. Performances were quarantined behind the proscenium arch. A huge tank of water was suspended in the ceiling above the stage. I think this is a good time for you to leave the stage and make your way up the stairs …

Within this section several key themes within the piece are brought to the fore. The playful mention of the water tank suspended above the performer's head, which is quickly followed by the instruction for them to 'leave the stage', is a light-hearted joke from the performer to the audience member. It is a reminder of the position of vulnerability on the stage, which the audience member has experienced, sitting alone and uncertain of what is to happen next, and as to whether they are being watched. The whole nature of the performance/spectator dynamic is brought into direct focus with the text stating that 'stage and audience had to be separated'.

Throughout the piece thus far the binary oppositions have been challenged, audience and performer becoming mutually interchangeable. They have not been 'separated' from each other; rather they are conjoined, together on stage, together as audience, together in one body. In this light, quarantining of the performer/performance from audience can be seen as tearing not only self from other but also self from self. 'Danger' then is implicit in this intertwining of performer and audience, and this danger is represented by fire, which is present in varying manifestations throughout the rest of the piece. This renegotiation of roles persists throughout the piece and trust between both audience member and performer becomes implicit.

Leaving the theatre space the audience member is guided up the stairs by the 'blind' performer – unable to see exactly where the audience member is at any moment. Yet at the same time she seems to be with them, following them and having gone before them:

> Have you passed the kitchen on your left? Then you are nearly there – just a few more stairs. If you'd like to make your way around the corner at the top of the stairs now, towards a room marked the Fire Room, you'll notice a series of wooden cupboards in the wall on your left. I'd like you to open the second cupboard along. Have you got it?

The low-tech/high-tech nexus, which permeates the piece, is in full swing here. The play of 'interactivity', the post modern techno buzz word pasted on computer games, CDs and Art alike is adhered to playfully within the performance format, encouraging the audience member to interact with the performer, and objects they encounter on the way, creating the performance itself.[8] The dialogue to explain activating the computer is deliberately low tech, as is the placement of the sleek state-of-the-art laptop, secreted in a small scuffed brown wooden cupboard. Four purple fluorescent light strips line the cupboard giving it a seventies style neon glow. The performer speaks:

> Now, in the cupboard you can see the computer and on the computer is a digitally rendered film. Just click on 'Animated Picture Studio' and the film will start to play. I'd like you to watch it; it's very short.

The computer runs off battery power and, like the phone, is wireless. In the film the audience watch three figures in Victorian garb, a finely dressed woman, a bearded man and an enthusiastic filmmaker. The woman has come to have her moving image captured and as the camera starts to roll she becomes highly animated, posturing and posing and eventually high kicking with abandon, etiquette momentarily quelled with the joy of performance. When the camera stops rolling, enthralled by the woman's display the bearded man makes amorous advances towards and persuades her to sit on his lap. Meanwhile, unbeknownst to the two of them the wily filmmaker has restarted the camera, and films their flirtation. He then leaves, returning with a mirror-like screen on which to project the moving images. At first the woman is delighted to see her image before her and revels in watching herself, clapping her hands in joy. Her joy turns to horror, however, as her playful posturing is replaced by the moving image of fraternization between herself and the bearded gentleman. Aghast and furious she dashes the screen to the ground, breaking it. The image however retains a quasi immortality and remains projected at their feet. They are forced to watch their lovemaking, their deed marked in imperishable replay.

The inclusion of this particular film serves several purposes within *Vena Amoris*. The play between early and modern technologies continues with the film footage, made in 1904 and digitized using the latest 1999 digital technology formatting the image into an aptly named 'Director movie'. The content of the film is significant to the themes within *Vena Amoris* concerning the reflection of self, the narcissism and the inescapability of the image. The filmmaker, both behind the lens and in front of it in the shape of Thomas

Edison himself is relevant to the performance. He inhabits different worlds divided by the frame of the lens and like the audience member and performer, is both spectator and artist, is present and absent. His presence as inventor ghosts the performance of *Vena Amoris* in the light bulbs in the theatre, the phone, the currents of electricity and within the text:

> **Performer:** Thomas Edison made the film you just watched in 1904. The same Thomas Edison who invented the light bulb. Or did he? There seems to be some controversy about this. At any rate, he at least liked to take the credit for it and was totally opposed to Nicola Tesla's dream of free wireless electricity. Particularly, he didn't like the way Tesla dressed. Unlike Tesla, Edison was unconcerned by appearance and in fact disapproved of washing, believing that too much cleanliness negatively altered the chemical on the surface of the skin. He began to smell so bad that his wife refused to sleep with him.

Electricity connects performer to audience member. This unbroken current is physically experienced. The audience member is requested by the performer to enter the door opposite, labelled 'Fire Room.' Gold curtains hang at the windows giving a theatrical atmosphere. Chairs are set out in neat rows as if for a lecture and as with the theatre space the chairs are empty. A small stage is at the far end of the room. On the stage is a white gallery style plinth, upon which stands a Van der Graaf generator, as if as art object. The generator is switched on and buzzes, making little sparks of electricity, visible from close up. The performer asks the audience member to approach the Van der Graaf and touch it – experiencing the charge of static electricity. For the audience member to do this they must trust the performer, whom they know only through her voice, guiding them on this unknown journey. The performer must now 'leave' the audience member as the mobile phone has to be switched off; continued contact through the phone in proximity to the generator being potentially dangerous; it is the 'fire' they have been warned about. Contact between performer and audience member has to be broken, in order for the performance to proceed, but it is a procession that ultimately leads the performer and audience member to meet 'in the flesh.' From the moment the audience member switches off their phone to approach the Van der Graaf they experience this part of the performance completely alone, witnessing the spark of electricity jumping between their body and the generator.

At the bottom of the plinth a tiny arrow and instructions direct the audience member to exit the 'Fire Room' through the door to the right of the Van der Graaf, on the opposite side of the room to where they entered. They find themselves in a narrow corridor, outside a door with a code lock. A tall blonde woman, elegantly dressed in a black velvet evening gown is standing outside the door. Upon the audience member's approach she enters the code, opens the door open a crack and gently pushes them through, while simultaneously whispering to her identical twin (figure 8.2), who appears on the other side of the door, whispering back:

Figure 8.2. Cath and Debs Sibbald in 'Vena Amoris'. Photo © Curious.com

Twins: I've missed you. I've been thinking of you. I've so wanted to see you again. I wanted to say something to you. I have to go now. I'll be thinking of you. I'll be waiting until we can be together again. Goodbye. Goodbye.

As the audience member passes through to the other side of the door, the twins kiss on the lips and whisper their good-byes through the crack in the door until the door closes again. Once more there is the concept of the audience member enabling the performance. Their journey through the door enables the separated twins to see each other, and each to see herself reflected in the other. The audience member enables the twins to kiss, to speak. The interior twin then closes the door and remains inside the studio with the audience member. For the first time the audience member has an audience with the presence of the twins. The twins act as ushers or facilitators as well as performers. Their performance presence is further convoluted by the fact that *their* performance is *themselves*. This layering of roles and images and their implicit meanings is further extrapolated by the presence of screens. As the second twin ushers the audience member in, another screen, an identical laptop, greets them with the digitally altered voice of Doris Day singing 'Make Someone Happy', the cursor scrolling slowly across baby blue vector waves on a pastel pink screen. The laptop is sitting on a white plinth, and echoes not only the Edison film played on the laptop in the cupboard but also the Van Der Graaf, both posing as art objects to be viewed. The pitch of the song has been digitally shifted so that it sounds oddly as if it is being sung by a man, the binary code of the computer enabling a transgendering.[9] Rebecca Schneider states that

> There is no way a woman can escape the historical ramifications of that representation unless she passes from visibility as a woman, passing as a man. As 'woman' she is preceded by her own markings, standing in relation to her body in history as if beside herself.
>
> (Schneider, 1996: 157)

This statement provides an interesting interpretation to the scene that the audience member has entered. The unmarked presence of the performer allows the freedom to engender a presence through the performance where there is almost a transcendence of gender.

At the far end of the room a door-sized mirror stands surrounded by dressing room lights. Another screen, another image. A chair is positioned in front of the mirror, which the audience member is invited to sit in by the 'interior twin' who then recedes to the far door. The audience member sees their own reflection in the brightly-lit mirror, unaware that the performer, in the dark on the other side can look directly through the mirror at them. The performer speaks from behind the mirror,[10] 'disembodied' like the voice on the phone:

> **Performer:** I'm glad you came.
> I didn't know if I would recognize you.
> I had a picture of you in my head.
> Did you miss me? I mean
> Did you ever think of me?
> Did you want to see me again? I mean
> Did I make any difference?
> Did you want to say something just to me?
> Did you want to catch hold of something that you thought you might have seen or at least thought you'd caught a glimpse of and at least, for a little while?
> Not want to let go?
> Was I too late?
> Did I say the right thing but at the wrong time?
> And what I'm really asking is do I get another chance while everything is changing skin, legs, flesh, hair, head, heart, chest?
> Did I lose part of myself – the part where I recognize myself but never had the chance to say goodbye?
> ...And did you did you NEED that tiny jolt of electricity just to know you were alive?

The text fragments are at once instantly recognizable and instantly unfamiliar; deliberately abstract and at the same time intensely personal and open to individual interpretation. There is a seeming randomness to the selection, to the way the fragments are pieced together. As it progresses the delivery of the text becomes more frantic, more desperate in its need to communicate, almost as if saying *anything* in order to say *something*.

This randomness raises the question of whether the text is in fact the *same* for each audience member. Is the whole journey they have taken unique to them? The live, real time, real space, nature of performance means that each performance is by definition unique. Thus the transient quality of live work is reflected by the fact that the audience member is unsure whether the next person will be directed to the same spaces, told the same things. As with the words of a lover there is a desire for what is spoken to be true for only one. 'Love is the answer, someone to love is the answer.' But the spoken text is enigmatic. Who is the performer really talking to? What is their gender? Is it the gender of the performer? Of the audience member? Does the performer direct the words to her own image, which she sees reflected in the mirror? The line, 'did I lose part of myself – the part where I recognize myself but never had the chance to say goodbye?' echoes Freud's statement of narcissism as identification with the lost loved object (quoted in Lacan, 1968: 169). Who is loved? Self or Other? What is the relationship between the inner and outer – and which is which?

All the while that the audience member has been making the journey, guided by the words of the performer, the performer has been sitting behind the mirror gazing at her own reflection. Has the performer then been talking to her own reflection all along? Is this the insight into the narcissism of the performer who has been frozen behind glass, immobilized by her own image, so entrapped/entranced she has not been able to leave, to take her place on the stage. The ownership of 'I' has shifted throughout the performance and within this text the subjectivity retains its ambiguity. Who then was the journey for? Who took it? The Performer? The Audience member? Both? Who was enabling whom? Or are the words spoken suggestions of the thoughts of the audience member? Uncanny illuminations of their own thoughts surfaced at some time or another? Seen with clarity through the glass, when confronted with their own image? Or is it in fact a direct communication from the performer to the audience member?

> Within a language pervasively masculinist, a phallogocentric language, women represent the *unrepresentable*. In other words, women represent the sex that cannot be thought, a linguistic absence and opacity. Within a language that rests on univocal signification, the female sex constitutes the unconstrainable and undesignatable. In this sense, women are the sex, which is 'not one' but multiple.
>
> (Butler, 1990: 9).

Once more there is the dilemma for the audience member as to whether the questions require an answer. In some ways the audience member is at last in the place *familiar* to them in which to witness a performance. The room is darkened, heavy curtains block out the light, they are seated and before them is the performer. Yet still the conventions of their role are confounded, as they have been throughout the journey. The way the mirror has been dressed, with open light bulbs framing it, can be seen to signify the traditional theatre dressing room mirror, the place where the performer sits before and after the show, before and after the audience, where she faces her reflection before presenting that image to another. Seeing herself before she is seen. If art holds a mirror up to nature, what is the intent when the artist holds the mirror up? Is this the Theatrical Fourth Wall, reflecting – 'imperfectly – what comes to it – imperfectly – from the other three walls and lets through – presently – the ghost of what it reflects, the shadow deformed and reformed according to the figure of what is called present: the upright fixity of what stands before me: "The inscriptions ... appear inverted, righted, fixed"' (Derrida, 1981: 314)?

The question that has been asked silently throughout the journey is most pertinent here. Has the audience member been under some sort of surveillance, like the body in cyberspace, 'tracked, traced, digitized and stored' (Hershman Leeson, 1996: 326). Who is being seen and who is seeing? Who listens and who speaks? Throughout the performance the audience member has felt watched on their journey, at times feeling a victim of an imagined voyeuristic gaze of the somewhere present performer. Ironically, the only time that the performer can in fact see them, the audience member feels unseen, unwatched. The audience member can guess at the gender of the performer through her voice and this is potentially all that they can surmise. In terms of a mind/body distinction it is important to note that in *Vena Amoris* the voice – the mind of the performer is free, but her body is trapped behind an image of itself. The audience member does not know when or if they will see her face to face, one to one. For the performer, there has been greater knowledge; she dials the numbers and places the calls. She knows the very moment others will join the performance. The performer has sightlessly guided the journey the audience member has taken, seeing it for and before them: 'just through the pink doors in front of you,' 'Can you see your light on the stage?' And yet she has not seen them. The moment of sight happens when the performer lights a cigarette from behind the mirror. The flame from the Zippo lighter brilliantly illuminates her face and she is visible to the audience member for the first time. 'You are getting hot as you approach that icy looking glass and the key to a certain clasp' (Derrida, 1981: 309). The moment comes and goes in a whisper, in a heartbeat. A presence. An absence. Fort! Da!

The moment the audience member sees the performer, their vision through the looking glass presents them with an equally strong image of themselves, still partially reflected in the glass. In this moment the mirror transposes the two illuminated faces onto each other, patina like, creating an almost other worldly effect, Blau's 'ghosted' presence, as the performer's eyes are imprinted on the audience member's eyes, mouth on mouth, forehead on forehead. The audience member has entered a double world, like Alice they have gone through the looking glass – but which side are they on? Whose image do they look to find? Their own? The performer's? Truly performer and audience member are meeting each other, flesh on flesh, shape on shape, feature on feature:

> As a representation of the real the image is always, partially, phantasmatic. In doubting the authenticity of the image, one questions as well the veracity of she who makes and describes it. To doubt the subject seized by the eye is to doubt the subjectivity of the seeing 'I'.

> (Phelan, 1993: 1)

Are Performer and Audience member engaged in an endless return as their gaze meets in the mirror and passes through, their reflections constantly altered, and returned? And in terms of gender, definitions already somewhat confounded by the ambiguity of the usage of 'I' and 'you' in the text spoken behind the mirror, what is suggested by double image of the layering of woman on woman, woman on man? When is the body unmarked or marked by gender? And which gender? What does the image represent when different ages, genders, and ethnicities merge? What identifications are made, and what narcissistic and scopophilic pleasure is found. Where is the desire? For self? For other? Who makes whom 'happy?' The innocent simplicity of the flame engendering the phantasmic representation of multiplicities belies the complexities of the representations and configurations it illuminates. Again there is the persistence of the low-tech/high-tech confluence, each mode seeming to switch roles, with the digital format used to manipulate grainy 100-year-old film as well as play Doris Day songs, and the elemental power of fire creating visual 'special effects': mirrors and smoke.

This final flame, rather than being the fire that separates performer and audience, spectator from stage – it is what enables them to meet, the heart of the piece. And yet they seem to meet only to say goodbye:

Performer: I'm glad you came. When will I see you again?
I'll miss you. I miss you already.
Goodbye.

The flame is blown out, the face of the performer disappears and the audience member is left staring at his or her own reflection once more. Rather than the moment when performer and audience member meet being a moment of demystification, it exists in a form as transitory as live performance itself, it does not signify an answer, a denouement, the reason for the journey. The audience has not been 'in search' of an author who they eventually see through a glass darkly. Rather, in the same way as an electric current must remain unbroken to be 'live', as the flow of the blood from the vein to the heart relies on a constant circulation, the meeting of the performer and audience member signifies a part of the journey, of the performance, not the conclusion. As the audience member enters the studio they are already passing through the mirror, as established by the identical twins, who – unlike the performer who is held permanently transfixed by her double-mirror image – see only fleeting glimpses of the reflected image of themselves in each other's faces. The audience member grants them the image they desire and they meet through the mirror moment, visually, physically, verbally.

In conclusion, in terms of the control, the detached viscerality and virtual closeness and the compliance which have been at play throughout the piece I would like to take Schneider's comment that:

For the feminist materialist 'reciprocity' becomes a project of recognizing the ricochet of gazes, and the histories of who-gets-to-see-what-where. The invested object will be, to some degree, *both* separate from *and* relative to herself in her general struggle with historical legacies of disembodiment – paradoxical *and* impossible as she is, being, herself, the previously unimaginable: philosopher and mother, prostitute and historical materialist, in one. One which is, of course, not one. Never only one.

(Schneider, 1997: 184)

There is a liberation within this comment that goes some way towards providing succour to initial performance concerns discussed earlier in this chapter, regarding loss of self within presenting certain images and discussed the desire as performer to supersede a marked, gendered, objectified role. This supersedence was engendered by the one-to-one format and the performer/audience invisibility/visibility. Schneider's final, affirmative, 'never only one' presents a freedom for the performer, fixed physically behind the mirror but fluid in role, spectator, mediator, non-performer, guide, ally, and able to reform, change, re-embody, shapeshift chameleon-like with every returned gaze of each audience member reflected before her and on her. The opacity and enigmatic quality of the exchange between performer and audience member, the embodiment of the audience member as spect–actor, have enabled both performer and audience member to be 'never only one'.

I'm glad you came.
When will I see you again?
miss you already.

References

1   The title refers to the Egyptian belief that the third finger of the left hand follows the *vena amoris*, the vein of love that runs directly to the heart. A direct 'digital' blood flow. *Vena Amoris* was supported by an Artsadmin Artist's Bursary and devised on site with collaborating artist Leslie Hill. Performances took place in Toynbee Hall, London, 1 and 2 July 1999.

2   See Rebecca Schneider who states that: 'The notion of a "returned" gaze or an object's eye seemed always to be reacting to an initializing challenge, always servicing a scene marked by the self-perpetuating and ultimately boring tango hold of patriarchal objectification, always complicit in a drama of submission. The impulse to find an "object's eye," like a "female gaze," seemed fraught with the impulse to create yet another de-objectified subject, caught in the binaried dance between subject and object that had set the stage for the shadow play of gender in the first place.' (Schneider, 1996: 160)

     Rather than joining in the reactionary two-step I wanted to find a way of establishing optimum contact whilst resisting the physical presence.

3   The reality is that they are *both* the performer and the audience. In Boalian terms they have become spect-actor, the single entity that subsumes both functions within a single body (See Auslander, 1997: 101).

4   During one of the performances, one audience member, a prestigious Live Art programmer when asked by the performer, 'can you see *your* light?' retorted, 'I can see *a* light', instantly aware of the meaning inherent in the question.

5   'Make Someone Happy', from the Musical production of *Do Re Mi* (B. Comden/A.Green/J. Styne). From *Two Classic Albums from Doris Day, Two On One, Bright and Shiny Compilation,* 1994 Sony Music Entertainment (UK) Ltd. MCPS/BIEM/SDRM.

6   There is a reference to Brecht's self-observing condition of the *verfremdung* technique in play here and the audience member self-consciously awaits the spectacle of the performer and the unfolding of the performance whilst simultaneously *being* that performer and performance.

7   'One always locates one's own image in an image of the other *and*, one always locates the other in one's own image' (Phelan, 1993: 18). It is interesting to note that throughout this section the audience member sustains a belief that in fact they are being watched by someone out there in the dark, in the space that they themselves usually inhabit in their role as spectator. The reality of the situation is that the voyeurism is imagined, however the strategies in place that encourage the audience member to *perceive* an element of voyeurism are deliberately positioned. These strategies are the means by which the specta-tor *becomes* performer, by which the voyeur becomes viewed. The play between seeing and being seen, watching and being watched runs through *Vena Amoris*. Here, alone on the stage the gazing audience member / 'performer' must try and *see* everything including their own image, as they are both, *being* and *seeing*. This 'mirror stage' reflects their image back on themselves.

8   Computer interactivity is an excellent example of a situation wherein the audience/spectator becomes the performer/participant/creator.

9   See Birringer on Laurie Anderson, 'Anderson is in control of the technological manipulation of the various (gender) identities constructed ...' (Birringer, 1991: 221–2).

10 It is interesting to note that nearly all of the audience members who witnessed the piece initially failed to recognize the presence of the performer in the room with them, because they were so accustomed to the disembodied voice of the performer through the phone. The presence and simultaneous absence and displacement provided by the disembodied voice parallels the disembodiment of digital technologies, 'Identity is the first thing you create when you log on to a computer service. By defining yourself in some way, whether through a name, a personal profile, an icon, or a mask, you also define your audience, space and territory ... Anatomy can be readily reconstituted. You do not need a body ... entering cyberspace encourages a disembodied body language.' (Hershman Leeson, 1996: 325–6)

11 Through the disembodied voice the only tangible identity established is that of gender, although with the 'transgendering' of the Doris Day song, even this is thrown into confusion.

9 Mouth Ghosts: The Taste of the *Os-Text*

Jools Gilson-Ellis

This chapter proposes a radical connection between femininity and orality. In particular it proposes the new term *os-text* to describe the relationship between writing and speaking one's own text in performance. The *os-text* incorporates the uttering mouth (the 'os'), the kissing (osculation) of words into being, and the oscillation between writing and speaking. Written, uttered, kissed and oscillatory, the *os-text* is a challenge to the conventional authority of the performance text. Its combination of textual and oral economies in a single corpus performs a resistance to and a revelling in *both*.

    I begin with the female mouth as a site of contested and contestable meanings. The filled, or obstructed female mouth is a recurrent image in literature, visual art, performance and film. Hélène Cixous writes in 'The Laugh of the Medusa' 'Our lovely mouths (are) gagged with pollen' (1981: 248). Caryl Churchill and David Lan have a female character in their play *A Mouthful of Birds* who feels that her mouth is stuffed with birds (1986: 71). Women's relationship to 'mouths full of talk' is a familiar one; they are consistently characterised as chatterers and gossips. Female insane asylums during the nineteenth century were regularly described as more noisy than their male equivalents (Showalter, 1985: 81). And yet the symptomatology of hysteria includes a loss of speech (Freud, 1895, 1905), and a lump in the throat at one time thought to be the womb rising towards the mouth (Veith, 1965). It is at this threshold of the body that many women play out the regulation of their self-worth through bulimic and anorexic economies (Orbach, 1986). These connections between femininity and orality are traced in this chapter, and the particular potentialities of the *os-text* is proposed as a strategy for transgressing such realms of oral occlusion, silence, and garrulousness, through a writing practice that weaves utterance in the breath of writing.

os *n.*, *pl.* **ora** *Anatomy.* A mouth or opening. [Latin *os*, mouth]

oscillate *v.* **1.** To swing back and forth with a steady uninterrupted rhythm. **2.** To waver between two or more thoughts or courses of action; vacillate. **3.** *Physics.* To vary between alternate extremes. [Latin *oscillare*, from *oscillum*, a swing, originally a mask of Bacchus hung from a tree in a vineyard to swing in the wind (as a charm) diminutive of *os*, mouth]

osculation *n.* **1.a.** The act of kissing **b.** A kiss

The *os-text* is a text that is neither written nor spoken, neither is it *both* written and spoken. This is a text that survives in oscillation not *between* but *because* of the mouth and the text. Its place is on the side of the feminine. It has no secure place in the oral or in the written, but flies instead in the face of both. This is a text which refuses stillness. A text marked by the grain of the voice. A text written in the mouths of writers.

What happens when the bite and taste of voicing is performed through the same body as the body of the writer? What does it mean to have your own writing in your mouth; your tongue in your text? The *os-text* describes this connection between orality and writing. Hélène Cixous (1993: 93) suggests that writing is writing what you cannot know before you have written. I suggest that to speak your own writing in performance is to speak what you cannot know before you have spoken. In this elaboration of Cixous' phrase is a claim about the extraordinary possibilities of voice in relation to writing, and writing in relation to voice. The *os-text* resists the suggestion that a voice speaking a text is a repetition of what has been written. I am interested in bodies which write *and* speak; in a voicing body which has also written; a writing body which also voices. I conjure a theory for the progressive ways in which vocality and 'writality' entwine:

> In the night, winds rise in her. They rush skin-close, and find the space of her. Warm blizzards arch in her chest, and her breasts swell and turn tender. Her belly answers the hefts of small gales – air filled with ochre leaves, turning on itself. She turns as the airs in her move. Leaf winds curve her a belly to meet her high breasts. Small breezes trace the surface of her skin, and when she wakes, she is plumly ripe and ready to birth. But before breakfast, she is tiny again. The flatness of her stomach inside her jeans. Her breasts are two handfuls again. And tenderless. This is an air haunting. She is nightly flooded with gusts that curve her from inside out. *wind ghost.*

Do such voices/such writing entwine or oscillate? Neither will quite do. Weaving and shivering between text and voice is the *os-text*:

> (finding the breath of writing)

> I write a text called 'wind ghost' for our work *The Secret Project*. I write it in the fall of 1998 in Northern Ontario. Leaves are blowing about me on my morning walks. And they are scarlet. I have been working on two ideas for the text of this work, one to do with falling, the other with ghosts. Another of the texts for the piece is called 'snow ghost.' In 1999, I try out some preliminary ideas for performing *wind ghost*, in Limerick and in Cork.[1] Strangely, my first idea is the one that makes it into the finished piece. The idea is to move from stage right to stage left, speaking the text and moving as if being swept internally by the winds and breezes and sudden gusts the text evokes. Finding the force of the text again in rehearsal is like digging for a precious thing I remember being there. I bury flesh in the blood of words so that I can return to them months / years later and find it there, pulsing. In performance, in the saying and moving of these words before an audience, I find the sinew of the text again. When I wrote *wind ghost* I placed something in it that I knew I could return to, without knowing what it was. Such a text oscillates in my os (my mouth); I send it curving flesh to text; font to voice. I kiss it to life. This is the *os-text*. I let the breath of flesh and

voicing arch in my chest. As I develop the piece, so I compose a score for the rhythms and intonations of the text. This is not anything I write down, but a musical pattern in my ear and mouth and body. I hear it resounding in my blood even as I write this. It rides on the waves of my moving longing flesh. It is one of the patterns on the turning cord of the performance. Listen. I hear my writing as I speak it; as I move in its tangled swept spaces; breathing in light's blush. In music's coil I conjure *wind ghost* into being, before you.

I bring you with me, slowly, from stage right to stage left.
Here we move. All of us. In breeze's arms.

wind ghost.

∂

In this next section I look at Ruth Salvaggio's *The Sounds of Feminist Theory* (1999) in relation to my proposal of the os-text. I use analyses of my own practice as a way to extend these discussions. This will lead into an examination of the work of Luce Irigaray and Hélène Cixous. It is the aim of this chapter to develop a productive understanding of the relationship between femininity, the body, writing and utterance in relation to a practice of women writing and performing their own texts (the *os-text*).

The Sounds of Feminist Theory is a dynamic engagement with orality, sounding and listening in relation to feminist critical writing. Salvaggio examines a range of contemporary feminist critical writing and identifies an enervating and motivating force within it which she identifies as inflected by the energies of oral language; something she calls 'hearing the O' (Salvaggio, 1999: 7). Although Salvaggio's analysis is always (finally) of writing, her argument is one of the most compelling in a development of the categories of the *feminine / oral* and the *os-text*, because she proposes a revolutionary potential for the meeting of orality and writing. In the following analysis of Salvaggio's book, I pay particular attention to her work on *aurality / listening*, and *motion*.

Salvaggio is interested in 'the way in which much feminist writing infuses the energies of oral language into a vibrant critical literacy' (1999: 7). She is careful to side-step an uncritical revelling in the liberatory possibilities of voice and orality: 'I stress both the distinctly oral and literate properties of the O because I do not want to seem as though I'm uncritically embracing a return to oral language and aligning it with feminine or feminist expression' (ibid.: 8). Salvaggio, like myself, is interested in the combination of oral and written energies; the difference between us is that Salvaggio is always speaking of a textual product, whereas I am proposing something which oscillates between writing and literal orality (the *os-text*). Why is Salvaggio careful to avoid an uncritical association of oral language with femininity? The main reason is likely to be that such a 'return' as Salvaggio calls it, risks excluding femininity from the culture of writing itself, and reifying notions of femininity. Nonetheless, Salvaggio's oft-repeated defences against the dangers of oralities suggest something of the apparently recidivist power of orality itself. The dangers Salvaggio describes lie in an 'uncritical celebration of so-called feminine modes of language that emphasise the personal, subjective, emotive and potentially liberatory dimensions of voice' (ibid.: 4). Whilst Salvaggio's reservations clearly refer to an early period of feminism,[2] it seems to me (and putting historical precedent, for the moment, aside) as possible to engage with the 'personal, subjective, emotive' and 'liberatory' in vocal as well as written language. I think the dangers of consciousness-raising groups defining feminine language / orality and the voicing of one's autobiographical truth have passed long enough for contemporary feminist thought to engage more rigorously and bravely in the possibilities of the oral.[3] Any political project undertaken uncritically is likely to fail. The proposal of the *os-text* is a proposal of an active engagement in the dynamics of writing and speaking, in which each is enervated by the other. The *os-text* links with Salvaggio's work on two levels; firstly because it connects writing and orality and secondly because it brings bodily poetics into writing and performance.

I want here to clarify how Salvaggio's work informs *os-textual* practice, and in what ways it exceeds it. I am aware that the work Salvaggio identifies as resounding with the 'O' is part of a discourse on the nature of critical / poetic / autobiographical *writing*. Therefore, any discussion of bodily practice in relation to this work is always a transformation of *writing* and reading. In relation to my proposal of the *os-text*; *writing* text and *speaking* it in performance does not in itself guarantee progressive *os-textual* practice. Just as too uncritical an embrace of orality in writing can fail ('Not some chaotic outburst, but a working and kneading of sound into written language and critical thought for the very purposes of expanding and multiplying possible meanings.' (Salvaggio, 1999: 132)), I want to suggest that progressive *os-textual* practice is best enabled through *both* an engagement with orality / aurality in the *writing* of these texts, *and* an oscillatory economy between voicing and writing in performance. It is my contention that something particular occurs when the writer is also the performer of such texts. This is not to say that someone other than the writer performing these texts is necessarily of less value, this is simply a *different* engagement with text and performance.

One of the strands of Salvaggio's argument is the importance of sound / listening in relation to 'hearing the O' in feminist critical writing. This is of particular relevance to the *os-text* firstly because it may contain such 'sonorous energy' in terms of the written text itself, and secondly because the *os-text* is doubly heard – by the performance writer herself as well as by the audience. Salvaggio is interested in 'the effects produced by the oral and aural reverberations of language as they infuse writing and thought' (ibid.: 14). I too am interested in such reverberations, but I am equally interested in the ways in which the oral / aural are affected by writing. Salvaggio writes of voices haunting written language (ibid.: 20), I want to ask how writing haunts *voice*; of writerly ghosts in mouths.

Salvaggio extends this discussion of the aural in contrasting the realm of sound to the realm of vision. She does this '... by turning (her) sensory antennae to what is audible rather than purely visible in critical language and thought' (ibid.: 22). Salvaggio cites Murray Schafer's work on 'soundscapes' in which he explains how 'the advent of writing and especially print in the west elevated vision over sound, resulting in our increasing lack of sensitivity not only to the sounds that surround us, but our very abilities to know the world through listening to its sounds as voices' (Schafer, 1980: 11, cited by Salvaggio, 1999: 137). In this scenario print replaces orality, steals its particular charge. In this process femininity is associated with the immersion of sound, and masculinity with the distance of vision. I want to associate femininity with a skilled heteroglossia – with an ability to weave both the sound of voicing and the vision of writing.[4] Salvaggio's engagement with these ideas take her into an analysis of certain critical / narrative strategies in which she identifies 'meaning on the move' – a resistance to dénouement in favour of troubling resonances, odd endings / cyclical structures. Salvaggio suggests that this is the consequence of sound / orality inflecting this writing, 'that the feminist engagement with bodies in writing works to sustain the effects of sound, meanings that resound beyond definitions and final determinations' (ibid.: 64). This is a well-made argument, but I am still struck by the actual silence of all this vocally inflected writing. No one speaks before me. No one moves before me. I understand Salvaggio's point that such writing conjures a kind of listening / reading, and an engagement with physicality, but if I heard this writing spoken, if these writers were present here on the cliffs at Cill Rialaig performing their texts before me, grounds would shift significantly.[5]

> **yarn** *n.* **1.** A continuous strand of twisted threads of natural or synthetic material, such as wool, cotton, flax or nylon, used in weaving or knitting.

> **2.** *Informal.* A long complicated story or a tale of real or fictitious adventures, often elaborated upon by the teller during the telling.

How does 'meaning on the move' become moved again by the exigencies of a performing speaking body before an audience? What is the connection between hearing a voice and moveable meaning? Michel de Certeau says that voice 'alters a place (it disturbs), but it does not establish a place' (1984: 155). I do not want to install meaning. I want to set it running. The *os-text* has the potential to engage Salvaggio's 'hearing the O' with the vivid presence of performance; to set meaning on the move:

> (inbreath) (inbreath) trip, shift to side. over slow, down. (breathe) runs, slipping up over. over down. (outbreath). fall (breath). down and wide. singing out over wide, to the left. wide. ocean. I have you. I'm falling. (outbreath) (two small sighs overlapping) sings, root of her, (outbreath). touchlight, falling, waterlight, over. ache. high, falling and over (escapes) (small breath). seeming. shift and echo to the side. twice turning. fly lightful, air wards, cleanly (breathe), small flicks passionful. keep sky, out over down. aches two. light folding over. small secrets, up over down. twice turning. stop (outbreath) (outbreath)

I write a text for *The Secret Project* called *twice turning*. My collaborator Richard Povall and I are working with technologies which connect movement with sound. The sound we use most often is samples of my voice speaking my text. When I write *twice turning*, I write it with the taste of this technology in my flesh.[6] The text attempts to *write* physicality; it is characterised by verbs, action, movement, and a parenthetical breathing. We design an intelligent environment for the text to be triggered in; we are interested in making something that you have to move vigorously within in order to trigger the text. Richard fragments the recording of the text, into short phrases.[7] He programmes an environment we design together; it operates like a little window over the text; early in the performance of the piece it is only possible to trigger the first phrase, and later a middle sentence, and so on. The text's fragmented quality is performed through the moving body of the dancer: she plays the text like an instrument. It is as if there are textual ghosts in the space which will speak their words if dynamic movement wakes them. And this is a text itself about dynamic movement. As a writer and performer, it feels as if this technology enables me to make my text three-dimensional. In the environment for *twice turning* it is possible to layer phrases of the text, as well as to slowly trigger the internal sound of a single word. Tumbles of text move with this fragmentation. Such cacophony and stillness engages with the moving dynamics of the text itself. Unlike many of the interactive environments designed for *The Secret Project*, *twice turning* does not involve the speaking of text in real time in relation to samples of text triggered by movement. This is not an *os-textual* piece because no one speaks before you in performance. But there is a voice, and it is mine, and I am speaking my writing. What does it mean then for another body to perform this piece? What does it mean when Cindy Cummings performs this piece in the final version of *The Secret Project*? Does she, in some sense 'speak' my writing? Does she, in another sense 'choreograph' my writing, as she controls its ebb and flow by her leaps, curves and stillnesses? What kind of 'O' would Ruth Salvaggio hear in such a piece? In the performance of *twice turning*, Cindy's working flesh – her breathing, arching, sweating body grazes and tangles the writing / voicing she triggers. In what sense is she the writer of this text? And in what sense am I its choreographer? The process of making this piece 'work' is one in which Richard develops the environment as Cindy works, as I watch, giving them both feedback. Cindy develops an improvisation which is structured in response to the environment. The environment becomes her dancing partner. This is neither completely open improvisation, nor set choreography. The ways in which Cindy triggers the environment will always be different (the movement / text score is always different). She (we) must *listen* in a way dancers are not used to listening because the soundtrack is usually the same.[8] If she (we) does not really *listen* and let the phrasing and phrases she triggers affect her improvisation, then the piece fails. Such a failure is a failure of the connection between fleshly and writerly longing. If there is a loop between *this* movement, *that* phrase and *this* movement, then such writing resounds with the 'O' put forth by Salvaggio. It becomes impossible to speak of this text and that body, it becomes instead a single thing, something like the 'bodies-language' proposed by Dianne Chisholm (1995), in a context of performance. Such a listening is always a double listening; a heightened fleshly hearing by the performer herself, that enables the audience to listen themselves through the heat of blood. *This* is meaning on the move.

> I choreograph writing; I leave it flickering with the beat of blood;
> I write dancing – I flesh it into loving speech –
> muscular sayings of consonant to vowel to inbreath.

∂

Amongst feminist critical theorists writing about femininity and writing, one of the distinctions regularly seen as definitive of their work is whether they develop their ideas in relation to *women* or *femininity*. These arguments are intimately connected to critiques of essentialism weighed fairly regularly against such writers, as I will discuss in relation to Luce Irigaray and Hélène Cixous later in this chapter. Such arguments turn on a fear of prescribing and reifying what it means to be a woman, and what femininity in turn might constitute. The two extremes (rarely seen so simply) either suggest femininity as clearly and directly connected to biological femaleness, or played out though a kind of liberal pluralism where any kind of difference is (apparently) 'OK.' In this fourth decade of contemporary feminism, feminist critical theory engages with a broad and complex spectrum of meaning. What constitutes biological femaleness is up for debate in the discourses of Queer and Transsexual theory and practice (see Butler (1990 and 1993) and Bornstein (1994)), just as much as liberal pluralism has been criticised in favour of a 'powerful infidel heteroglossia' (Haraway, 1991: 181). Early readings of French Feminist texts as essentialist and therefore philosophically recidivist have been re-thought in favour of readings which emphasise the importance of playfulness, mimicry and 'tactical essentialism' (see later). Feminist thought remains a powerfully dissonant discourse, however, even as its occasional polyvocal playfulness suggests intelligent irreverence might be the way forward for such infidels.

In relation to this discourse within feminist theory about the relationship between femininities and femaleness, I am proposing that the *os-text* is *not* exclusively linked to *women* and their texts / performances. The *os-text* is certainly *on the side of* the feminine. I have no interest in claiming *os-textual* practice for women alone, but I do want to suggest that women (on the whole) are the artists making this kind of work. It seems to me that women are *more likely to* engage with writing and performance in this way. This is not to say that men are unable to make this kind of work, rather that if they do so, they engage in the dynamics and energies of femininity. Whilst this particular distinction is not the focus of my argument here, it seems to me that contemporary women artists make this kind of work because they are often in a political, social and sexual position to engage with writerly and oral energies in performance transgressively: symbolically they have little to lose from disturbing settled philosophical and artistic categories with an *os-textual* practice.

∂

Before moving on to analyses of Irigaray and Cixous, I want to examine the relationship between vision and sound from another perspective; the perspective of

159

being seen to speak. In an *os-textual* practice, part of the scenario of writing and performing one's text, is that one is *seen to speak*. I first became interested in this 'witnessed' speaking of text during the making of a screenic work; the CD-ROM *mouthplace* (Gilson-Ellis and Povall 1997). I was interested in the consequences of a particular dissonance between visual images (sometimes animated video stills / sometimes just stills), and the utterance of my writing. By an accident of design, and despite forty sites of text and performance – I was never *seen to speak* in this work. There were technical reasons why it was difficult to synchronise video and audio on a CD-ROM in 1995,[9] but such limitations still impact on meaning, even productively so. In a CD-ROM which was entirely focused on the feminine / oral, and which contained a plethora of images of my mouth, and many spoken texts focused on feminine orality, *none* included mouths which were seen to speak. In *mouthplace* I am not seen to speak, but I speak incessantly nonetheless, and I am in almost every image. I came to this CD-ROM project interested in women writing and then speaking that writing, and yet we made something that was not able to witness this in any image of a female body that was a *speaking* female body. Although this characteristic started its life as a technical difficulty, it becomes resonant of the cultural, political and psychic context of women writing and speaking their writing in performance.[10]

In *The Secret Project* which we premiered in Cork, Ireland a few people at the rear of the audience said that they couldn't see when we were speaking, and when we were triggering pre-recorded texts by our movement.[11] Because of this, something failed for them. Re-reading the website text written about *mouthplace* in 1996, I realise how this echoes with my concerns then about not being seen to speak.[12] *The Secret Project* is a dance-theatre production. This means that our bodies are breathlessly before an audience. We speak; it's unmistakable. But because we have our voices amplified through headset microphones, and play with environments which enable us to trigger pre-recorded samples of voice with our movements, and then to improvise vocally in relation to them, *who* is speaking, and *when* becomes intentionally confused. If you are not close enough to *see me speaking*, something fails. I speak a text in counterpoint to a text I trigger with my movement. This is a loop which an audience needs to be able to witness in order to engage with. Unlike the CD-ROM, if the audience is unable to bring the realm of vision (the *seeing* of speaking) into play with the realm of sound (the *hearing* of speaking) then something particular about live performance is lost for them.

What is the nature of this difference between speaking / performing in a recorded medium (CD-ROM) and speaking / performing in a live medium? The dissonance between voices and images in our CD-ROM *mouthplace* produces a work in which her (my) voice is lost in the darkness, or a counterpoint to a visual image. Such a work performs the troubled relationship between *being seen* and *being heard* for femininity, and it uses a writerly strategy to do this. These are ghosted, difficult connections between *this* body and *this* voicing, through *this* writing. It makes a resonant sense that we have made a work which never witnesses a speaking female body. Instead this is a work of mourning and wickedness, in which voices are wrested from bodies, only to be laid beside them in careful canon.

This powerful difference between *mouthplace* and *The Secret Project* lies in the unmitigated *presence* of live performance. Such a difference performs itself through the trope of the feminine body speaking text, and being *seen to do so*, or not. In conjuring 'meaning on the move' within *The Secret Project*, it is *dancing* bodies which speak; a fleshly articulateness bringing the bite of text into utterance. This is no coincidence of skill. In the CD-ROM *mouthplace*, 'meaning on the move' is choreographed in the way we design navigation from this site to that, so that the user's movements construct the patterns of viewing. In *The Secret Project*, we wanted to bring the muscular knowledge of dancing bodies into a speaking presence. In itself this is an interleaving of the discipline of watching (dance) and the discipline of listening (theatre). So that *speaking* as much as *writing* the 'O' would be a bodily thing. To see her (me / us) speak, is to assert the utterance of blood; such is the charge of performance. The ghosts we set running here are half-seen things in the darkness; the recorded story *snow ghosts*, woven in the textures of my voice, the haikus that repeat themselves,[13] the two performances of *lingua* (one by Mary Nunan and one by me) that graze English against French, Irish against Irish. This is meaning on the *move*.

$$\partial$$

Luce Irigaray

Irigaray's radical and far reaching critique of the symbolic structuration of Western philosophy has produced a troubled response amongst critics. One such response has been the regular dismissal of her as an essentialist. Margaret Whitford (1991) argues that Irigaray has often been mis-read on this count, suggesting instead that what has been read as essentialism is part of a tactical 'double-gesture', an 'intervention' setting change in motion; not the theoretical 'answer', but a process *enabling* of dynamic cultural shifts. Irigaray's expulsion from the Department of Psychoanalysis at Vincennes after the publication of *Speculum* in 1974 was the result of censure for being politically committed. This aspect of Irigaray's work makes her writing both tantalising and difficult because it engages with both material and symbolic realms.

Irigaray suggests that the 'feminine' is not available under present masculinist hegemony, as well as arguing for the importance of women's symbolic representation. This aspect of her theory is often regarded as utopian in its willingness to imagine a post-patriarchal future. Such imaginative zeal is tempered by her regular assertion that such a female symbolic is unknowable under patriarchy. Nonetheless she scratches at its possibilities. Part of this project is to attempt to collapse the division between feminine pleasure and language. She *enacts* as well as *calls for* such a collapse. She characterises the un-knowable possibility of this female symbolic as fluid and plural, and defines it by refusing, in a radical and playful gesture, the underpinnings of what it means to define. Whatever it might be, and it is (literally) unimaginable, such a symbolic will be multiple and resistant to categorisation. Understandably then, under such a philosophical conundrum, Irigaray has been read as suggesting a feminine symbolic that is essentialist (see for example Moi, 1985: 127–49); one that is to do with the determinism of female bodies, rather than a profoundly alternative symbolic, achievable (perhaps) through provocation, and by playing at such positionality. Some clusters (cultural, geographic, temporal) of women *do* have significant shared experience, but it is possible to think of such experience as culturally produced rather than ensuing from the flesh of femaleness. It is at this juncture where feigning at essentialism for a political project and essentialism itself become confused.

The relationship of femininity, bodies and language is a troubled one. The thrall of Irigaray's project is that she engages in the grand gesture of trying to imagine the impossible. She teases methodically, ruthlessly and playfully at the edifice of Western Thought, its foundational implications, preoccupations and exclusions. Although Irigaray is regularly clumped in the trio including Julia Kristeva and Hélène Cixous and labelled with them as a theorist of *écriture féminine*, she never uses this term in her work (Whitford, 1991: 38). Instead she uses the term *parler-femme* (speaking (as) woman). This has been variously interpreted as a regression to the pre-Oedipal moment, hysterical / incoherent / irrational / a direct connection between women's bodies and a 'woman's language'. Whitford suggests: 'we might understand the idea of a woman's language as the articulation of the unconscious which cannot speak about itself, but which can nonetheless make itself heard if the listener is attentive enough.' (1991: 39) This resistance to the authority of metalanguage's explanatory zeal is an important characteristic of *parler-femme*. It is a basic presupposition of psychoanalysis that the unconscious makes itself heard through speech. The concern of Irigaray is how such utterance is gendered. I am interested in the negotiation of such speech through writing and performance. Is the work of Irigaray productive in relation to the *os-text*?

Perhaps the most important and distinctive aspect of Irigaray's term *parler-femme* is that her concern with both the material and symbolic realms means that she argues for the possibility of a female symbolic which would result in a different kind of language for *real women*, as opposed to a notion of a femininity within language achievable by men or women (see for example, Cixous, 1981). This has been a regular stumbling block in the response to Irigaray; since she is *not* an advocate of a pre-given identity / essence, and yet talks about the possibility of women's accession to a different language. Again, the response to this aspect of Irigaray's work is located in the elision of essentialism and sexual difference.[14]

Margaret Whitford suggests that Irigaray uses psychoanalysis as a model in her writing. Just as the parole of the psychoanalyst provokes change in the analysand, so Irigaray's writings also act as a provocation for change. It is important to note that such change (within the psychoanalytic scene and within the intervention of Irigaray's writing) is never programmatic, static or conclusive, but contextually dynamic and contingent. Within this context, Whitford's suggestion is a compelling one because it links Irigaray's written texts with a speaking scene. In a variation on the idea of the *os-text*, Irigaray's written texts engage with readers to provoke the cultural possibility of *parler femme*; of a feminine speaking. Irigaray's texts operate in an oscillatory and troubling relationship to dominant culture and language. With their irritant playfulness, they have their power in their very shiftiness, in their refusal to prescribe what might constitute *parler-femme*, at the same time as their insistence on its possibility.

It is within language that one becomes a subject. According to Irigaray, therefore, the subject is male. Whitford terms this 'the monosexual structuration of subjectivity' (1991: 38). In her early work on senile dementia (*Le Langage de déments,* 1973), and later work on the language of the schizophrenic, hysteria and obsession, it became clear that Irigaray was attempting to establish a connection between psychic and linguistic phenomena. The term enunciation (*énonciation*) is used within these writings to refer to the position of the speaking subject in the discourse or statement. Whitford (1991: 41) suggests that *parler-femme* must refer to enunciation in this sense. She goes on to elaborate that:

> This would also explain why *parler-femme* has no meta-language, since in the moment of enunciation the enunciation is directed towards an interlocutor (even if this direction is in the mode of avoidance), and cannot speak about itself.
>
> (ibid.)

In this scenario speaking (as) woman is always spoken *to* someone, in a way that precludes meta-linguistic discourse on the speaking scene. What is interesting to note here is that *parler-femme* is seen to refer to the act of *speaking* rather than writing. Certainly Whitford's point about meta-linguistic resistance of the *parler-femme* only makes sense if the language is spoken, i.e. is positioned within discourse in 'real time' in relation to an interlocutor. She can't speak two languages at once (although she might try). Such contingent acts of utterance suggest this moment of enunciation. It is also such kinds of utterance which constitute performances involving the spoken voice.

It is important to distinguish between *parler-femme* within patriarchy in which the voice is not heard / listened to and *parler-femme* within a different symbolic order which does not yet exist. Because women are used to construct language, it is not available to them. Irigaray uses the metaphor of the mirror in this regard, suggesting that women are the tain, and function as reflective material with no possibility of seeing themselves. Irigaray wants women to enter the symbolic as female subjects, and in this way forge the beginning of a different symbolic order.

In this yet un-signified female symbolic, grounded not in the destinies of anatomies, but in the material processes of cultural operation, Irigaray calls for a different kind of difference, not the 'minus A' to man's 'A', but a 'B'. Elizabeth Grosz suggests that Irigaray's insights regarding the primacy of the phallus indicate 'not a truth about men and women, but the investments masculinity has in disavowing alterity' (Grosz, 1990: 172).

To elaborate on the ways in which women are used to construct language, one can think of 'Woman' as a 'universal predicate' (Whitford, 1991: 46) i.e. just as the predicate within grammar expresses something about the subject, so women function to elaborate something about men within language. However, if 'Woman' is configured as a universal predicate, it suggests that the price of bringing 'Woman' to language is the end of signifying itself. Another tack would be to shift the enunciatory position. Irigaray suggests that there could be a two-way predication, or an enunciation not yet qualified by a predicate (Whitford, 1991: 46). Perhaps another way to 'shift the enunciatory position' would be to engage in the grammatical and oscillatory trouble of *writing* as well as *speaking* one's own text (*os-textual* practice), without recourse to a beginning and ending for such a scenario. Will she predicate nonetheless?

In *Lingua* from *The Secret Project*, I speak the etymologies and dictionary definitions of the words 'secrecy,' 'secret,' and 'secretive.' This is a text adapted from that definitive of all texts; the Oxford English Dictionary. This is a text characterised by its attempts to install meaning; to capture the sense of words. I work with such a text for that very reason; I want to set meaning running within its definitive phrases. We design an environment in which I can trigger samples of my voice speaking French. The French words and phrases are all associated with secrecy; mysteries and hidden things. And then I move. I nudge French text, and counterpoint it with my English definitions. I use physical phrases which suggest hidden things, but with an assurance that whatever secrecies I conjure here, they are *on the move*. This is a pleasure in metonymy. I want to tell you that this skill of interlacing text to text to physical effort is an *un-thought* thing, a thing enabled by much rehearsal and discussion, but that is finally – if it *listens* aurally, physically and vocally, a forgotten thing. In rehearsals when we are working on our structured improvisations in these environments, when the work is good, we finish performing and have little sense of what we did. Cindy expects this. I finish a rehearsal of *Lingua*, with Mary and Cindy watching; they both say the work is hugely better than earlier, but I can't remember what I did. Cindy says 'Of course! That's the sign of good improvisation.' What does this mean? And what does it mean for an audience as well as the performer? Mary and Cindy help me recall what I did, not so that I can reproduce it, but so that I can find the taste of the possibilities of the piece, the kinds of gesture pools, the spatial dynamics, the particular playfulness with layering and repetition. In performance, when this works, when we are listening, speaking, moving alive things, then the complexity of our endeavour becomes a clear and single thing, wrought from our steady attentiveness to each moment. There is something I struggle to tell you which is to do with this attentiveness, which results in a radical forgetting. I want to say it is the operations of the unconscious in performance, except that is not quite it, or not quite possible. Let me leave it then, that I want to say it nonetheless. I want to suggest that this is why the work is forgotten, because it is both vividly present in the moment yet engaged with a particular level of consciousness. I recall Whitford on Irigaray's *parler-femme:* 'we might understand the idea of a woman's language as the articulation of the unconscious which cannot speak about itself, but which can nonetheless make itself heard if the listener is attentive enough.' (1991: 39) I stumble in text to articulate something, which by its very resistance suggests something of Irigaray's *parler-femme*. I want to suggest that within such *os-textual* practice, what is heard is the consequence of a skilled performative listening which facilitates the attentive listening of the audience. I re-read Irigaray *This Sex Which is Not One* (1986), and find this:

She steps ever so slightly aside from herself with a murmur, an exclamation, a whisper, a sentence left unfinished … When she returns, it is to set off again from elsewhere. From another point of pleasure or of pain. One would have to listen with another ear, as if hearing *an 'other meaning' always in the process of weaving itself, of embracing itself with words, but also of getting rid of words in order not to become fixed congealed in them.*

(Irigaray, 1986: 29)
[Irigaray's emphasis]

Strangely, this reads like a description of our work on *The Secret Project* ('She steps ever so slightly aside from herself with a murmur, an exclamation, a whisper, a sentence left unfinished … When she returns, it is to set off again from elsewhere'). One of the effects of weaving text with text through physicality is both a claiming of and a moving-through language worlds (*'embracing itself with words, but also of getting rid of words'*). In this work 'listening with another ear' becomes a collaborative discourse, played out between performers and audience. This ear which is not one.

Irigarayan philosophy has radical implications for language, utterance and signification. Irigaray never discusses performance or concrete strategies for bringing about her vision of such a powerfully alternative symbolic. She does, however, perform a strategy in her mimesis of the critical voices of philosophy and criticism. I take this gesture, that of mimesis, and place it here.[15] Just as *parler-femme* has no meta-language, so Irigaray's strategies are performative rather than descriptive. I will not tell you what you should do, because I do not know. You must find your own ways. But I do it here. In my voice. Inflected through my knowledges, and acted like the wise actresses feminine things can be.

In her essay 'When our Lips Speak Together' (Irigaray 1986: 205 - 218), Luce Irigaray writes a performative text conjuring the relations and possibilities of feminine sexuality and orality. Her title purposely elides oral and genital feminine lips, mirroring the symbolic slippage common in Western discourse. In this revolutionary text, Irigaray suggests a feminine orality characterised by plurality: it is not possible for simply one word to pass here:

Open your lips; don't open them simply. I don't open them simply. We - you/I - are neither open nor closed. We never separate simply: a single word cannot be pronounced, produced, uttered by our mouths. Between our lips, yours and mine, several voices, several ways of speaking resound endlessly, back and forth. One is never separable from the other. You/I: we are always several at once. And how could one dominate the other? Impose her voice, her tone, her meaning?

(Irigaray, 1986: 209)

Here Irigaray evokes a multiple feminine orality in *text*. She does not speak it; I read this rather than listen to it. Tenors of textuality and orality playfully mingle here in a provocation of the possibilities of a feminine language. Irigaray writes to me, she doesn't kiss me, though perhaps she might if she were here. I write / kiss to you, here

165

again, as I visit this kissing loving text. Irigaray's text of plural voices, of unceasing layering, repetition and reworkings is made concretely and productively possible in the engagement of writing, technologies and performance. Our work is an example of this. None of our mouths open simply; we speak and move to call up another speaking. Such voices might be our own, or one of the other two, or both of them. We always play anew in the thrall of them: 'several ways of speaking resound endlessly.' None of us can dominate the meaning because we don't have it – we make it every time we perform, *differently*.

> **lip** *n.* **1.** *Anatomy*. Either of two fleshy, muscular folds that together surround the opening of the mouth.
>
> **2.** Any structure or part that similarly encircles or bounds an orifice: as *Anatomy*. A labium.
>
> **3.** *Slang*. Insolent talk. – **bite one's lip.** (i) To hold back one's anger or other feeling. (ii) To show vexation. – **button one's lip.** *Slang*. To stop talking. – **smack one's lips**. To relish or gloat over something anticipated or remembered.

∂

Hélène Cixous

Hélène Cixous is among those theorists commonly included under the rubric 'French Feminism' and associated with *écriture féminine* (feminine writing). Although widely known outside of France as a theorist, the majority of Cixous' publications have been fiction. Importantly for this study, Cixous' recent fiction includes play texts written for a context of live performance. Much of Cixous' work is concerned with writing and sexual difference. Whilst Irigaray is also concerned with the possibilities of articulating sexual difference, she does so in terms of a specifically female language. Cixous in contrast to this articulates her terms of sexual difference in relation to a femininity which can be enacted by men or women. Cixous has also been accused of ahistorical essentialism, and in a similar movement to the critical response to Irigaray, recent commentators have re-thought this relationship between theories of sexual difference and essentialism in relation to her work.[16]

For Cixous, writing is a revolutionary practice. One of the main reasons for this is its potential to undo binary structures. Writing is also powerfully corporeal for Cixous. The combination of these two gestures – the bodily undoing of binary opposition within writing results in a practice of fiction / theory concerned with destabilising narrative / lived subjectivity, and re-inscribing somatic experience. Cixous' association with *écriture féminine* may seem contradictory to a practice concerned with undoing the opposition feminine / masculine (see Sellers, 1994). For Cixous, however, *écriture féminine* is 'feminine' in two senses. Firstly she believes women are presently closer to a feminine economy than men. Consequently she sees in women's writing both the possibility of including other experience and the subversion of existing structures. The relationship to the mother's body is also important in this context. For Cixous the rhythms and articulations of the maternal body continue to affect the subject into adult life, and this provides a connection to the pre-symbolic union between the self and m/other. The subject's relation to the self, the other, language and the world is affected by this connection. Secondly (according to Cixous), a feminine subject position is not constructed around mastery, and does not, therefore, appropriate the other's difference. Because of this, Cixous suggests that feminine writing will bring into being alternative forms of perception, relation and expression.[17]

Cixous' most well-known work is the essay 'The Laugh of the Medusa' (1981) first published in 1975/6. In this essay Cixous calls for a feminine writing that will be powerfully physically located, radically transgressive and pleasured / pleasurable. Elin Diamond suggests that the writing called for in this essay is as much revolutionary myth as practice. This seems to me a useful way to think about this essay and Cixous' work in general.

I am particularly interested in Cixous' use of the feminine voice as a trope / referent within her fiction and theory. This is not always a use of the term 'voice' as a metaphor for a writing practice. Feminine vocality also functions as an 'inspiration' in these texts, a lived / imagined experience 'to be brought' to such writing, something like Salvaggio's 'O'. Interestingly, the opposition between speaking and writing is one of the binaries Cixous lists at the beginning of 'Sorties' (Cixous and Clément, 1986). How then, can an undoing of such opposition only be sought in writing itself? It is as if Cixous uses the extraordinary possibilities of the feminine voice to inscribe such vocality in her writing, but never approaches what the possibilities of using such writing to inscribe vocality in literal voices might be.

In the following quotation from 'Sorties' Cixous weaves such a writing practice from vocal and textual femininity:

> First I sense femininity in writing by: a privilege of voice: writing and voice are entwined and interwoven and writing's continuity / voice's rhythm take each other's breath away through interchanging, make the text gasp or form it out of suspenses and silences, make it lose its breath or rend it with cries.
>
> (Cixous and Clément, 1986: 92)

In this extract, writing and voice exchange breath and rhythm. Cixous writes of a text which has vocality – it gasps and cries. Yet I hear nothing. There is no body before me breathing into writing, moving rhythmically flesh to text. Cixous powerfully theorises and practices a feminine writing which calls up feminine vocality / corporeality. Implicitly Cixous' work invites the theorisation and practice of the *os-text*, a practice which inscribes the transgressive possibilities of writing within vocality / performance. A site in which she can breathe into text before me / beside me / inside me.

What does it mean for an *os-textual* practice that women (according to Cixous) are closer to the pre-symbolic connection with the mother? Here the maternal voice figures undifferentiated plenitude. There are certainly dangers of essentialism ghosted in this terrain; ghosts that promise privileged access (for women) to a site where the 'other' is not yet separate from the subject. If this connection is only figured in this way then it is a philosophical and political failure. For this realm to be productive, it must operate as a half-truth. It must figure as a 'revolutionary myth' (Diamond, 1997: 83) inciting radical departure from the patriarchal structurations of language, whilst at the same time opening up the possibilities of *difference* for subjects figured as feminine in relation to the maternal. Women have a different relation to the maternal because they have the potential for maternity themselves, as well as being closer (according to Cixous) to the 'equivoice' – a voice that brings into being / is processual in opposition to the subject / object monoliths. Importantly, this is partly through their material exclusion from cultures:

> Text, my body: traversed by lilting flows; listen to me, it is not a captivating, clinging 'mother'; it is the equivoice that, touching you, affects you, pushes you away from your breast to come to language, that summons your strength; it is the rhyth-me that laughs you; ... Voice: milk that could go on forever ... Eternity: is voice mixed with milk.

> (Cixous 'Sorties' in Cixous & Clément, 1986: 93)

Cixous' imagery of a 'voice mixed with milk' powerfully inscribes the maternal agency in the subject's shift from pre-symbolic to symbolic realms. Later in 'Sorties', Cixous writes "She writes with white ink." (Cixous and Clément, 1986: 94) suggesting that such bodily and fluid agency is a writerly as well as vocal influence. In these revolutionary scenarios, the maternal body (her voice and milk in particular) figures a practice of writing which mixes up oralities – the suckling of milk and utterance, and confuses who it is that utters, the mother or her child. Such fluid tectonics find their way into textuality in the metaphor of the woman writing in milk.

$$\partial$$

In our 1997 CD-ROM *mouthplace* there is a section on insanity. You can find it under an icon of cut stitches. When you click [this icon,] 'Special Mark' appears on your screen, written in my handwriting. At the opening of the insanity section, there is a video loop of my face moving, milk slowly dripping from my mouth. As you move the cursor over the surface of this moving image, so quiet whispered texts can be heard:

I'm bruised
I've got bruises
they're deep and slow
like drugged hornets
I'm body-stuck
and hurt in slow motion
your little kisses
little half-kisses
ached-for breaths of skin to skin
I am half-surprised
you ever came to me
woman.

and when you click, you hear the following words in a clear voice:

I jumped in with my lips clenched, gasped at the cold,
and a swarm of hummingbirds flew out of my mouth.

As milk moves from my lips in the field of vision, so flowing visions move from my mouth here in the realm of sound. I write this to nudge you towards witnessing this seeing and hearing spun from milky trajectories of mouths and writing.

∂

In the extract from Cixous' 'Sorties' quoted above, the maternal and the child's voice, suckling / maternal voice, suckling / speaking and suckling / writing are webbed together in non-hierarchical connection. This could be figured as a Deleuzian assemblage in which subject and object are understood not as discrete opposites but as a series of flows and intensities, linked in heterogeneous ways (Deleuze and Guattari, 1987). This is a useful way of thinking these relations, since it resists staging any of these scenes as necessarily productive of any others. This is important because Cixous is not only interested in describing a psychoanalytic scene but in provoking a writing practice. The following quote is from 'Breaths' (1975):

The voice says: 'I am there.' And everything is there. If I had such a voice, I would not write, I would laugh. … (it) rises from the greatest dilation of her breast, without listening to herself. Does not assume airs … If I had such a voice, I would not write, I would fight.

(Cixous in Sellers, 1994: 50–1)

Here Cixous again inscribes maternal plenitude as voice. This is a voice which suggests a circumvention of writing – a kind of imaginary pure access to jouissance and revolution. What is important here is that Cixous' fictional voice is inscribed here in *writing*, in a writing pleasured and motivated by such a voice. It is not *voiced*.

Elizabeth Grosz in her study of corporeality, *Volatile Bodies* (1994) analyses orality and sexuality in relation to a range of theorists. According to psychoanalysis, during the development of the sexual drive, the sensuality of sucking milk shifts to other bodily parts (Grosz, 1994: 54–5). However, the mouth remains especially privileged in terms of its sensitivity to sensations – introceptively and extroceptively – 'a primordial link … connecting perceptions from inside to the outside of the body' (ibid.). In the following quote, Grosz refigures oral sexuality as a kind of connective zest:

oral sexuality can be re-transcribed in corporeal terms. Instead of describing the oral drive in terms of what it feels like, as an endogenously originating psychical representation striving for an external, absent or lost object (the fantasmatic and ultimately impossible object of desire), orality can be understood in terms of

169

what it does: creating linkages with other surfaces, other places, other objects or assemblages. The child's lips, for example, form connections (or in Deleuzian terms, machines, assemblages) with the breast or bottle.

(ibid.: 116)

It seems to me that whilst the participants of such assemblages might change, the essential structure of their connective operations does not. In adult life and in the context *os-textual* practice, such connections / machines / assemblages involving orality matrix writing, utterance, performance instead of breasts or bottles.

In 'To Live the Orange' (1979) Cixous elaborates her experience of the voice as a trace of the articulate body:

> I can adore a voice: I am a woman: the love of the voice: nothing is more powerful than the intimate touch of a veiled voice, profound but reserved coming to awaken my blood; the first ray of a voice that comes to meet the newly-born heart. My heart is in the belongingness with a voice fashioned out of shining darkness, a nearness infinitely tender and reserved.

(Cixous in Sellers, 1994: 84)

In this extract, Cixous speaks simply of her love of the voice. This is not the maternal voice, yet her description certainly recalls her writings on the maternal. Such a voice (part of a prelude to a tribute to the Brazilian writer Clarice Lispector) is marked by its nearness and tenderness. She goes on:

> There are those of whom I cannot speak outside with words that come out making noise. Out of love for the infinite delicateness of their voices. Out of respect for the delicateness of the nearness. Those whose speaking is so profound, so intense, whose voices pass gently behind things and lift them and gently bathe them, and take the words in their hands and lay them with infinite delicateness close by things, to call them and lull them without pulling them and rushing them. There are women who speak to watch over and save, not to catch, with voices almost invisible, attentive and precise like virtuoso fingers, and swift as bird's beaks, but not to seize and mean, voices to remain near by things, as their luminous shadow, to reflect and protect the things that are ever as delicate as the newly-born.

(Cixous in Sellers, 1994: 84)

In this second passage, it is quite clear that Cixous uses the maternal metaphor to figure her love of this voice, as if such moving voicing were an uttered act of mothering. Certainly there are dangers here in reifying a romanticised version of the maternal (a site of material oppression for women, as well as pleasure), but of importance here, is that once again the maternal is figured in webbed relation to the voice and writing. This extract also recalls Irigaray's *This Sex Which is Not One*, cited earlier: 'And how could one dominate the other? Impose her voice, her tone, her meaning?' (1986: 209). And here is Cixous: 'There are women who speak … not to seize and mean, (these are) voices to remain near by things' (Cixous in Sellers, 1994: 84). Both suggest a voicing that sets meaning in motion.

∂

Hélène Cixous' radical textual practice has been enormously influential in re-thinking writing in relation to the body, and the female body in particular. Yet it is in *performance* that writing's transgressive possibilities might be staged in an altogether different paradigm. It is my contention that the choreographer / writer / performer has the potential to bring into being alternative forms of perception, relation and expression; a particular access to making '*the text gasp … make it lose its breath or rend it with cries*' (Cixous 'Sorties' in Cixous & Clément, 1986: 92). With the addition of technology, this relation of physicality and vocality in choreography / performance can be textured in new ways, troubled into unlikely alliances.

Most structures of contemporary performance training separate voice / text work from physical / choreographic work. Dancers, in my experience, often stumble at voice work, despite their articulate bodies. Yet it is precisely this detailed physical knowledge, which, with training, also makes them extraordinary performers of vocality. Such physical knowledge also brings something particular to digital technology. Perhaps our epistemologies are more likely to refuse a separation between the technologies that become our tools and our dancing / uttering bodies.

In the work of weaving bodies, writing, utterance, sound and technology, it is the troublings of improvisational grazes that most profoundly recall Cixous' work. Her crying out for a plural writing, one marked with bodies and their voices (Cixous, 1981) seems to me to lie here in the playful entanglement of digital technology and the voice / body / writing / sound. Here in the linear lines of theory, I must place my elements one after the other, in different orders divided by slashes, to evoke a sense of their mingling. There is much in performance which resists analysis, but I continue to try and articulate what happens in sweat and light. I too want to write a writing that will antagonise resistance.

The Banff Centre for the Arts, Canada
Out of the Box: The Future of Interface
September 1998

Air Canada is on strike. The Sample Cell and BigEye have not arrived from Ohio. It's Saturday, and I'm performing this evening. This is the first time I've performed without Richard setting up the environments. Nothing on the 8 a.m. bus, or the 9 a.m. At 9.30 [a.m.] Bill walks into the studio with a grin on his face and a parcel in his hand. Scott and I set to work. It takes us all day, a move of studios and several borrowed lamps to get set. 'Chorda' is the last one. It's nearly 6 [p.m.] and the performance is at 8 [p.m.]. We run the choreography and tweak the settings. My knowledge of the piece is a corporeal one. I know clearly how it feels to perform when the settings are right, but light levels, camera proximity, and what I'm wearing affect these settings. I try to guide Scott with my physical understanding of the piece, but I struggle for a language – 'It felt much richer' 'It needs to have a clear threshold here that I can move beneath' 'I need to be able to build up the layers more.' Between us we weave a space for me to perform in conjured from the memory of flesh and the pressure of fingers on keys.

In this work, we make spaces for entanglement. These are precisely designed to be imprecise. Their textures are composed from choreographic fragments, made to conjure sound / text from its motion in particular ways. This practice demands that I am alive to every moment of performance; I weave with pools of choreography, utterance, and recorded text / sound. What I trigger with my motion affects what I say / sound / how I move again. Listening, speaking and moving become a related series of energies. I push at language to tell you what this is.

The movement of air in bodies variously occluded to produce sound, is not profoundly different to the movement of information within digital technologies. Exchanges between these two (the uttering body and technology) is not a radical conceptual leap, especially if the relation between writing, utterance and physicality is already one of connective flows and intensities. Perhaps the most productive body of theory in relation to these ideas is Deleuze and Guattari's 'assemblages' in which one element is never dominant over another, but are combined in terms of energies, processes, durations, corporeal substances and incorporeal events (Deleuze and Guattari, 1987).

Elizabeth Grosz suggests that Deleuze and Guattari's reconception of corporeality in these terms is key to re-thinking bodies, the body is

> understood more in terms of what it can do, the things it can perform, the linkages it establishes, the transformations and becomings it undergoes, and the machinic connections it forms with other bodies … In place of plenitude, being, fullness or self-identity is not lack, absence, rupture, but rather becoming.
>
> (Grosz, 1994: 165)

Such 'becoming' is a productive way of thinking what happens in the physical – vocal – written – digital performance I am describing here; a processual matrix, in which the performer, her writing, her live voice, her recorded voice, the digital tools, the programmer and composer comprise a webbed series of liaisons, which shift and mark each other with durational pulses. Such liaisons are

> composed of lines, movements, speeds, and intensities, rather than of things and their relations. Assemblages or multiplicities, then, because they are essentially in movement, in action, are always made not found. They are the consequences of a practice.
>
> (Grosz, 1994: 167)

Thinking corporeality in discourse has pressing implications for a choreographic practice which involves bodies which write, dance and speak. Cartesian dualisms of mind and body (read writing and dancing / writing and speaking), are simply not productive in relation to these practices. Woman's troubled relationship to bodily symbolics means that she is positioned differently to men in these economies; her body has been represented / constructed as 'frail, imperfect, unruly, unreliable' (Grosz, 1994: 13) and is symbolically associated with the body in the mind / body pair. For femininity then, re-working such weary dualisms becomes a necessary tenet. The *os-text* does this with noisy texts in its arms. In the trouble, mess and grubbiness of performance, with technology and theory as partners, such re-thinking, such thinking again seems to me to make possible the kinds of perception, relation and expression Cixous has so often cried out for, and femininity's unruliness is a twinkling skill for such a troubling.

References

1 At a lunchtime concert in the Irish World Music Centre, at the University of Limerick, Ireland 15 April 1999; and at the Triskel Arts Centre, Cork, Ireland for the opening of the Intermedia Festival, 1 May 1999.

2 During the first ten years of contemporary feminism (approx. 1965–1975), there was a movement both within grass roots and theoretical feminism that did exactly what Salvaggio describes herself as avoiding here; it engaged in an uncritical celebration of 'feminine' modes of language, that emphasised the personal, subjective, emotive and liberatory dimensions of voice. In relation to performance practice this manifested itself as a staging of 'positive' voices of women. This is Lynda Hart on this period of feminism in relation to performance practice:

> The optimism of the 1970s, in which feminist theatre companies were operating with the idea that presenting 'positive' images of women would counteract the misogyny of masculinist representations of women, gave way to the realisation that differences between, among, and within women precluded any direct access to what constitutes 'positivity.' … In the histories of these collectives we can observe the process of feminists wrestling with what Derrida has called 'women as truth' and 'women as untruth,' both remaining 'within the economy of truth's system, in the phallogocentric space.' (Derrida, 1978: 97) Such oscillation between competing claims for a definition of 'woman,' raises the problem of essentialism and the necessity of performing gender and sexuality in a register that disrupts a metaphysics of presence. (Hart and Phelan, 1993: 6–7).

3 During the early years of feminism, particularly in the United States, there was a 'consciousness raising' (CR) movement. This consisted of groups which encouraged and validated the telling of personal histories/stories and fantasies as a way toward 'women's liberation.' This is not to denigrate the importance of speaking one's experience in a supportive context, but such groups tended to do so uncritically, and validate anything that was said because it was uttered by a woman. Part of the consequence of this was (i) that the tenets of CR became powerfully associated with the broader meanings of feminism, and (ii) that in trying to dislodge and problematise these meanings, contemporary feminism has become overly sensitive to being accused of essentialism. The pleasures and possibilities of the oral operate within this historical context within feminist history. 'In the 1960s and 1970s, "consciousness raising" stressed the importance of women sharing their experiences in order to understand that these experiences were not only personal and individual but were political, produced and affected by the prevailing social and cultural structure and systems.' (Harris, 1999: 145–6).

4   Heteroglossia is a term used by Bakhtin (1984), to describe the mixing of discourses within carnival. I use it here to suggest the uttered and written nature of what I want to associate with femininity, and the contingent, politically-inflected meanings that might be wrought from such apparently dispersed discourses.

5   The Cill Rialaig Project, Ballinskelligs, Co. Kerry, Ireland is an International Artist and Writers Retreat.

6   half/angel spent several years developing expertise in motion-sensing systems in relation to text and choreography. This work took place largely during residencies at STEIM, Amsterdam (July & September 1996), Firkin Crane, Cork, Ireland (November 1997) and The Banff Centre for the Arts, Canada (April and September 1998/August and September 1999).

7   These 'intelligent environments' are made using a software programme called 'BigEye.' Performers are not required to wear any identifying costumes/nodes, or to 'hit' particular triggers in the space. Instead movement information is fed into the computer through a simple video camera which surveys the space. This means that performers are physically unencumbered by the technology. This also means that it is possible to have a fluid relationship with each environment because it is sensitive to qualities of movements, in ways that all of us (performers and programmers) design and navigate together.

8   This profoundly corporeal listening became a key process for all of us (Cindy Cummings, Jools Gilson-Ellis and Mary Nunan) performing within the intelligent environments designed for *The Secret Project*.

9   In the production of our CD-ROM work *mouthplace*, we found that files which contained audio as well as visual information were prohibitively large, and would take overly long to load when viewing the work. It was difficult as a consequence to video me speaking and then use the audio and the visual information on screen. Instead we made a decision to counterpoint visual and aural worlds by design. A consequence of this is that the CD-ROM contains no sound that was recorded at the same time as the images were filmed. Most of the video loops in the CD-ROM are animated stills: we reduced the amount of 'frames per second' in order that they might load more easily. This gives these loops a distinctive staccato quality that contrasts with the high quality of the sonic worlds that accompany them.

10 See Laurie Anderson's performance from 'For Instants', for another example of performance practice in which seeing and speaking are dissonant (Anderson, 1994: 114–15).

11 *The Secret Project*, a dance theatre production by half/angel, European Première, Firkin Crane, Cork, Ireland 4 November, 1999.

12 This text was written as part of the *mouthplace* website: www.halfangel.org.uk

13 These were heart, palm and echo:
    heart
    my small heart
    flying towards
    the finish line
    without me
    palm
    if you're falling
    so is the snow
    perhaps
    you will also
    melt
    in my palm
    echo

I have

your echo

in me

14 Such 'difference' is not a difference from a pre-given norm, but 'pure difference' - difference in itself, difference with no identity. Such 'pure difference' refuses to privilege either term. See Grosz 1995: 53

15 Irigarayan use of the term 'mimesis' refers to a process of miming dominant discourses, as a way of engaging with and troubling such dominance. Its most contentious manifestation, is as a mimicry of dominant discourses of the feminine, a process intended to puncture their descriptive force. Critics of Irigaray's tactics usually profess unease at the possibility of negotiating traditional realms of femininity with resistant flair. Such discussions have been developed further in the discourse on camp, cross-dressing and Queer theory. See Meyer (1994), Garber (1992) and Case (1996a).

16 See introduction to Sellers (1994) re: Cixous, and Whitford (1991) re: Irigaray.

17 I am indebted to Susan Sellers' introduction to *The Hélène Cixous Reader* (Sellers 1994) for this summary of Cixousian theory.

Afterword – Shape-Shifters and Hidden Bodies

Jane de Gay

The chapters in this book have explored a variety of ways in which female performers have sought to take systems (both verbal and visual) which threatened to speak *for* them and re-shape them so that performers could speak for themselves. Although the book was first conceived some eight years ago amidst discussions as to whether there might be such a thing as a 'woman's language in the theatre', the case studies of performance work considered in this collection would suggest that there is no 'women's language' as such. However, each chapter and each performance piece documented provides evidence of a common desire to use theatre languages creatively to elicit new meanings.

As was stated at the outset, this book has not attempted to present an overview of theatre work being by undertaken by women today, and so any conclusions to be drawn from the pieces discussed must be tentative, and any common strands which emerge would need to be tested against a wider selection of performance work. However, the performance pieces discussed here call the lie to any lingering notion that women theatre-makers may be mainly or exclusively interested in exploring 'women's issues' or 'women's experiences'. Perhaps only the oldest piece discussed here, *Lear's Daughters* (1987) foregrounded questions of social and economic equality, family relationships and birth control as issues likely to be of interest to female audience members. More recent pieces address the particular social or cultural situations in which gender is only one of a number of axes of difference or inequality. Some pieces spoke to quite different questions or situations: *The Day Don Came with the Fish* brings in the experience of HIV-positive men and *Vena Amoris* may be seen in part as a reflection on mobile phone culture. Gender has not disappeared from the agenda, but explorations of its workings have become far more complex and an increasing amount of attention has been given to the interrelation of gender and other social and cultural factors.

This collection also suggests that the various theoretical positions articulated around concepts of *écriture féminine* are still useful and relevant but, crucially, that they can and should be uncoupled from essentialist implications. As Jools Gilson-Ellis demonstrates, the primacy given to physicality in Irigaray's *parler-femme* and Cixous's *écriture féminine* means that such languages are ideally suited to be *performed*. Both are predicated on *movement* or revolutionary change: thus, they can not only be performed but, in performance, such language may enable new ways of thinking and living. Reading back from Gilson-Ellis's piece through the preceding chapters, it is possible to see the work of other performers in reshaping theatre languages as 'feminine' strategies.

The emphasis given to *shape* in the title of the book is significant. *Ecriture féminine* has often been caricatured as advocating confusion or muddle, a challenge to the linear structure of written language, but many of the performances discussed here are highly structured, although the structures used are not necessarily literary or linguistic ones. Thus, Jane Prendergast shaped *I, Hamlet* around the musical structure of an octave in which the final note is silent: the story of Hamlet is reshaped and framed in a way that encourages contemplation and participation. Similarly, Adeola Agbebiyi, Patience Agbabi and Dorothea Smartt partly structured *Fo(u)r Women* around jazz rhythms: a form of music in which melodies are systematically reshaped and which, crucially, has long been associated with Black performers.

New media technologies have the potential for offering both structure and flexibility. CD-ROMS and websites tend to offer logical pathways based around series of menus, whilst allowing the user to explore different parts of a work in varying sequences enabling endless play and re-play, the freedom to experience alternative versions of the same sequence, and oscillation between states as the user 'toggles' between windows. The potentials for new technologies to realise the ideals of *écriture féminine* are still being explored: examples discussed in this book include Fiona Shaw's presentation of alternative cuts of *King Lear* on CD-ROM and Jools Gilson-Ellis's *Mouthplace* CD-ROM.

While many early feminist theories of language were sceptical of the value of text, many of the examples discussed here show female performers working with text – writing their own texts and rewriting those by other people. And yet those examples remind us that a theatre text is not single or simple: several of the performances discussed in Part 1 had a paratextual element, in which a new text debated or explored issues raised by an earlier one. Timberlake Wertenbaker's *The Love of the Nightingale* (discussed in chapter 1) is a good example, as is Jane Prendergast's performed commentary on Shakespeare in *I, Hamlet*. Metatheatre plays part in this: for example, Fiona Shaw's video workshops on *King Lear* offered a reflexive commentary on video production, as she 'broke the frame' to show technicians and camera operators at work. These are also examples of how criticism and theory can be *performed*.

Gaps, silences and spaces have often been seen as features of feminine language and, indeed, space has been a recurring theme in this book as contributors articulate quests for space, and discuss the processes of living with space and giving space. The need for new performance spaces is clearly high on the agenda. Many of the performance pieces documented here have taken place outside traditional theatre spaces: some have been staged in workshops or studios, or in buildings constructed for another purpose but used as theatres; others have sought to explore feminist spaces opened up by radio, video, and multimedia. However, there is also evidence of an interest in opening up space within play-texts and other source materials. Thus, punctuation (or syncopation, to invoke another musical metaphor) has also been a theme. For example, we saw image and action punctuating text in *I, Hamlet* and *Ophelia;* music punctuating text in *I, Hamlet* and *Fo(u)r Women;* percussion and silence (the scratch in the record) punctuating the voice in *The Day Don Came With the Fish.* The non-linear approaches possible within multimedia offer female performers radical ways of punctuating current understandings – many new ways of becoming shape-shifters.

The quest for space goes hand-in-hand with a desire for inclusivity: a reaching-out to the audience to invite their participation too. For example, Jane Prendergast saw the missing note at the end of the octave structure of *I, Hamlet* as 'a free space in the performance where audience and actors could meet, after the performance, continuing the performance in a shared forum.' Lindsay Bell also champions the audience (or reader), when she describes her adaptation of *To the Lighthouse* as answering Virginia Woolf's call for 'comment, not action'. And yet, as the missing 'fourth woman' in *Fo(u)r Women* reminds us, space may articulate exclusion as well as participation. While recognizing ourselves as audience members in the 'fourth woman', it is important also to know when space has to be respected and interrogated for what it is.

Alongside questions of absence, this collection reflects a concern to make the body present in performance – speaking and not spoken for. A number of contributors have explored, in their written and performance work, ways of 'hiding the body' from the 'male gaze', and chapters have documented how bodies have been transmitted into cyberspace, or how they have departed from a radio studio leaving no visible trace. Yet, at the same time, contributors like Helen Paris have reminded us of the value of bringing the body into physical proximity with the audience and Jools Gilson-Ellis reminds us that the body matters for it, too, may be able to make theory. Helen Paris's use of sign-language and Jools Gilson-Ellis's inclusion of performing bodies to activate textual components of *Secret Project* are examples of making the body speak. That is, the body plays an active role in articulating languages rather than having meanings inscribed upon it. So, as the *discussion* of these issues continues in cyberspace and in print, the body must be given its place too. We need to keep returning to performance spaces to make new work and to share in it as audience members. We need to keep up the dialogue between text and body, between performance and theory/critique/analysis (call it what you will), to find new ways of breaking down those dualisms. As many of the contributors to this book have urged us, in different ways, let us keep practising performance, practising theory and theorizing our practice.

Bibliography and Further Reading

Acker, K. *Bodies of Work*, London and New York, Serpent's Tail, 1997.

Agbabi, P. 'My Mother' in Agbabi, P. *R.A.W.*, London, Gecko Press, 1995.

—— 'Ufo Woman' in McCarthy, K. (ed), *Bittersweet*, London, Women's Press, 1998.

Agbebiyi, A., 'Fo(u)r Women: The Art of Collaboration' in Rapi, N. and Chowdhry, M. (eds) *Acts of Lesbian Passion: Sexuality, Gender and Performance*, (Binghampton, N.Y.: Haworth Press, 1998), also published as *Journal of Lesbian Studies* 2: 2/3

——, 'Ident', in *Journal of Lesbian Studies*, 3/4.

Anderson, L., *Stories from The Nerve Bible*, New York, HarperPerennial, 1994.

Aston, E., *Feminist Theatre Practice: A Handbook*, London, Routledge, 1999.

Auslander, P., *From Acting to Performance: Essays in Modernism and Postmodernism*, Routledge: London and New York, 1997.

Bakhtin, W. M., *Rabelais and His World*. trans. H. Iswolsky, Bloomington, Indiana University Press, 1984.

Barber, F., 'Ophelia in *Hamlet*', in Jackson, R. and Smallwood, R. (eds) *Players of Shakespeare 2: Further Essays in Shakespearean Performance by players with the Royal Shakespeare Company*, (Cambridge, Cambridge University Press, 1988), pp. 137–49.

Barton, Robert, 'Voice in a Visual World', in Marion Hampton and Barbara Acker (eds) *The Vocal Vision: Views on Voice* (New York, Applesauce, 1997), pp. 79–92.

Baudrillard, J., *Simulations*, New York, Semiotext(e), 1983.

Baym, N., 'The Madwoman And Her Languages', in Warhol, R.R. and Herndl, D.P. (eds) *Feminisms: An Anthology of Literary Theory and Criticism* (New Brunswick & New Jersey, Rutgers University Press, 1991), pp. 156–67.

Bennett, S., *Theatre Audiences: A Theory of Production and Reception*, London, Routledge, 1991.

——, *Performing Nostalgia: Shifting Shakespeare and the Contemporary Past*, London and New York, Routledge, 1996.

Birringer, J., *The Postmodern Body in Performance, Theatre, Theory, Postmodernism*, Bloomington and Indianapolis, Indiana University Press, 1991.

Blau, H., *To all Appearances: Ideology and Performance*, London and New York, Routledge, 1992.

——, *The Audience*, Baltimore and London, Johns Hopkins University Press, 1990.

Bornstein, K., *Gender Outlaw: On Men, Women and The Rest of Us*, London and New York, Routledge, 1994.

Braidotti, R., *Nomadic Subjects: Embodiment And Sexual Difference in Contemporary Feminist Theory*, New York, Columbia University Press, 1994.

Brown, J., *Feminist Drama: Definition and Critical Analysis*, Metuchen, N.J.: Scarecrow Press, 1979.

Butler, J., 'Performative Acts and Gender Constitution: an Essay in Phenomenology and Feminist Theory,' *Theatre Journal*, 40: 4 (1988), pp. 519–31.

——, *Gender Trouble: Feminism and the Subversion of Identity*, London and New York, Routledge, 1990.

—— *Bodies That Matter: On the Discursive Limits of 'Sex'*, London and New York, Routledge, 1993.

—— *Excitable Speech: A Politics of the Performative*, London, Routledge, 1997.

Cameron, D. (ed.) 'Pieces of Eight: Interviews with 8mm Filmmakers', in *Big As Life: An American History of 8mm Films*, a special issue of *Cinematheque*, San Francisco, 1998.

Campbell, P. (ed.), *Analysing Performance: A Critical Reader*, Manchester, Manchester University Press, 1996.

Camper, F., 'Qualities of Eight', in *Big As Life: An American History of 8mm Films*, a special issue of *Cinematheque*, San Francisco, 1998.

Canning, C., *Feminist Theaters in the USA: Staging Women's Experience*, London and New York, Routledge, 1996.

Carlson, M., *Performance: A Critical Introduction*, London and New York, Routledge, 1996.

Case, S.-E., *Feminism and Theatre*, Basingstoke, Macmillan, 1988.

——, *Split Britches*, New York and London, Routledge, 1996a.

——, *The Domain-Matrix: Performing Lesbian at the End of Print Culture*, Bloomington and Indianapolis, Indiana University Press, 1996b.

Chisholm, D., '"The Cunning Lingua" of Desire: Bodies-language and Perverse Performativity', in Grosz, E. and Probyn, E. (eds), *Sexy Bodies: The Strange Carnalities of Feminism* (London and New York, Routledge, 1995), pp. 19–41.

Churchill, C. and Lan, D., *A Mouthful of Birds*, London, Methuen, 1986.

Cima, G. C., *Performing Women: Female Characters, Male Playwrights, and the Modern Stage*, Ithaca, Cornell University Press, 1993.

Cixous, H., 'The Laugh of the Medusa' (first published 1975 (in French); 1976 (new version in English)), in Marks, E., and de Courtivron, I. (eds), *New French Feminisms* (Brighton, Harvester, 1981), pp. 245–64.

——, *Three Steps on the Ladder of Writing*, New York, Columbia University Press, 1993.

——, and Clément, C., *The Newly Born Woman*. trans. Betsy Wing, Minneapolis, University of Minnesota Press, 1986.

Coldwell, J. 'The Beauty of the Medusa: Twentieth Century', *English Studies in Canada*, 9 (1985), pp. 422–37.

Cousin, G., *Women in Dramatic Place and Time: Contemporary Female Characters on Stage*, London and New York, Routledge, 1997.

Curb, R. K. *The Amazon All-Stars*, New York and London, Applause Books, 1996.

Cutler, A., 'Abstract Body Language: Documenting Women's Bodies in Theatre', *New Theatre Quarterly*, XIV, 2, 54 (May 1998), pp. 111–118.

de Beauvoir, S. *The Second Sex* (1949), tr. and ed. H. M. Parshley, London, Everyman, 1993.

de Certeau, M., *The Practice of Everyday Life*, trans. S. Rendall, Berkeley, University of California Press, 1984.

Deleuze, G., and Guattari, F., *A Thousand Plateaus: Capitalism and Schizophrenia*, tr. B. Massumi, Minneapolis, University of Minnesota Press, 1987; repr. London, Athlone Press, 1996.

Dempsey, S., and Millan, L., excerpt from 'Mary Medusa', in Goodman, L. (ed.) *Mythic Women/Real Women: Plays and Performance Pieces by Women* (London, Faber, 2000), pp. 247–57.

Derrida, J., *Spurs: Nietzsche's Styles*, trans. Barbara Harlow, Chicago, University of Chicago Press, 1978.

——, *Dissemination*, trans. B. Johnson, Chicago, University of Chicago Press, 1981.

Diamond, E. 'Brechtian Theory / Feminist Theory: Toward a Gestic Feminist Criticism', *The Drama Review*, 32 (1988), pp. 82–94.

——, 'Mimesis, Mimicry and the "True-Real"', *Modern Drama*, 32 (1989), pp. 58–72.

——, *Unmaking Mimesis*, Routledge, London and New York, 1997.

—— (ed.), *Performance and Cultural Politics*, London, Routledge, 1996.

Doanne, M., *Femme Fatales*, London, Routledge, 1991.

Dobson, T. (1998), '"High-Engender'd Battles": Gender and Power in "Queen Lear",' *New Theatre Quarterly*, 54 (1998), pp. 139–45.

Dolan, J., 'In Defence of the Discourse', *The Drama Review*, 33 (1989), 64–65.

——, *The Feminist Spectator as Critic*, Ann Arbor, UMI Research Press, 1988.

——, *Presence and Desire: Essays on Gender, Sexuality, Performance*, Ann Arbor, University of Michigan Press, 1993.

Dunderdale, S., 'The Status of Women in British Theatre and Survey', *Drama*, 152 (1984), pp. 9–11.

Egervary, B., 'Another Con-Text', in Rapi, N. and Chowdhry, M. (eds), *Acts of Passion: Sexuality, Gender and Performance* (New York, Hawthorn Press, 1998), pp. 34–44.

Esslin, Martin, 'The Mind as a Stage', *Theatre Quarterly*, 1:3 (1971), pp. 5–11.

Evaristo, B., *Lara*, Speldhurst, Angela Royal, 1997.

Feldman, T., *An Introduction to Digital Media*, Routledge, London, 1997.

Ferris, L., *Acting Women: Images of Women in Theatre*, Basingstoke, Macmillan, 1990.

Findley, Timothy, 'Voices in the Dark: The Magic of Words', *CanPlay*, 7:2 (1980), p. 7.

Fonoroff, N. 'Riff-Raff and Hooligans: Super 8 and Mass Art', in *Big As Life: An American History of 8mm Films*, a special issue of *Cinematheque*, San Francisco, 1998.

Forte, J. 'Women's Performance Art: Feminism and Post-Modernism', *Theatre Journal*, 40, 2 (1988), pp. 217–35.

Freud, S., *The Standard Edition of the Complete Psychological Works of Sigmund Freud*. 24 volumes, trans. and ed. J. Strachey, London, Hogarth Press, 1953–74.

——, 'Studies on Hysteria' (1895), *Standard Edition*, vol. 2.

——, 'Fragment of an Analysis of a Case of Hysteria' (1905), *Standard Edition*, vol. 7.

Garber, M., *Vested Interests: Cross-Dressing and Cultural Anxiety*, New York and London, Routledge, 1992.

Gay, P., *As She Likes It: Shakespeare's Unruly Women*, London, Routledge, 1994.

Geritz, K. 'I Came into an 8mm World', in *Big As Life: An American History of 8mm Films*, a special issue of *Cinematheque*, San Francisco, 1998.

Goodman, L., *Contemporary Feminist Theatres: To Each Her Own*, London, Routledge, 1993a.

——, 'Women's Alternative Shakespeares and Women's Alternatives to Shakespeare in Contemporary British Theatre' in Novy, M. (ed.) *Cross-Cultural Performances*, (Chicago, University of Illinois Press, 1993b), pp. 206–26.

——, 'La Figura della Donna in Shakespeare' (The Figure of Woman in Shakespeare), in Lanati, B. (ed.) *Divina Vicende Di Vita e Di Teatro*, (*Divina: Facts of Life in Theatre*) Volume Two, (Torino, Tirrenia Stampatoris, 1994a), pp. 83–100.

——, 'Sexuality and Autobiography in Performance (Art)', *Women: A Cultural Review*, Special Issue on Women and Performance, 5: 2 (1994b), pp. 123–36.

—— (ed.), *Feminist Stages: Interviews with Women in Contemporary British Theatre*, London and New York, Harwood Academic Publishers, 1996a.

——, 'Feminist Performance: Canon Fodder and Cultural Change', in Campbell, P. (ed.) *Analysing Performance* (Manchester University Press, 1996b), pp. 19–42.

——, 'AIDS and Live Arts', in Campbell, P. (ed.) *Analysing Performance* (Manchester University Press, 1996c), pp. 203–18.

——, 'Who's Looking at Who(m)?: Re-viewing Medusa', *Modern Drama*, 39: 1 (1996d), pp. 190–210.

——, 'Performance Language as Art Form and Communicative Gesture', in Maybin, J. and Mercer, N. (eds) *Using English: from Conversation to Canon*, (London, Routledge, 1996e).

——, 'Representing Gender/Representing Self: A Reflection on Role Playing in Performance Theory and Practice', in Boireau, N. (ed.) *Drama on Drama* (Basingstoke, Macmillan, 1996f).

—— (ed.) *The Routledge Reader in Gender and Performance*, London and New York, Routledge, 1998.

—— (ed.) *Mythic Women/Real Women: Plays and Performance Pieces by Women*, London, Faber and Faber, 2000.

—— *Sexuality in Performance: Replaying Gender in Theatre and Culture,* London, Routledge, forthcoming.

—— with Coe, T., and Williams, J. H., 'The Multimedia Bard: Plugged and Unplugged' *New Theatre Quarterly,* 14: 53 (1998), pp. 20–42.

—— and de Gay, J. (eds) *The Routledge Reader in Politics and Performance,* London and New York, Routledge, 2000.

Graves, R., *The Greek Myths,* 2 vols. (1955), Harmondsworth, Penguin, 1960.

Gray, Frances, 'Carry on, Echo: The Dissident Sound Body', *Sound Journal,* online
    <http://www.ukc.ac.uk/sdfva/sound-journal/gray001.htm>, accessed June 8, 2001.

Griffin, Gabrielle and Elaine Aston, eds. (1991). *Herstory,* two volumes, Sheffield: Sheffield Academic Press.

Grosz, E., *Jacques Lacan: A Feminist Introduction,* London, Routledge, 1990.

——, *Volatile Bodies: Towards a Corporeal Feminism,* Bloomington and Indianapolis, Indiana University Press, 1994.

——, *Space, Time, Perversion,* New York and London, Routledge, 1995.

Gubar, S., 'Mother, Maiden and the Marriage of Death: Women Writers and an Ancient Myth', *Women's Studies* 6 (1979), pp. 301–15.

Guild, E., '*Écriture Féminine*', in Wright, E. (ed.) *Feminism and Psychoanalysis* (Oxford and Cambridge, MA, Basil Blackwell, 1992), pp. 74 - 6

Hanna, G., *Monstrous Regiment,* London, Nick Hern Books, 1991.

Haraway, D. J., *Simians, Cyborgs and Women, The Reinvention of Nature,* London, Free Association Books, 1991.

Harris, G., *Staging Femininities: Performance and Performativity,* Manchester and New York: Manchester University Press, 1999.

Harrison, J. E., *Prolegomena to the Study of Greek Religion,* Cambridge, Cambridge University Press, 1922.

Hart, L. (ed.) *Making a Spectacle: Feminist Essays on Contemporary Women's Theatre,* Ann Arbor, University of Michigan Press, 1989.

——., 'Motherhood According to Finley: The Theory of Total Blame', in *The Drama Review,* 36: 1 (1991), pp. 124–34.

—— and Phelan, P. (eds), *Acting Out: Feminist Performances,* Ann Arbor, University of Michigan Press, 1993.

Helms, L., 'The Weyward Sisters: Towards a Feminist Staging of *Macbeth*', *New Theatre Quarterly,* VIII, 30 (1992), pp. 167–177.

Hershman Leeson, L. 'Romancing the Anti-Body, Lust and Longing in Cyberspace', in Hershman Leeson, L. (ed.), *Clicking In, Hot Links to a Digital Culture,* (Seattle, Bay Press, 1996), pp. 325–37.

Hutcheon, L., *A Theory of Parody: The Teachings of Twentieth-Century Art Forms,* London, Methuen, 1985.

Irigaray, L., *Speculum of the Other Woman* (1974), trans. G. C. Gill., Ithaca, New York, Cornell University Press, 1985.

——, *This Sex Which is Not One,* trans. Catherine Porter, Ithaca, New York, Cornell University Press, 1986.

Jenson, J., '8mm: American Images and the Art of the Everyday', in *Big As Life: An American History of 8mm Films,* a special issue of *Cinematheque,* San Francisco, 1998.

Jones, L., *Bulletproof Diva: Tales of race, sex and hair,* New York and London, Anchor/Doubleday, 1994.

Just, R., *Women in Athenian Law and Life,* London, Routledge, 1989.

Kozel, S., 'Multi-Medea: Feminist Performance Using Multimedia Technologies', in Goodman, L. with de Gay, J. (eds) *The Routledge Reader in Gender and Performance* (London, Routledge, 1998), pp. 299–302.

Kristeva, J., *Revolution in Poetic Language,* trans. by M. Waller, intro. by L. S. Roudiez, New York, Columbia University Press, 1984.

——, *The Kristeva Reader,* ed. T. Moi, Oxford, Blackwell, 1986.

Bibliography and Further Reading

Lacan, J., *The Language of the Self: The Function of Language in Psychoanalysis*, trans. A. Wilden, Baltimore, Johns Hopkins University Press, 1968.

Lavery, B., 'But Will Men Like It? Or Living as a Feminist Writer Without Committing Murder', in Todd, S. (ed.) *Women and Theatre: Calling the Shots* (London and Boston: Faber & Faber, 1984), pp. 24–32.

Levinson, P., *Soft Edge: A Natural History and Future of the Information Revolution*, New York and London: Routledge, 1997.

Makward, C., 'To Be or Not to Be ... A Feminist Speaker', in Jardine, A. and Eisenstein, H. (eds) *The Future of Difference* (Boston, G. & K. Hall, 1980).

Marks, E. and de Courtivron, I. (eds) *New French Feminisms: An Anthology*, Brighton, Harvester, 1981.

Martin, C., *A Sourcebook of Feminist Theatre and Performance*, London and New York, Routledge, 1996.

Mellencamp, P., *Indiscretions*, Indianapolis, Indiana University Press, 1990.

Mercer, K., *Welcome to the Jungle*, London and New York, Routledge, 1994.

Meyer, M. (ed.) *The Politics and Poetics of Camp*, London and New York, Routledge, 1994.

Miller, N. K., *Subject to Change: Reading Feminist Writing*, New York, Columbia University Press, 1988.

Mitchell, J. and Rose, J. (eds) *Feminine Sexuality; Jacques Lacan and the Ecole Freudienne*, trans. J., New York, W. W. Norton & Company, 1982.

Moi, T., *Sexual/Textual Politics: Feminist Literary Theory*, London, Methuen, 1985.

Mulvey, L. 'Visual Pleasure and Narrative Cinema', *Screen*, 16 (1975).

Nicholson, L.J. (ed.) *Feminism/Postmodernism*, London: Routledge, 1990.

Novy, M. (ed.), *Women's Revisions of Shakespeare: On the Responses of Dickinson, Woolf, Rich, H.D., George Eliot, and Others*, Urbana and Chicago, University of Illinois Press, 1990.

—— (ed.), *Cross-Cultural Performances: Differences in Women's Re-visions of Shakespeare*, Urbana and Chicago, University of Illinois Press, 1993.

Oddey, A., 'Devising Women's Theatre as Meeting the Needs of Changing Times', in Goodman, L. with de Gay, J. (eds), *The Routledge Reader in Gender and Performance* (London and New York, Routledge, 1998), pp. 118–24.

Olauson, J., *The American Woman Playwright: A View of Criticism and Characterization*, Troy, New York, Whitson, 1981.

Orbach, S., *Hunger Strike: The Anorectic's Struggle as a Metaphor for our Age*, New York, Norton, 1986.

Ostriker, A., 'The Thieves of Language: Women Poets and Revisionist Mythmaking', *Signs*, 8 (1982), pp. 68–90.

Paglia, C., *Sexual Personae: Art and Decadence from Nefertiti to Emily Dickinson*, London, Penguin, 1991.

—— *Sex, Art and American Culture*, New York, Vintage Books, 1992.

Phelan, P., 'Feminist Theory, Poststructuralism, and Performance', *The Drama Review*, 117 (1988), 107–27.

——, *Unmarked: The Politics of Performance*, London and New York, Routledge, 1993.

——, *Mourning Sex: Performing Public Memories*, London and New York, Routledge, 1997.

Putzel, Steven, 'Virginia Woolf and "The Distance of the Stage"', *Women's Studies*, 28 (1999), pp. 435–70.

Rabillard, S. (ed), *Caryl Churchill: Contemporary Representations*, Winnipeg, Blizzard Press, 1998.

Rapi, N., 'Hide and Seek: The Search for a Lesbian Theatre Aesthetic', *New Theatre Quarterly*, 9: 34 (1993), pp. 147–58.

—— and Chowdhry, M. (eds), *Acts of Lesbian Passion: Sexuality, Gender and Performance*, New York and London, Haworth Press, 1998.

Robson, C., Georgeson, V,. and Beck, J. (eds) *Women Writers' Handbook*, London, Aurora Metro, 1990.

Ronnell, A., Interview in Juno, A. and Vale, V., *Angry Women*, New York, Research, 1991.

Rose, G., 'Performing Space' in Massey, D., Allen, J., and Sarre, P. (eds), *Human Geography Today* (Malden, USA, Blackwell, 1999), pp. 247–59.

Rutter, C. with Cusack, S., Dionissotti, P., Shaw, F., Stevenson, J., and Walter, H., and Evans, F. (ed.) *Clamorous Voices: Shakespeare's Women Today*, London, Women's Press, 1988.

Salvaggio, R., *The Sounds of Feminist Theory*, New York: State University of New York Press, 1999.

Savona, J. L., 'French Feminism and Theatre: An Introduction', *Modern Drama*, 27 (1984), pp. 540–44.

Schafer, R. M., *The Tuning of the World: Toward a Theory of Soundscape Design*, Philadelphia, University of Pennsylvania Press, 1980.

Schlueter, J. (ed.) *Modern American Drama: The Female Canon*, London and Toronto, Associated University Presses, 1990.

Schneider, R., *The Explicit Body in Performance*, London and New York, Routledge, 1997.

——, '*After Us the Savage Goddess*', in Diamond, E. (ed.), *Performance and Cultural Politics*, London and New York, Routledge, 1996.

Scoliniocov, H., *Women Theatrical Space*, Cambridge, Cambridge University Press, 1994.

Sedgwick, E. K., 'The Rats and the Democrats', *The Drama Review*, 37: 3 (1993), pp. 171–85.

Sellers, S. (ed.) *The Hélène Cixous Reader*, London & New York, Routledge, 1994.

Senelick, L., *The Changing Room*, London, Routledge, 2000.

Showalter, E., 'Representing Ophelia: Women, Madness, and the Responsibilities of Feminist Criticism', in Parker, P. and Hartmann, G. (eds) *Shakespeare and the Question of Theory* (New York and London: Methuen, 1985), pp. 77–94.

——, *The Female Malady: Women, Madness and English Culture, 1830–1980*, London, Virago, 1987.

Silver, Brenda R., '"Anon" and "The Reader": Virginia Woolf's Last Essays', *Twentieth Century Literature*, 25 (1979), pp. 356–441.

Smartt, D. 'Crossroads : Junction 17 from 22', in *Cutting Teeth* 12 (1998)

—— 'Forget', in *FEED: An Arts Magazine of Communion*, 2/3 (1994); and *Kunapipi*, XVII, 2 (1995).

—— 'Faultlines' in *Writing Women* (1995) and Ross, J. and Anim-Addo, J. (eds), *Voice, Memory, Ashes* (London, Mango Publishing, 1999).

—— 'Medusa? Medusa Black!', in Goodman, L. (ed.) *Mythic Women/Real Women: Plays and Performance Pieces by Women* (London, Faber, 2000), pp. 259–62.

Smith, Z. *White Teeth*, London, Hamish Hamilton, 2000.

Solomon, A. *Re-dressing the Canon*, London, Routledge, 1997.

Suleri, S., 'Skin Deep', in Appiah, K.A. (ed.) *Identities*, Chicago and London, University of Chicago Press, 1995.

Turner, B., 'Heiner Müller's Medea: Towards a Paradigm for the Contemporary Gothic Anatomy', in Byron, G. and Punter, D. (eds) *Spectral Readings: Towards a Gothic Geography* (Basingstoke, Macmillan, 1999), pp. 202–16.

Ugwu, C., 'Keep on Running', in *Let's Get it On: The politics of Black performance*, London, ICA, 1995.

Veith, I., *Hysteria: The History of a Disease*, Chicago: University of Chicago Press, 1965.

Wagner, J. A., 'Formal Parody and the Metamorphosis of the Audience in Timberlake Wertenbaker's *The Love of the Nightingale*', *Papers on Language and Literature*, 31 (1995), pp. 227–54.

Walter, H., 'The Heroine, the Harpy and the Human Being', *New Theatre Quarterly*, IX: 34 (1993), pp. 110–20.

Wandor, M. (ed.) *On Gender and Writing*, London, Pandora, 1983.

—— *Carry On Understudies*, revised edition, New York, Routledge and Kegan Paul, 1986.

—— *Look Back in Gender: Sexuality and The Family in Post-War British Drama*, London, Methuen, 1987.

Warner, D., 'How do you solve a problem like Medea?', interview with L. Gray, *Independent on Sunday*, Culture Section (21 January 2001), p. 7.

Wertenbaker, T., *Plays: One*, London: Faber, 1996.

Whitehead, Gregory, *Out of the Dark: notes on the nobodies of radio art*, online <http://www.somewhere.org/NAR/Writings/Critical/whitehead/Main.htm>, accessed June 8, 2001.

Whitford, M., *Luce Irigaray: Philosophy in the Feminine*, London and New York, Routledge, 1991.

Winston, J., 'Re-Casting the Phaedra Syndrome: Myth and Morality in Timberlake Wertenbaker's *The Love of the Nightingale*', *Modern Drama*, 38 (1995), pp. 510–19.

Winterson, J., *Art Objects: Essays on Ecstasy and Effrontery*, London, Vintage, 1996.

Woolf, Virginia, '*The Cherry Orchard*' (1920) in Andrew McNeillie (ed.), *The Essays of Virginia Woolf, Vol. 3* (London, Hogarth Press, 1988), pp. 246–49.

——, 'Congreve' (1921) in Andrew McNeillie (ed.), *The Essays of Virginia Woolf, Vol. 3* London, Hogarth Press, 1988), pp. 295–97.

——, 'Congreve's Comedies' (1937), in *Collected Essays, Vol. 1* (London, Hogarth Press, 1966), pp. 76–84.

——, 'The Narrow Bridge of Art' (1927), in *Collected Essays, Vol. 2* (London, Hogarth Press, 1966), pp. 218–29.

——, 'Notes on an Elizabethan Play' (1925), in *Collected Essays, Vol. 1* (London, Hogarth Press, 1966), pp. 54–61.

——, 'On Not Knowing Greek' (1925), *Collected Essays, Vol. 1* (London, Hogarth Press, 1966), pp. 1–13.

——, *To the Lighthouse* (1927), Oxford, Oxford University Press, 1998.

——, '*Twelfth Night* at the Old Vic' (1933), *Collected Essays, Vol. 1* (London, Hogarth Press, 1966), pp. 28–31.

Unpublished sources

Battaglini, R., *La Nozze* and *Altri Tempi*, performed at the Magdalena Festival, Cardiff, September 1994.

Bell, L., Adaptation of Virginia Woolf's *To the Lighthouse*, first performed at Royal George Theatre, Shaw Festival, on August 3, 2000, as part of the Bell Canada Reading Series.

Lavery, B., *Ophelia*, first performed at Stantonbury Campus Theatre, Milton Keynes, 1996. Extract published in Goodman, L. (ed.) *Mythic Women/Real Women: Plays and Performance Pieces by Women* (London, Faber, 2000), pp. 325–42.

Rodwell, S. and McNamara, M. (the Toad Lilies), *Crow Station*, performed at the Magdalena Festival, Cardiff, September 1994, and on tour in Wellington, Coventry, Amsterdam and Berlin, May–July 1996.

Electronic sources

Agbebiyi, A., 'Crystal Visions', on *Crystal Visions* CD (Shango Music, 1993)

—— 'Wrap You Up', at http//:www.shango.demon.co.uk

Bardwell, Jenny, producer (2000). *Lear's Daughters*, audio CD (Milton Keynes: Open University/BBC).

Coe, Tony, producer. (2000) *King Lear*, video. (Milton Keynes: Open University/BBC).

Gilson-Ellis, J., and Povall, R., *Mouthplace*, CD-ROM, Hanover, NH, Frog Peak Music, 1997.

Williams, Huw, programmer. (2000) *Shakespeare: Text and Performance*, CD-ROM (Milton Keynes: Open University/BBC).

Index

189

Index